Science Supplement

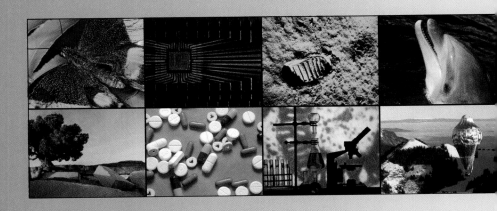

Spring | 1998

Published By Webster's Home Library
99 White Plains Road
Tarrytown, New York 10591-9001

ISBN 0-87475-089-X

Printed in the United States of America

Designed by Patricia Moritz, Moritz Design

Science Supplement

Spring | 1998

Publisher's Note

Scientific knowledge continues to advance at an astonishing rate, and we remain fascinated with "how it works." In the Spring 1998 edition of the *Science Supplement*, we explore topics that recently have captured the attention of scientists and those with curiosity for scientific discoveries and explanations. A major breakthrough was the successful artificial cloning of a sheep, fueling both a scientific as well as an ethical and theological controversy over genetic engineering. This topic is reported by Roger Smith in "The Trouble with Clones" (page 12). A less controversial area of scientific investigation is nutrition, and Elizabeth D. Schaefer surveys the historical and current research on whether diet can influence human intelligence, an easier way than cloning to manipulate our future offspring (page 318).

Our attention also has been riveted on space recently, and we are entering a productive era of space exploration and discovery. As we go to press, the bold discovery of strong evidence for frozen water on the Moon, as reported by Joseph L. Spradley (page 124), is being overshadowed by the dramatic success of Mars Pathfinder's roving exploration of the red planet, an event we look forward to reporting in the Fall *Science Supplement*.

We are pleased to once again bring to you a collection of diverse scientific reports and hope they continue to interest you.

Contributors

Marcia Bartusiak

Alvin K. Benson

Paul R. Boehlke

Bruce Bower

William J. Broad

Jane E. Brody

Malcolm W. Browne

Mark Caldwell

Donald Dale Jackson

Jeffry Jensen

Christopher Keating

Kevin Krajick

Robert Kunzig

Brian J. Nichelson

Ivars Peterson

John R. Phillips

Mary Roach

Wendy Sacket

Elizabeth D. Schafer

Roger Smith

Joseph L. Spradley

Russell R. Tobias

Dan Vergano

David L. Wheeler

John Noble Wilford

Corinna Wu

Carl Zimmer

Contents

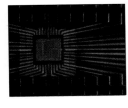

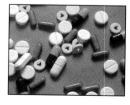

The Trouble with Clones

ROGER SMITH

When *Nature*, the top British science journal, announced on February 27, 1997, that an adult female sheep had been successfully cloned, clever headlines flowed fast and, sometimes, furious from the media: "Ewegenics," *The New Republic* scoffed angrily. *Newsweek* coyly echoed the nineteenth-century poet William Blake—"Little Lamb, Who Made Thee?"—and several others, punning on a 1970's hit tune, sang, "Bring in the clones!" *The Chronicle of Higher Education* pondered the ethical ramifications of the discovery. No wonder an editorial in the British medical journal *Lancet* sighed, "One lamb, much fuss."

However, most scientists and religious leaders were not laughing. The clone, a ewe named Dolly, stood in the eye of a stormy controversy. Distrust of genetic engineering gave the controversy energy and much wind, as did the modern fear of technology-spawned monsters. Politicians soon listened to the worries of ethicists and theologians, and acted. President Bill Clinton banned federally funded research in cloning pending further review. Republicans introduced bills into Congress to forbid human cloning, period. State legislatures followed these political winds, and parliaments worldwide instituted restrictions or formed study committees. Most signal of all, the government of Great Britain withdrew its grant to the Roslin Institute, where cell biologist Ian Wilmut and his colleagues had done the impossible in creating Dolly —for cloning mammals, real cloning, was supposed to be impossible according to the received wisdom of developmental biology.

Twinning can be thought of as a type of cloning too. In this sense, there is nothing new or unnatural about human clones either.

CLONES AND CLONING

There is nothing surprising or unnatural about clones. Derived from the Greek word for "twig," the term itself first appeared in English when biologist H. J. Weber used it in 1903 to mean a group of plants propagated from "vegetative parts," such as cuttings or runners. The meaning had become a little more specific by the 1960's: replication of an organism asexually. Bacteria, most yeasts, and even a few plants reproduce by natural cloning, as do animals that use some forms of parthenogenesis—development of adults from unfertilized eggs. Twinning can be thought of as a type of cloning too. In this sense, there is nothing new or unnatural about human clones either.

There is nothing surprising or unnatural about clones. Derived from the Greek word for twig, the term itself first appeared in English when biologist H.J. Weber used it in 1903 to mean a group of plants propagated from "vegetative parts," such as cuttings or runners. ▼

Nobody objects to natural clones. Artificial cloning presents the problem. Yet even it is not new. For decades scientists have known that it is possible to create twins, triplets, and other multiple births artificially. After sperm fertilizes an egg, it becomes an embryo cell, which then divides. All embryo cells contain nuclei whose deoxyribonucleic acid (DNA) preserves identical genetic information. Such cells, in scientific terminology, are totipotent, equally capable of development. Merely separate embryonic cells, and one has the beginnings of artificial twins.

There is another, more sophisticated, exquisitely delicate technique as well: nuclear transplantation. First scientists remove and discard the nucleus of an egg cell in a process called enucleation. They draw out the nucleus from a totipotent cell and insert it into the egg cell, which then is implanted in a host mother's womb. If all goes well, normal embryo cell division, fetal development, birth, and maturity follow. The technique first succeeded in 1952 with frog embryos and has since produced mice, rabbits, pigs, cows, and monkeys. In 1996 Wilmut announced that he had produced sheep with nuclear transplantation of embryo nuclei. Another group of experimenters even created human embryos with nuclear transplantation, although they destroyed the modified cells soon after the procedure.

Still, twinning embryo cells or swapping around their nuclei does not quite correspond to the original idea of cloning: taking a cutting of a mature plant and growing a new plant from it. The key word is "mature," that is, adult. Most biologists believed that nuclear transplantation would not work with cells from adult animals, and for good reason. After dividing several times—the exact number depends upon the species—animal embryo cells begin to specialize. Some becoming brain tissue, for example, while others grow as muscle or liver or toenail. The varying developments occur because cells "differentiate." For reasons still not well understood, certain chemicals bind permanently to segments of the DNA, covering and censoring the information encoded in those segments, and the chemicals involved vary from cell to cell during differentiation. As a result, while all of an animal's cells have the same DNA, the portions available for use differ. It was believed, therefore, that a clone of one cell type would automatically differ from a clone of another cell type; no single mature nucleus would deliver the genetic information needed to replicate the entire donor.

Below: DNA helix model.

DOLLY AND THE TRANSGENICS

Then Keith H. S. Campbell devised a way to "uncensor" differentiated cells. Essentially, he cleans the DNA of proteins. The crucial step is to starve the cell. After removal from the donor animal, it is deprived of nearly all nutrients for five days. Its normal growth cycle stops, and it becomes dormant. Some of the chemical modifications to the genes reverse, and the nucleus reverts to a condition similar to that of an embryo cell nucleus.

When Campbell told him about this "deprogramming," Wilmut seized upon it for his cloning experiments with sheep. He scraped cells from the udder of a six-year-old finn Dorset ewe and cultured them *in vitro*, where he starved them into inactivity. Then he fused these donor cells with enucleated egg cells from a Scottish Blackface ewe by pulsing an electric current through them. These composite embryos were implanted in the uterus of a surrogate mother. In some cases the initial embryo cells divided into cells that differentiated, and fetuses developed. After a pregnancy of 148 days, one fetus survived birth as a 6.6-kilogram lamb, a little large for a finn Dorset but otherwise normal. And so, Dolly, the first mammal cloned from adult DNA, was born. When Wilmut and his colleagues Campbell, A. E. Schnieke, J. McWhir, and A. J. Kind revealed her existence in *Nature*, she was a six-month-old sheep with six-year-old DNA.

However, she is not a perfect clone in every possible way. The mitochondria in her cells, tiny factories producing an essential fuel, have their own DNA, and it is inherited from the egg cell, not from the udder cell of the finn Dorset donor. Still, this tiny flaw in Dolly's clonehood hardly matters, because species-specific characteristics come from nuclear DNA. All sheep — all humans, too — get their mitochondrial DNA from their mothers. What distinguishes Dolly is that she had two mothers, and no father.

The process was difficult and far from flawless. It took Wilmut 277 attempts to produce Dolly, far less efficient than sexual reproduction. He still cannot be sure that Dolly is a normal sheep, either. He is monitoring her development to see if she matures sexually, is fertile, can bear lambs of her own, and lives a normal life span. Most important, until someone successfully repeats his experiment, there is always the possibility that Dolly is a fluke. Good science requires independent verification.

Controversy, however, does not. The *Nature* article started it. A week later, scientists at the Oregon Regional Primate Research Center announced that they had cloned rhesus monkeys, and the tone of the controversy rose a notch in pitch and intensity. It did not seem to matter that the cloned rhesus came from an embryonic cell, not an adult cell. Nor did most commentators pay much attention to the purpose of Wilmut's experiments with sheep. Suddenly, it struck people that if sheep and monkeys can be cloned, then the most sophisticated and dangerous of all mammals — humans — might be cloned too. The prospect scared some and revolted others.

Wilmut himself came out strongly against human cloning. Like his employer, the Roslin Institute, Wilmut works to improve breeds of domestic animals. In particular, he is trying to make it easier to produce "transgenic" animals. A transgenic animal is one whose DNA combines the DNA of its own species with DNA snippets from some other species. These snippets add information to the genetic code that enables cells to produce chemicals otherwise foreign to the animal, but helpful to people.

So far scientists have produced transgenic animals only by a very inefficient method. They snip out a useful bit of human DNA and inject it into the animal embryo

All sheep— all humans, too— get their mitochondrial DNA from their mothers. What distinguishes Dolly is that she had two mothers, and no father.

Cell biologist Ian Wilmut of the Roslin Institute, whose cloning experiments with sheep resulted in the birth of Dolly – the first mammal cloned from adult DNA.

It took Wilmut 277 attempts to produce Dolly, far less efficient than sexual reproduction.

nucleus and hope it gets incorporated. Usually it does not. Sometimes, however, the human snippet does work itself way into the embryo DNA, and the mature animal becomes a living factory for useful chemical compounds. Using this method, scientists have produced a goat whose milk contains therapeutic proteins and a cow whose milk is especially nourishing. The prospect of medicine-spiked milk — or better meat and pelts — is only the beginning. Researchers hope to grow transgenic pigs that can supply organs for transplant into humans without tissue rejection; other "designer animals" could test new drugs or model the progress of diseases. Such developments would drastically lower the cost of sophisticated drugs and surgical procedures. Meanwhile, the profits for successful genetic engineering companies would be enormous.

Wilmut collaborated with scientists from PPL Therapeutics, a British pharmaceutical company pursuing transgenic research. Part of their purpose was to develop a reliable method of gene transfer. If an adult animal's

DNA is extracted and useful genes are added or harmful ones deleted, it can then be inserted into an egg cell, using Wilmut's method, and grown into an adult animal. Such a transgenic animal would be guaranteed to produce the desired product. Herds (or flocks) of its offspring would turn out the product in quantity.

While some ethicists have grave doubts about exploiting animals this way and animal rights advocates have denounced transgenic experiments, few scientists recoil from it. That the nuclear transplantation could be used on humans is a different matter entirely. Nevertheless, some scientists believe that cloning humans is possible. Human embryo cells differentiate earlier than do the equivalent sheep cells, so the procedure would be more difficult, and many experiments would be required to refine the technique. However, nothing in Wilmut's work, or that of other researchers, forbids human cloning.

FORBIDDEN KNOWLEDGE

What the laws of nature do not forbid, scientists have a knack for creating. Therefore it appears to be only a matter of time before humans are cloned. Such a creative act seems too much like "playing God," and therefore immoral and arrogant, to many religious leaders and some scientists. Theologians wonder if clones can have souls and ponder what cloning will do to the essence of humanness. The Catholic Church opposes cloning because it wants to "safeguard those values that constitute the human being and its existence" and insists there is a fundamental human right to be born to parents rather than to laboratory technicians, that *father* and *mother* are more conducive to healthy childhood memories than *donor* and *surrogate*. Others see in cloning a technology that has as much power to destroy civilization as nuclear weapons. To these critics, science is asking questions that it should leave alone; cloning research of any kind is a quest for forbidden knowledge.

Most commentators, though, have fretted about applications rather than morality. If humans *can* be cloned, *why* will they be cloned? Who will control the cloning? The initial answers to these questions expressed two basic worries.

First is what might be called the "replacement" syndrome. Scientists themselves have speculated that human

The cloning of Dolly:

1. Udder cells are scraped from the udder of a Finn Dorset ewe.

2. The cells are placed in a culture but given a minimum of nutrients and become dormant.

3. Eggs are taken from a Scottish Blackface ewe and the nucleus extracted from each.

4. Eggs and dormant cells are fused with pulses of electricity to produce embryo cells.

5. The embryos are cultured.

6. Embryos are implanted in host ewes, surrogate mothers.

7. One grows into a viable fetus.

8. Dolly is born.

organ tissue might be cloned in a factory to supply transplant surgeries. If farfetched and eerie, the cloned-organs idea has not been proved impossible. An even more gruesome possibility is the cloning of a complete human to provide spare parts for the donor. Two similar suggestions cannot help but tug on the heartstrings of even staunch cloning opponents. If a man and woman yearn for a child but cannot conceive or if they run the risk of randomly passing on a genetic disease through sexual reproduction, they could resort to cloning. And what if a child, long desired and dearly loved, were about to die? Could a clone be made to replace that child? These possibilities have ramifications that disturb many commentators. The wealthy might try to clone themselves in a bid for immortality. (In fact, in March, 1997, Valiant Ventures, a company in the Bahamas, announced its intention to build cloning facilities for paying customers.) A woman might dispense with a male's input altogether and clone children from her own tissue and egg, or those of another woman. (This would not work for men, because they do not produce eggs.)

Second is the "brave new world" syndrome. Aldous Huxley's 1932 novel *Brave New World* bitterly satirized industrial civilization. The major premise of its futuristic plot is that types of identical people can be produced artificially, as needed, to fill specific functions in society, from janitors to rocket scientists, and each type amounts to an inescapable social class. The idea so horrifies readers accustomed to democracy and individuality that the novel has long symbolized the dehumanizing effects of technology. Cloning appears to realize the novel's premise perfectly, and so the most apprehensive of today's commentators fear that a dictator could turn out hordes of worker and warrior drones and soon conquer the world. Or unprincipled "mad" scientists might tinker with genes and develop clones that are physically and intellectually superior, a super race. In the low-comedy version of this fear, sports announcers have joked about a basketball team of Michael Jordan clones.

These human cloning speculations rest on two faulty assumptions. The first is that a grown-up clone would be identical to the adult donor. Since the 1960's, scientists and reputable popularizers have pointed out that adults are the product of their genes *and* their environment.

Researchers hope to grow transgenic pigs that can supply organs for transplant into humans without tissue rejection; other "designer" animals could test new drugs or model the progress of diseases. Such developments would drastically lower the cost of sophisticated drugs and surgical procedures. Meanwhile, the profits for successful genetic engineering companies would be enormous.

Environment includes how and where someone is raised. For a clone to match the donor exactly in every physical, intellectual, and psychological detail, both would have to grow up in the same place under the same influences with no chance variations, a prospect so unlikely as to be a fantasy. Actually, the clone and donor should grow up at the same time too—an outright contradiction if the donor is an adult.

Scientists themselves have speculated that human organ tissue might be cloned in a factory to supply transplant surgeries. If far-fetched and eerie, the cloned-organs idea has not been proved impossible. ▼

The second misleading assumption is that cloning could be faster and cheaper than regular sexual reproduction. It would not be faster, not without extraordinary advances in rearing children rapidly. Cloned humans would take just as long to grow up as traditionally produced humans. In the immediate future, cloning does not appear to be cheaper either. If human cloning is allowed and if the technique is perfected—very big ifs indeed— the cloned hordes would require expensive laboratory equipment and technicians on a large scale. Even the most ambition-crazed dictator might pause at the investment of time and money required before a useful horde is available.

Unfortunately, hope-filled speculations and paranoid fantasies have obscured a notable scientific discovery. With Dolly, Campbell and Wilmut have demonstrated that the differentiation of cells, even mammalian cells, is reversible. Biologists long debated the point. Now the debate is over. Whether the media laugh at it, moralists deplore it, or drug companies profit from it, the fact advances basic knowledge.

The Dolphin Strategy

CARL ZIMMER

Dawn Noren hoists oxygen tanks onto her back, places an air regulator in her mouth, grabs a plastic box and slate, and falls out of the motorboat into the ocean. Through 50 feet of pale blue Bahamas water she can see the ten other divers kneeling in a circle on the sandy, ribbed seafloor. She swims down to the group and positions herself at its edge. Two more divers arrive and glide into the middle of the circle, carrying with them long white drums full of dead herring. They are followed by the animals that brought everyone here: two Atlantic bottle-nosed dolphins named Bimini and Stripe.

The circled divers are tourists who have paid dearly—about $100—to spend half an hour in the dolphins' element. The two divers with the dead fish are Patrick Berry and Eden Butler, trainers who work with a company called the Dolphin Experience, which keeps 13 animals in a nine-acre lagoon outside Freeport. Berry and Butler have spent years getting the dolphins to interact with customers on command. Berry points to a diver, who puts out his palm, and Bimini swims to it, curving his path so the diver can touch his rubbery skin. The dolphins snatch rings and spin divers like turnstiles by pushing against their outstretched arms. The favorite is the kiss: a diver takes the regulator out of his mouth and the dolphin puts its beak-shaped mouth to the human's lips.

It is easy to forget that the dolphins also need an air supply; but every few minutes they casually stop what they're doing, make a few quick upward kicks, and ascend to the surface. Each time they do, they make clear that the real performance lies not in a dolphin's stunts but in its astonishing grace. When dolphins swim, they don't look like they're doing anything. Berry twists his hand and Stripe twists his whole body with as much effort as a

Whales, porpoises, and dolphins belong to a family of mammals known as cetaceans.

thought. Sometimes on their ascent the dolphins disappear beyond the water's ceiling, leaping into the air and then plunging down again. With a corkscrewing flourish, they come to a stop upside down in front of Berry or Butler, hoping for fish.

At 230 feet, the pressure of the surrounding water becomes so great that a dolphin's lungs collapse. The animal is squeezed into a smaller, denser shape and drops through the ocean like a rock. ▼

For the tourists this half hour is paradise. For Noren it is hell. Noren, a graduate student in marine biology at the University of California at Santa Cruz, is the one person in this group for whom the dolphins' stunts are peripheral. She is here to take measurements of dolphin physiology, and neither the animals nor her equipment is being particularly cooperative. Kneeling on the sand, she slams her plastic box around in underwater slow motion. The machine inside the box is supposed to register the flow of heat coming off the warm-blooded dolphins. She needs to get her probe, a flat plastic disk on the end of a spring, onto the dorsal fin and tail of the dolphins for about a minute at a time. At best, she can hope for a mere handful of readings on each dive—the trainers help her only when there's a break in the paying action. "I can't say, 'This is what I want, and I want it now,'" she says. "Taking notes is the only thing I can control."

To measure the heat of a dolphin, either Berry or Butler must first hold out a hand. The dolphin places the tip of its mouth in the cupped palm and holds itself still. Then the trainer works his way down to the dorsal fin and holds out his free hand like a surgeon waiting for a scalpel. Noren hands him the probe, then settles back down to watch her meter. If all goes well, the dolphin holds still until the reading is done.

This time all does not go well. A bad wire in the probe is screwing up the readings, and soap opera squabbles among the dolphins back at the Experience headquarters have left Bimini and Stripe cranky and skittish. When Berry cups his palm, Bimini pulls away. He is willing instead to deliver the ring to a few divers. After a moment, Berry tries to use the probe again, and for a few seconds Bimini goes along. But then he decides he's had enough and snaps away. The summer is headed for hurricane season and Noren needs data badly, but today, as the tourists bring home stories and videotapes, all she brings home is a blank slate.

This is how science typically goes for those who study how cetaceans—whales, porpoises, and dolphins—do what they do. Despite our long familiarity with these creatures and our common mammalian heritage, we really know little about them. We barely even understand how they move through the watery environment they returned to some 50 million years ago. The tools we use for understanding the movement of land animals—the treadmills, the sealed atmospheric chambers, the high-speed videos—are hard or impossible to use on an animal that breathes by surfacing every few minutes to blast open its blowhole, then disappears underwater.

Few people know this better than Noren's adviser, physiologist Terrie Williams. Williams has been trying to get a handle on her slippery subjects since 1990, when the U.S. Navy first offered her an opportunity to study the physiology of free-swimming dolphins. The Navy's interest traces back to a decades-old belief that there is something almost magical in a dolphin's swimming abilities—something in its design that, by greatly reducing drag, allows the animals to achieve a speed and maneuverability that physics says should be impossible. Around the beginning of the cold war, both the American and Soviet navies imagined that by divining dolphin secrets, they would be able to design submarines that could slip through the water with unheard-of efficiency and silence. Guesses as to what the key dolphin secret was were plentiful. Perhaps, some suggested, the heat coming from a warm-blooded animal made the surrounding water less viscous. Or maybe a dolphin's skin had ridges that could channel the water down its flanks. The U.S. Navy even invented rubberized paints on the suspicion that a dolphin's rubbery skin could damp out tiny waves that ultimately create drag.

By the time Williams came along, it was clear that none of these hypotheses would lead to a stealth submarine. Still, the Navy thought dolphins might prove useful if they could at least be trained to patrol underwater installations and hunt for mines. "The Navy wanted to know, are the things we're asking the dolphins to do easy

Despite our long familiarity with these creatures and our common mammalian heritage, we really know little about them. We barely even understand how they move through the watery environment they returned to some 50 million years ago.

Dolphins are wrapped in a sheath of connective tissue, which along with their blubber, may add spring to their swimming strokes.

or hard?" says Williams. "If we ask a dolphin to dive 200 meters, is that a tough thing for it to do?"

Williams and her Navy co-workers tried to figure out a way to measure a dolphin's oxygen consumption while it swam alongside a motorboat. "To have a metabolic unit out there was just too difficult," she says. "You'd have to have a big hood in the water and an oxygen analyzer and pumps with a ton of gear—about $50,000 dollars worth of stuff you don't want to sink on a boat. And if the wind came up with diesel, it would throw everything off. So we tried having them breathe into a metabolic balloon. These things look like potato chip bags. The dolphins would come up, and we'd put this little cone down and they'd exhale into it, and then we could take it back to the lab and analyze it. But I didn't like that because the dolphins thought they had to exhale as forcefully as they could, and because they'd also take in a big breath, you'd get the oxygen consumption looking abnormally high."

What finally worked, Williams discovered, was measurement by proxy. On the wall of a pool she set up a force-sensitive disk and had trained dolphins swim against it. Then, with a hood set on the water, she measured how much oxygen they breathed. At the same time, she measured their heart rate with a suction-cup electrocardiogram. She found that as a dolphin burned more oxygen, its heart rate always increased in a beautifully linear way. And since she could attach suction cups to dolphins and measure heart rate in open water, she could then calculate how much oxygen they were burning while swimming.

Williams used this data to calculate the dolphins' "cost of transport." Technically, this is milliliters of oxygen consumed per kilogram of body weight per kilometer, but essentially what it tells you is how much energy it takes to move a given weight of animal a given distance. Williams soon discovered that a dolphin's cost of transport is the lowest ever measured for a swimming mammal, and only two or three times as high as that of a like-size fish. Seals have a cost four times as high as fish. Yet when she compared a swimming dolphin with a running terrestrial mammal—comparing the animals as they move in their own elements—she found that it was about as impressively efficient as a zebu (an African ox). "There was nothing I saw that made them look amazing," she says.

Dolphins harbor no great physiological secret, Williams has concluded, beyond a fine adjustment to a life at sea. And that adjustment consists of a host of tricks and shortcuts. Dolphins are famous, for example, for surfing on the bow waves of ships, sometimes just below the surface, or bouncing along on a wave's crest. Though they may seem to be doing it for fun, Williams has shown that the practice is cost-cutting good sense: a dolphin surfing at eight miles an hour has about the same cost of transport as it does swimming at four miles an hour. Most likely dolphins had been grabbing cheap rides long before the first boat cut a wake. "If it's a wave off a whale, if it's wind waves—if a dolphin has any opportunity to snag a ride, it'll do so," says Williams.

Dolphins cheat underwater as well, Williams subsequently discovered. Before they take a plunge, they gulp a few breaths of air and swiftly pull the oxygen into hemoglobin in their blood and then into a muscular equivalent called myoglobin. To conserve the oxygen, researchers have long assumed, the animals cut off circulation to their skin and their extremities, leaving only vital organs and tail muscles working. Obviously, on long dives—which can easily last several minutes at depths of up to 600 feet—these physiological responses are crucial. Yet when Williams plugged in her numbers for oxygen consumption, she found that even with such cost-saving measures, and despite blatant evidence to the contrary, it was simply physiologically impossible for dolphins to do what they do. "I had all my predictions ready, telling me this is how much oxygen the animal will consume on a dive," she

The largest muscle on a dolphin is the longissimus — it looks like a fat snake. On a blue whale, the longissimus stretches 80 feet, the longest muscle on Earth.

says. "Boy, I had it wrong." By her calculations, a dolphin should run out of oxygen and drown in mid-ascent.

Her mistake was made clear when Texas A&M biologist Randall Davis presented her with a camera that a diving dolphin could carry on its back. The instrument consists of a velocity meter, a depth gauge, a light, and a video camera, all strapped to a dolphin and pointed at the animal's tail. She sent dolphins on deep dives and reviewed the tapes they brought back. Each recording was the same. As the depth gauge readout appears in one corner of the screen, the dolphin's tail moves up and down. Before long the water grows dark, the tail illuminated only by the camera. "You're watching the depth gauge, and it hits the 70-meter [230-foot] mark, and the tail just stops. You think the film has stopped, but when you look at the depth gauge, it's just rolling and rolling—100 meters, 150 meters, 200 meters, and nothing has moved in the picture."

Williams had assumed that dolphins dive by swimming, but actually, she found, they fall. At the 70-meter mark the pressure of the surrounding water becomes so great that their lungs collapse. Williams thinks that by squeezing the animal into a smaller, denser shape, the pressure makes the dolphin less buoyant and allows it to drop through the ocean like a rock. Since it doesn't need to move a muscle, it doesn't need to burn any oxygen and can thus slip out of Williams's limiting calculations. At the bottom of a deep dive, a dolphin's heart races for a few seconds as it starts kicking into an ascent. When it comes back up to a depth of 70 meters, its lungs open, its body becomes buoyant, and it glides the last leg to the surface.

But even as this revelation resolved one paradox, Williams realized, it created another. A dolphin is wrapped in a thick, insulating layer of blubber to preserve heat. However, in some cases it can provide too much insulation and make the animal overheat. Thus, for cooling purposes, a dolphin also has blood vessels that poke out of the blubber and run under the surface of its dorsal fin and tail flukes; from there heat is easily transferred to the ocean. We have a similar set of vessels in our arms and legs. When we're warm, blood is shunted to these surface vessels, which give off their heat to the air and return the cooled blood to our body core; if we're cold, these vessels are shut off. The surface vessels of dolphins

The U.S. Navy even invented rubberized paints on the suspicion that a dolphin's rubbery skin could damp out tiny waves that ultimately create drag.

are thought to work the same way. But if to conserve oxygen dolphins pinch off blood flow to their fin and tail flukes, then their need to stay cool, Williams realized, collides head-on with their need to avoid suffocation.

Williams attempted to resolve this conflict on her first trip to the Dolphin Experience in 1995. Although Patrick Berry had prepared the dolphins for her experiments, it was not a promising visit. "We had a bad hurricane season and we couldn't go out in deep water," she recalls. "It was just horrible."

She thought she could salvage her trip by taking some measurements in shallow water. After all, a dolphin has to hold its breath whether it's 15 feet underwater or 50 feet. "So we took the dolphins to a shallow area, and we were taking all our little measurements. Patrick was holding the probe on one dolphin's tail. You're underwater, and as you're working the box, you basically have to stare at the meter till it stabilizes and you can tell Patrick to stop." As she watched the meter, it stabilized at 60 watts per square meter. Then without warning it suddenly lurched up to 120 watts for a few seconds, then fell back down again.

Williams signaled to Berry to head up to the surface. "I said, 'End of dive! The thing's busted—water got into it, I don't know how, but it's a total washout.' We packed everything up and brought the animals back to the pen." On land she tested her meter to find the trouble, but instead she found it was working perfectly.

Berry could see that she was at a loss. "Patrick said, 'Didn't you see what the animal did?' I said, 'No, I was watching the stupid meter.' Well, Patrick was standing in only 15 feet of water holding the tail, and the animal is 9 feet long, and so it came up and took a breath."

Williams knew that when dolphins hit the surface, they get a lot done fast. They exhale and inhale quickly, during which time they clear out carbon dioxide, rebalance their body's pH, and load oxygen into their blood and muscles. Dolphins spend as little time as possible on the surface, because there they have to battle surface waves and waste strokes that push air instead of water— altogether making their swimming inefficient. Perhaps, she began to wonder, they also take these brief opportunities to suddenly open up the blood gates, fill up the surface vessels in their fin and flukes, and in a torrent let loose all the heat they had built up on their dive. If that

The real performance lies not in a dolphin's stunts but in its astonishing grace.

There is something almost magical in a dolphin's swimming abilities—something in its design that, by greatly reducing drag, allows the animals to achieve a speed and maneuverability that physics says should be impossible.

were the case, dolphins would be the camels of the sea. Camels don't try to cool themselves by sweating, because they can't afford to use so much water in the desert. Instead they store heat during the day and unload it in the cool of the night. If Williams was right, dolphins would have taken this strategy to its extreme, unloading heat in a matter of seconds. "I think that's what happened. It was a onetime observation, but I think it might be real."

When dolphins hit the surface, they get a lot done fast: they exhale and inhale quickly, during which time they clear out carbon dioxide, rebalance their body's pH, and load oxygen into their blood and muscles. ▼

That's one of the things Dawn Noren tried to test last summer. Whenever Berry had time, they would take a dolphin out on a shallow dive and try to reenact the events that had triggered Williams's weird spike. Barracudas, bad weather, and the fussiness of dolphins slowed her research, but one afternoon near the end of the summer a female named Cayla let her take half a dozen measurements in a row. And every time, the heat flow more than doubled when Cayla took a breath.

Apparently then, Williams was right, and the dolphin's remarkable physiology had devised an elegant solution to the conflicting problems of oxygen conservation and heat buildup. The only puzzle is that the dolphin's equally remarkable anatomy seems to argue that such a solution is, to say the least, problematic.

In a lab at the University of North Carolina at Wilmington, Ann Pabst and Bill McLellan stand by a steel table, edged with troughs, a bucket hanging at one end. Pabst snaps on powdered surgical gloves and McLellan sharpens a dissection knife with flicks along a steel rod by the table, on which lies the corpse of a little bottle-nosed dolphin, its eyes half shut, still smiling as it starts to thaw.

Six weeks earlier this baby dolphin's corpse washed ashore at Virginia Beach. A crew from the Virginia Marine Science Museum Stranding Project arrived quickly with a truck and drove it to their facility, where it was frozen and sent on to the North Carolina lab.

By rights, Pabst and McLellan ought to be a pretty grim couple. They take apart a dead dolphin almost every week, and a fair number of whales each year. Yet they have a sparky rapport as they do their work. They talk easily about dissection workshops the stranding network has, about their first dates on beaches up and down the mid-Atlantic, slitting open bottle-nosed dolphins, spotted dolphins, beaked whales, pilot whales, and sperm and baleen whales.

"This is a really cool little animal," Pabst says, rolling it onto its side.

"What do you want to do?" McLellan asks her. "You want to do just the standard?"

"Yeah, and we'll weigh it up. And get samples of blubber and liver."

McLellan executes quick long cuts down the length of the dolphin's back, the scalpel making a faint creasing sound as it goes. With tiny nicks so fast that they sound like the whir of a cicada, he detaches long flaps of skin and blubber from connective tissue. The flesh below is pink, except for a gooey patch of red near the head, the remnant of a remarkable piece of cetacean anatomy. When a diving dolphin hits the lung-collapse depth, its rib cage collapses also. If it had the normal mammalian carotid artery running to its brain, the blood squirting out of its squeezed heart would rush through the vessel with so much pressure that it would literally blow the dolphin's brains out. Instead the blood flows from the aorta into a mesh of capillaries called a rete mirabile—Latin for "miraculous net." The effect is like water from a faucet pouring into a sponge; as the blood surges into the fine vessels, it slows down. Only then does it gently flow into an artery that dives into the spinal canal and up to the brain.

The hemorrhaging in the neck is so bad that McLellan is pretty sure he knows how this baby died. "We know there was some sort of blunt trauma, but we don't see any fishing net marks on the head, which is a good indication that this was natural. But it could have taken a hit from somebody." By now the table is slippery, so McLellan has to pull the dolphin back toward him by the flipper. He slices off the dorsal fin and amputates the flippers at the shoulder. Soon the face is a gray mask on a barrel of meat.

A dolphin's cost of transport is the lowest ever measured for a swimming mammal, and only two or three times as high as that of a like-size fish. Seals have a cost four times as high as fish.

Skinned, even this baby dolphin flaunts the architecture of power carried by cetaceans 30 times its size. The muscles attached to the front and back of the spine — used by land mammals like ourselves simply to hold our body up — are the crankshafts of the body's motor. Cables of muscle run from the neck to the base of the tail; when McLellan cuts loose the biggest muscle, the longissimus, it looks like a fat snake. On a blue whale, the longissimus stretches 80 feet, the longest muscle on Earth.

Although the dolphin's gut is still frozen, rude gases escape as McLellan takes apart the viscera. Pabst weighs the esophagus, intestines, stomach, and liver. The uterus is a drab purple swath of flesh. McLellan pores over it, pointing out details to a grad student holding a video camera. McLellan and Pabst are particularly interested in dolphin wombs these days; they have discovered to their surprise that when a dolphin swims, even this organ at the core of the animal's anatomy is affected.

Their interest in wombs was actually triggered not by dissections of female dolphins but of males. "We were taking apart male animals bit by bit," says Pabst. "At the end of each dissection, we would have the testes, and there would be two kilograms of stuff around it. We thought, two kilograms of anything in a hundred-kilogram animal is significant. It was vasculature." More than that, it was a particular kind of vasculature: fine veins ran closely alongside arteries branching off the aorta. As they dissected more males, Pabst and McLellan pumped milk or latex into the veins around the testes to trace their path, and the white trail led to the dorsal fin and the tail flukes — the areas where dolphins cool their blood.

Suddenly something very obvious — and totally uncontemplated in decades of dolphin research — occurred to them: swimming should make a male dolphin sterile. Sperm can grow and survive only at temperatures a few degrees below that of a mammal's body, and so most males keep their testes in a sac that hangs away from the body. For a swimming mammal, though, this clever arrangement would be a disaster. The last thing you'd want to put on a streamlined, hydrodynamic body is a dangling bag. Instead dolphins lodge their blimp-shaped testes snugly in their bodies. Now they can swim quickly, but it would seem they couldn't have children. The testes sit between massive muscles that work continuously as

Basically, a dolphin is a pressurized cylinder wrapped with crisscrossing sets of helically wound fibers. This kind of structure has some valuable properties for an animal. Like a garden hose, such a cylinder won't kink when it bends and the angle of the fibers lets it resist twisting. Squid, earthworms, and sharks are only three of the many animals that wrap their bodies in helically wound fibers.

the dolphins swim, and are nourished by vessels coming off the nearby aorta, full of hot blood. Arranging things this way makes as much sense as putting a tub of ice cream on an engine block.

There was a way, Pabst and McLellan realized, that a dolphin could escape this dilemma. When blood is cooled on the surface of a dolphin's tail and dorsal fin, it doesn't simply cool the core of the body in general. Instead it heads to the region around the testes. There the veins split up into finer vessels that run side by side along the hot arteries. The arrangement functions as a counter-current heat exchanger, warming blood in the veins and cooling blood in the arteries. Thus the blood that bathes the testes should, in theory, be cool enough to save the dolphin's sperm.

Sentiel Rommel of the Marine Mammal Pathobiology Laboratory in St. Petersburg, Florida, came up with a way for Pabst and McLellan to test the idea. They built a 16-inch probe to be inserted into a willing dolphin's colon; once in place it would give them temperature readings along its length. Rommel, Pabst, and McLellan then went to Hawaii and joined Terrie Williams at the Navy's lab. There three very amiable male dolphins were trained to have their temperatures taken. The region around the dolphins' testes turned out to be 1.3 degrees cooler than the surrounding body. Moreover, the refrigerator was so powerful that when the dolphins took long, fast swims — heating their bodies even more — the testicular temperature actually dropped half a degree more.

Soon afterward Pabst and McLellan realized that female dolphins had an even more desperate need than males did for a cool core. "The fetus is a little furnace," explains Pabst; its metabolic rate is one and a half or two times higher than the mother's. "That heat has to be removed or it can cause damage — anything from fetal distress to terrible developmental disorders to death. In terrestrial mammals, 85 percent is conducted away through blood flow. Fifteen percent is conducted across the abdominal wall into the environment. You know that when you touch a pregnant lady's belly and it's hot."

A female dolphin, on the other hand, doesn't have that window. The dolphin uterus is in the same part of the body as the testes, which means that between the fetus and the ocean is a hard-working, heat-producing layer of

The dorsal fin and tail flukes are the areas where dolphins cool their blood.

abdominal muscle, and beyond that a layer of insulating blubber. "It seems like a dangerous place to have a kid," says Pabst.

Female dolphins, Pabst and McLellan have now shown, use the same anatomical trick that males do. McLellan pokes at the baby dolphin's uterus to show the dark web of veins that cover the uterus. Cooled blood flows directly to the womb from the tail and fin.

Last summer, Pabst and McLellan began taking measurements of wild dolphins off the coast of North Carolina. Pabst would sit at a computer on board the boat while McLellan handled the animals, shouting to Pabst when the thermometer was in position. One of their subjects was a pregnant female in her first trimester, and she turned out to have the coldest temperature they had ever measured inside a dolphin. "I couldn't believe it," says Pabst. "All I kept doing was shouting to him, 'Is it on? Is it turned on?'"

How can their results be reconciled with those of Williams? How can a dolphin both refrigerate its uterus and yet release its body heat only when it surfaces for a breath? Pabst hopes to pursue this question soon by studying blood flow in female dolphins immediately after a long dive. But she suspects that the cooling flow may not be regulated by a simple on-off switch—it may be a graded response, diverting blood to the uterus (or testes) as needed, throughout a dive.

For years Pabst and McLellan cut right past some of a dolphin's most well-kept secrets. "I would be doing dissections and peeling off the blubber and saying, 'What is this thing underneath the blubber layer?'" says Pabst. To get the blubber off, she had to slice through a sheath of connective tissue. Anatomists knew that it had evolved from a sheet of gristle that covers the lower back of mammals (we have it as well), but no one had given it much more thought than that. To Pabst, though, the beauty of the densely woven mesh of crisscrossing fibers suggested that it must have importance beyond a glue for blubber.

She ended up spending five years mapping the sheath's marvelous complexity. From the back of the dolphin's head to the base of its tail, the subdermal sheath wraps completely around the muscles. It doesn't simply encase them; the muscles attach some of their tendons to it just as they would normally attach to bone. It took Pabst a while to figure out what all the connections were for,

A dolphin is wrapped in a thick, insulating layer of blubber to preserve heat. However, in some cases it can provide too much insulation and make the animal overheat. Thus, for cooling purposes, a dolphin also has blood vessels that poke out of the blubber and run under the surface of its dorsal fin and tail flukes; from there heat is easily transferred to the ocean.

scribbling diagrams and tugging on the tail of a dolphin skeleton with dozens of strings. She finally concluded that when dolphins swim, they first contract a set of muscles that tighten the sheath until it's stiff. Then another set of muscles use the stiffened sheath as a skeletal anchor, almost like a second spine; other muscles use it as a tendon to transmit their forces down the length of the animal's body.

The sheath was obviously mechanically important, but Pabst wondered if it had another, more subtle function. Basically, a dolphin is a pressurized cylinder wrapped with crisscrossing sets of helically wound fibers. This kind of structure has some valuable properties for an animal. Like a garden hose, such a cylinder won't kink when it bends and the angle of the fibers lets it resist twisting. Squid, earthworms, and sharks are only three of the many animals that wrap their bodies in helically wound fibers.

Tangential section of dolphin fat.

Chalk-and-blackboard models of these objects suggest that, for a given length of fiber, the angle of the fibers can change the properties of the cylinder. To enclose the maximum volume, for example, sets of fibers should be fixed at a 55 degree angle relative to the long axis of the cylinder—any smaller than that and the cylinder will be too narrow; any bigger and it will be too squat. And at angles above 60 degrees—depending on the materials that a cylinder is made of—it becomes so springy that it bounces back when bent. In other words, the energy that goes into the bending is stored in the fibers and then released again.

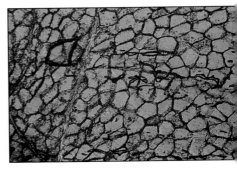

Cow fat.

Thus Pabst listened very closely when Terrie Williams told her about strange results that had come out of her work. In her lab she had studied dolphins swimming against a force sensor, pushing as hard as they could. As the force they delivered increased, so did their consumption of oxygen, which is normal for any animal. When they got up to a load of about 85 kilograms (187 pounds), their oxygen consumption leveled off, which again is perfectly unamazing—animals have limits to their aerobic metabolism, and to generate any more force, they have to resort to metabolic chains of chemical reactions that don't use oxygen—that is, anaerobic metabolism. For humans, as with most other animals, this anaerobic energy is short-lived because it generates lactic acid as waste, which builds up in the muscles. But Williams found that her dolphins could keep pushing against the sensor — up to nearly 200 kilograms in the case of one dolphin. After these exercises, trainers would instruct the dolphins to turn upside down and present their tail so that a blood sample could be taken. Even at 200 kilograms, Williams found, they had paltry levels of lactic acid in their blood.

That, Pabst knew, puts dolphins in the company of some highly efficient land animals, the prime example of which is the kangaroo. Kangaroos, once they reach their aerobic capacity, can still double their hopping speed without burning any additional fuel in their muscles, and they do so by letting the springlike tendons in their legs take over. With each jump, they stretch the stiff strands of collagen and store much of the energy of their fall; when they spring out for the next hop, the tendons return 93 percent of the energy put into them. Williams's dolphins were showing signs of doing the same thing in water. Perhaps at a certain frequency the upstroke of a dolphin's tail would load energy into the subdermal sheath, which would then spring back, helping push the tail through its downstroke. At the right frequency, the dolphins would resonate as they swam, ringing like bells. If they did, their impressive swimming with the physiology of an ox would make more sense.

Pabst knew that a number of researchers had speculated that dolphins might swim with springs, but their findings have been ambiguous. Part of the trouble is that dolphins are not the simple cylinders that theoretical biologists use as models; their tails narrow and flatten, and the sheath does confusing things like anchor to the spine. Still, Pabst was tantalized by the finding that the angle of the fibers around the chest (where the dolphin's body is rigid and large) was a volume-filling 55 degrees, while closer to the tail (where a spring would be useful) the angle went over 60 degrees.

The most direct way to test this idea, of course, is to measure the resilience of the sheath. Pabst tried clamping pieces of it into a machine that carefully stretched material, but it was a bust. "I grab onto it and I pull on it, and because I'm not pulling on every fiber, I'm reorienting them because of the looseness of the weave, and I create a new material." There was no way to know if the properties she registered in her machine were the same in a dolphin.

Most people think of blubber as plain fat, but it is blubber alone that creates a cetacean's slippery shape.

As she was testing the sheath, however, Pabst began to think a lot about blubber. Most people think of blubber as plain fat, but it is blubber alone that creates a cetacean's slippery shape. She decided to compare blubber with normal fat under a microscope. Under polarized light, the fat of a cow is an expanse of purple blobs. When Pabst put blubber under the scope, she saw the same purple blobs, but woven into them were gorgeous blue and gold stripes of connective tissue. "It was like the most beautiful Japanese tapestry I've ever seen," says Pabst.

She realized that she had found a second cross-woven material encasing a dolphin. And when she had a student of hers measure the angles of the fibers in the blubber along the length of a dolphin's body, he found that the angles were identical to those of the sheath fibers. Like the sheath, the blubber is stiff around the ribs but stretchy closer to the tail.

Now Pabst could ask the same questions of blubber that she could of the sheath: Is it a good spring? And since blubber, unlike the sheath, holds its shape when clamped and stretched, she could finally get some hard numbers on resilience. "Resilience is just a measure of the amount of energy you get out of a system relative to the amount you put in," says Pabst. "Collagen is the best spring—it's got a value of 93 percent. So 93 percent of the energy you put in, you get back. Spider silk is a good shock absorber because you don't want your fly ricocheting out of the web. And 35 percent is its value. Blubber has a value of 87 percent. So, despite the fact that it's fat, it's a fine spring."

Whether an entire dolphin acts like a spring is another matter, one that Pabst will have to consider by working on living dolphins rather than a patch of blubber. With Williams and other dolphin experts, she is now studying how blubber stretches in relation to the kicks of a dolphin's tail. They may have a few ideas of how dolphins swim, but they're trying to be careful not to assume too much. Better to let the dolphins guide them to the truth.

"That's been the fun part," says Williams, "looking for the tricks. They use so many of them. You go in thinking you know so much about them, and then they say, 'No, no, no, we'll let you know what's really going on.'"

Horses, Mollusks and the Evolution of Bigness

All evolutionary roads may not lead to increased size.

JOHN NOBLE WILFORD

Paleontologists in the 19th century kept digging up fossils of early horses no bigger than a diminutive mouse deer. Over the expanse of evolutionary time, they came to see, the horse lineage showed tendencies to increase in body size, leading to the sole surviving genus Equus, which includes such imposing animals as Kentucky thoroughbreds and Clydesdales capable of pulling wagons heavy with beer barrels.

Other discoveries seemed to confirm a trend toward bigness. Many of the giant dinosaurs were coming to light at this same time. Even the tiny Foraminifera, single-cell plankton so common in the marine fossil record, appeared to follow a pattern of lineages starting with small founding members and then evolving larger body sizes.

With such observations in mind, the American paleontologist Edward Drinker Cope formulated in 1871 a "law" of biology: the body size of organisms in a particular evolutionary lineage, whether horses or mollusks or plankton, tends to increase over the long run. This principle, known as Cope's rule, ascended to conventional wisdom in biology. It is cited in textbooks to this day.

For all these years, however, scientists had never bothered to put Cope's rule to a rigorous test. A few apparent exceptions had been exposed, and over the last decade, some prominent scientists questioned the rule's general validity. Now a University of Chicago paleontologist has marshaled the most comprehensive evidence yet to challenge Cope's rule.

Completing a comprehensive study of mollusks over a 16-million-year period, Dr. David Jablonski concluded that there is no more tendency for organisms to become bigger as they evolve than there is for them to become smaller. Even in the lineages showing size increase for

American paleontologist Edward Drinker Cope formulated in 1871 a "law" of biology: the body size of organisms in a particular evolutionary lineage, whether horses or mollusks or plankton, tends to increase over the long run. This principle, known as Cope's rule, ascended to conventional wisdom in biology. It is cited in textbooks to this day.

the largest species, he noted, the smallest species often decrease in size over the same interval. The result is an expansion of the overall range of variation, both large and small, and not, as Cope had surmised, a directed trend toward increasing general size.

The study is based on an analysis of fossil clams, snails, whelks, scallops and other mollusks that lived on the coastal plain from New Jersey to Texas in the last 16 million years of the Cretaceous geological period, which ended with the mass extinction 65 million years ago that killed off the dinosaurs. Dr. Jablonski spent the last decade, with a caliper always at the ready, examining museum fossil collections of 191 evolutionary lineages, including precise measurements of over 1,000 species.

Equus przewalskii.

"This is the first time anyone has taken a quantitative look at a large enough data base to really draw a general conclusion," Dr. Jablonski said.

Dr. Douglas Erwin, a paleontologist at the Smithsonian Institution in Washington, praised the care and methods of Dr. Jablonski's study, saying it "set the standard" for future research into broad trends of evolutionary biology. He suggested that there were probably "many other trends that paleontologists think they see in life, think are true, but often don't have rigorous tests to prove them."

Dr. Daniel McShea, a Duke University paleontologist, said that similar studies should be conducted on a wider variety of life in different time intervals. "That would really test Cope's rule," he said. But he agreed that the new findings showed that the rule is by no means an invariable law of nature.

The results of Dr. Jablonski's research were published in the current issue of the journal Nature. In an accompanying article, Dr. Stephen Jay Gould, a paleontologist at Harvard University, wrote that the findings provide "no support for Cope's rule as a preferential bias in the evolution of size."

Indeed, Dr. Gould and other scientists said the research revealed that evolutionary biologists had long allowed themselves to be deluded by a general bias in the way they often viewed nature. Like most people, they have been unduly impressed by bigness.

"Might not our conviction about the validity of Cope's rule," Dr. Gould asked, "be a psychological artifact of singling out lineages that display size increase because we all know that 'bigger is better'?"

Dr. Gould in 1988 first spoke of the need for reconsidering Cope's rule and in his latest book, "Full House," published last year by Harmony Books, elaborated on weaknesses in some of the rule's supporting evidence. And in the Nature article, he wrote that the new findings also called attention to "another pervasive and lamentable bias of human reasoning: our tendency to focus on extremes that intrigue us, rather than full ranges of variation."

Such has been the case in studies of the horse. The horse is often cited as the classic example of Cope's rule. But in fact, Dr. Jablonski pointed out, horses show a broad range of sizes through most of their evolutionary history — until the end, when all became extinct except for one of the larger lineages.

"The last survivor just happened to be a large one," he said. "If you connect the small starting point with the big final survivor, you seem to get a straight line of size increase, but the real pattern is much more complicated."

No doubt Cope was impressed by bigness because he was a vertebrate paleontologist working at the time that Diplodocus, Stegosaurus and other huge dinosaurs were being excavated in the American West. A wealthy Philadelphian, Cope financed his own fossil-hunting

An undated picture of the skeleton of a horse discovered in an archeological site in Sinai is the first ever physical evidence of a horse in Egypt, dating from the Hyksos invasion of Pharaonic Egypt around 1700 B.C. The discovery suggests that the Hyksos, invaders from Asia, brought the first horses to ancient Egypt.

expeditions, usually in bitter competition with Othniel C. Marsh of Yale University, and was an impetuous genius who never shied from speculation.

When in 1987 he decided to test Cope's rule, Dr. Jablonski concentrated on mollusks, the group of marine organisms he had already been studying. Rich collections of mollusk fossils were available, especially at the American Museum of Natural History in New York City, the Smithsonian's National Museum of Natural History in Washington, and the United States Geological Survey in Reston, Va.

He further chose to examine late Cretaceous specimens because the mass extinction at the end of that period served as a sharp cutoff of normal evolutionary processes. At least half of the mollusk species became extinct then, though many of the clams and snails of that period have relatives living today. For his measurements, he examined adult sizes of each genus at the beginning and end of the study interval.

Left to right: fossil Xiphactinus and Gastropods.

Analyzing the data, Dr. Jablonski found that 27 percent to 30 percent of the lineages showed a net increase in body size over the 16-million-year period. But just as many lineages displayed an overall body size decrease, while 2.8 percent showed an increase at both ends of the size scale. Only a few lineages showed a decrease in the total range of body sizes. A directional net increase in body size is thus no more frequent than an increase in the range of sizes among species, or even a net evolutionary size decrease.

In short, he said, the results are "very much in opposition to the classical Cope's rule."

What are the implications for evolutionary biology? "We will have to be more skeptical about assertions that natural selection favors this or that body size," said Dr. McShea of Duke.

Under the influence of Cope's rule, many scientists have assumed that large body size somehow bestowed critical evolutionary advantages: the attraction of mates, self-defense, resistance to temperature extremes and mobility over a greater foraging and hunting range. Consequently, larger organisms would have a better chance of passing on their genes, which would eventually translate into a pattern of ever-increasing body sizes within a lineage.

But in at least one fateful case, it may have paid to be small. Early mammals, many of them no bigger than shrews, managed to survive the Cretaceous mass extinction. Among the advantages often ascribed to small-body organisms is rapid reproduction and the ability to hunker down to avoid predation or survive environmental change. While big dinosaurs were dying, many small mammals hung on to evolve into scientists who would contemplate the merits of being small or big.

"My data show that although body size may be tremendously important in an ecological sense," Dr. Jablonski said, "there is no simple extrapolation to size being important in a long-term, large-scale evolutionary sense."

Among the advantages often ascribed to small-body organisms is rapid reproduction and the ability to hunker down to avoid predation or survive environmental change.

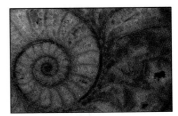

Fossil mollusk.

Snow Geese Survive All Too Well, Alarming Conservationists

JANE E. BRODY

The striking sight of thousands of snow geese flying north in waving skeins across the spring sky is an annual thrill for midcontinent birders, and it should be, too, for environmentalists, who fret constantly about threats to waterfowl survival.

Instead, the ever-growing flocks of snow geese inspire deep conservation concerns, fears that after the voracious feeders reach their summer subarctic and arctic breeding grounds, thousands of square miles of delicate tundra will be destroyed, perhaps never to come back.

Thanks to an eclectic appetite and a brain that seems more flexible if not larger than might be expected, the snow goose has been so successful at adapting to human destruction of its southern winter home that the bird now threatens its summer home.

The goose population is now nearly three times as abundant as it was when first studied decades ago, and it is still growing. A colony that breeds at La Pérouse Bay near Cape Churchill, Manitoba, and winters from the Gulf Coast to Kansas, had 2,000 nesting pairs in 1968. By 1990 it had grown to 22,500 pairs, an average annual increase of nearly 8 percent.

A team of prominent conservationists has proposed to halve the population by 2005, largely by reducing restraints on hunting throughout North America and by allowing the Inuits of Canada to gather their fill of goose eggs.

For the sake of the entire ecosystem—the delicate arctic vegetation and the other birds and vertebrates it supports—the conservationists say they have no choice but to reduce the number of geese that are fast tearing up the tundra. And the sooner the better.

Researchers estimate that more than three million geese, up from one million in the late 60s, spend the win-

Opposite page: Once endangered, snow geese like this flock have adapted so well to encroachment on their wintering grounds that their proliferation threatens the tundra of their summer home.

ter in the central states, and return each summer to the shores of Hudson Bay and Foxe Basin to breed.

But what seems to be a runaway success in conservation in the United States is fast turning into an environmental disaster where the birds nest in Canada. It is a disaster that could ultimately lead to the loss of other species, as well as the demise of countless geese and goslings. "This is a very unusual problem, an overabundance of birds," said Dr. Bruce Batt, chief biologist for Ducks Unlimited, the largest waterfowl conservation organization in the world. "Our profession is not used to this kind of problem with migratory birds."

Dr. Batt is chairman of the international Arctic Goose Habitat Working Group, which studied the problem and has come up with some solutions that it believes fit with conservation goals. The group is to present its findings next week at meetings of the Texas Parks and Wildlife Department near Houston.

Satellite photos taken in Canada over the years and analyzed by Andrew Jano, a specialist in remote sensing at the Ontario Ministry of Natural Resources, "helped us see the big picture, and it wasn't pretty," said Dr. Robert F. Rockwell, a professor of biology at the City University of New York and a research ornithologist at the American Museum of Natural History. "The photos show spreading rings of destruction by the geese. In the areas where the geese summer, 35 percent of the habitat is overgrazed, 30 percent is damaged, and 30 percent is destroyed."

Because of the short cold growing season in the arctic and subarctic, Dr. Rockwell said, it would take two or three decades for damaged habitat to come back. And because of sharp increases in the salinity of the soil, destroyed habitats may never come back, Dr. Batt said.

As a result of runaway consumption, known in conservation circles as a "trophic cascade," Dr. Rockwell said, "the geese are turning the tundra into a spreading slum." As they denude one area of edible vegetation, they simply move on to a place where the pickings are better.

"These are very opportunistic birds," said Dr. Robert L. Jefferies, a botanist at the University of Toronto who studies the interaction of the geese and vegetation. "We've marked young goslings before they could fly and found that they would walk up to 60 kilometers from their hatch site to exploit a new feeding area." (Sixty kilometers is about 37 miles.)

In conservation circles, runaway consumption is known as "trophic cascade."

Dr. Rockwell, co-author of an article on the problem in the winter issue of *The Living Bird Quarterly*, a journal of the Cornell University Laboratory of Ornithology, traced the origins of this crisis from two phenomena of modern life that in more usual circumstances, lead to the demise of species, not to population explosions.

Those are the loss of marshes along the coasts of Texas and Louisiana as a result of urban and agricultural development and the conversion of grasslands north of the coast into huge farms.

A close-up view of the wing of a snowgoose.

The marshes had been the birds' traditional wintering grounds, where a finite resource of reeds, roots and tubers in the brackish water controlled the size of the goose population. The limited nutrition in the vegetation could not sustain ever-expanding flocks. Not every adult could stash away enough nutrients to make the 2,000-mile trip north in spring and still have enough left to produce a brood of healthy, robust chicks.

But in the two decades after World War II, many of the coastal marshes were lost or severely degraded by urbanization. At the same time, farmers, aided in some cases by Government subsidies, greatly expanded crop production on adjacent lands. The farmers in turn gave the birds a food subsidy.

Geese breed for an average of 8 to 10 seasons.

"Now the geese had hundreds of thousands of acres of cropland to live on," Dr. Rockwell said.

With their serrated beaks, they had little trouble ripping out what farmers left in the ground to keep the land from eroding. The stubble and spillage of rice, corn and soybeans proved far more nutritious fare than Phragmites, Spartina, Scirpus and other marsh reeds, and the birds flourished on their new high-energy, high-protein diet.

The results, Dr. Rockwell said, included "a higher reproductive rate, a much higher adult survival rate, and offspring that were larger and in much better shape to survive."

As if that were not enough, Federal and state agencies, with nothing but the best intentions, established wildlife refuges along migration routes to provide wetland habitats for breeding and migrating waterfowl. Many refuges provide corn and other grains to keep birds on the refuge.

And in the 1970s, lobbying by conservationists led to the establishment of no-hunting zones in areas adjacent to the refuges, as well as strict limits on the hunting of geese generally.

Dr. Rockwell and his co-authors, Dr. Jefferies and Dr. Kenneth F. Abraham, a biologist at the Ontario Natural Resources Ministry, wrote that those measures "contributed to a nearly 50 percent reduction" in deaths among adult snow geese.

And because the geese breed for an average of 8 to 10 seasons, surviving adults produced many more young, which in turn were more likely

Snowgeese are denuding their arctic breeding grounds.

to grow up and reproduce successfully. And so the population grew and grew in classic Malthusian fashion.

Climate, too, has played a role. Walter Skinner, a climatologist with Environment Canada in Toronto, analyzed about 200 years of climatic data for all of Canada. A temporary warming trend in the late 1960s and early 70s in the Hudson Bay-Foxe Basin region, where many of the geese nest, produced an earlier spring melt, permitting earlier nesting and increased reproductive success, Dr. Rockwell said.

More recently it has been unusually cold in the high arctic, prompting migrating geese headed for northernmost breeding sites to spend extra time with more southerly colonies, adding to the environmental pressure at the southern sites.

"In 1984," Dr. Rockwell said, "100,000 extra birds stayed about five days at La Pérouse Bay, and in that short time destroyed about six kilometers of coastal marsh."

The effects of heavy foraging on fragile arctic soil have been well documented in the 28-year study of the La

Pérouse Bay colony. Adult geese arrive each spring before the vegetation begins growing, Dr. Rockwell and his co-authors wrote. The birds feed by grubbing beneath the surface for roots and rhizomes of their salt-marsh forage plants.

That destabilizes the thin arctic soil and results in erosion by melting snow, spring rains and wind. Ponds form, growing every year as the birds grub along their edges.

On the remaining land, with the vegetation gone, evaporation increases, and salts from underlying sediments surface. As soil salinity increases, reaching levels three or more times higher than sea water, the forage plants decline, leaving behind few edible plants for goose meals and no live willow bushes for the geese to nest in.

The desecration is having effects on other species. At Cape Churchill, the yellow rail has declined, and Jim Leafloor, a biologist at the Ontario Natural Resources Ministry, has documented a drastic decline in the breeding of small Canada geese in areas where the foraging of snow geese has been intense.

The geese themselves are beginning to suffer from their success. Dr. Batt of Ducks Unlimited said there were early warning signs of a gradual loss in the health of adult geese and their ability to reproduce in some colonies.

"Now the goose population is so high," Dr. Batt said, "it is on a collision course, with destruction of the ecosystem surpassing its ability to support these birds, leading to a protracted decline."

Dr. Batt acknowledged that the solutions being suggested "won't be palatable to a lot of people."

"But," he added, "we have to kill birds, for their own good in the long run as well as for the good of the other birds and animals that are being shut out."

Ducks Unlimited rejected all solutions that would result in "wasting these terrific birds," he said. Instead, the group's suggestions would increase the use of snow geese for human food. The recommendations include extending hunting limits and allowing hunters to harvest three times more birds than now permitted.

"Some of us are considering writing a cookbook of goose recipes," Dr. Rockwell said, noting that wild geese are much less fatty, albeit gamier, than domestically raised geese. "You can do everything with a snow goose that you can do with chicken," he pointed out. "It's really delicious."

Because of the short cold growing season in the Arctic and subarctic, it would take two or three decades for damaged habitat to come back.

The Wired Butterfly

The world's tiniest radar tags are making a Rocky Mountain butterfly—
and its ecology—a lot easier to follow.

MARK CALDWELL

On first acquaintance, the Apollo butterfly seems improbably ethereal for a harbinger of breakthrough technology. A scant two inches from wing tip to wing tip, it flaunts a bold delicacy of design more Miro than Microsoft, the wings translucent white flecked with glowing circles and confident brushstrokes of crimson, black, and brown. And striking though it is in close-up, Apollo (or, officially, *Parnassius sminthius*) is an easy creature to overlook outdoors. It lives in isolated upland meadows, surviving largely on one inconspicuous low-growing alpine plant, called stonecrop.

Yet for the past two summers, a few of these unpretentiously elegant creatures have been fluttering around the Kananaskis Range of Alberta's Canadian Rockies outfitted like trend-crazed backpackers with the latest, the lightest, and the techiest of equipment; milligram for milligram, it's also the priciest. The butterflies carry tiny radar probes that allow University of Alberta ecologist Jens Roland and his colleagues to track them across the meadows of Jumpingpound Ridge at altitudes of 7,000 feet and higher.

The Apollo butterfly lives a complex life—and, as an example of a species dependent on delicate environmental supports, a significant one. While it's not endangered, it is an object lesson in ecological fragility, requiring an exact and rarefied environmental mix: Alpine meadow, yellow-flowered stonecrop, hot summer temperatures, and ample sunlight. Apollo is no traveler, and it can't manage a long-distance search for optimal conditions. Though its ancestors found their way to North America from Asia, they must have done so in incremental stages, generation after generation. Individuals pupate, mate, and reproduce over a single summer, dying

Above: Stone crop is the main food for an Apollo butterfly, parnassus phoebus. *Opposite page: A diode is on the back of a female Apollo butterfly, which allows people to track it.*

with the onset of cold weather. Only the eggs and the pupae winter over. Buried in the gravelly soil, they replace the water in their bodies with glycerol, a substance also used in antifreeze. The butterflies tend to stay put, content to live and die within the confines of a single meadow. Even there, Roland says, "they like the hot little valleys, where there's lots of stonecrop." So their well-being is highly contingent, fluctuating as meadow conditions change.

All in all, the Rocky Mountain site offers an ideal natural lab for studying the interaction between a vulnerable species with very particular needs and an environment that's subject to change. Homebodies though they are, the 10,000 or so Apollo butterflies that live in the chain of high-lying meadows along Jumpingpound Ridge can and do sometimes migrate from meadow to meadow.

That means a population isn't necessarily doomed if, for example, the stonecrop in its home turf dies off; it also means that a freak summer snowstorm that kills off all the Apollos in one meadow can open up an attractive niche for pioneering migrants from a neighboring habitat. The Jumpingpound meadows form a beautifully linked miniature ecosystem, almost like a little Galápagos archipelago, with individual habitats separated by a few hundred yards of forest rather than miles of turbulent water. And that forest, while easy for humans to cross, is a real obstacle course for the butterflies. Their isolated populations and quick generational turnover mean that separate colonies can start to show genetic divergence with gratifying speed.

All these factors conspire to make the Apollo butterflies an inviting index species. They're like a self-contained, easily studied test market for the investigation of ecological problems that may also turn out to bedevil longer-lived, wider-ranging, harder-to-handle animals. "In a way," Roland explains, "the Apollos are a little like grizzlies. Their habitats are shrinking and increasingly isolated. Will they be able to survive in the habitats they've got, and move if they have to?"

The beauty of Roland's research lies in its completeness: he can easily monitor large populations over a

Above left: A diode and antennae the size of a hair is attached to Apollo butterflies so they can be tracked. Right: Professor Jens Roland attaches a diode to an Apollo butterfly.

genetically significant time period while also tracking potentially fateful changes in their habitats. Unlike grizzlies, Apollo butterflies don't get testy when you net them and don't balk at having you write on them with a felt-tip pen. "One of the reasons I started working on them," Roland admits, "is that they're easy to catch: relatively big, slow, and easy to spot." Much of Roland's research depends on doing just that: ranging the meadows with his colleagues and students, catching the butterflies, marking them with identifying letters, and whenever they recapture a previously marked individual, recording the location and date. This mark-and-recapture technique allows them to monitor butterfly populations and track the broad outlines of their movements.

What it does not allow them to do, however, is monitor individual behavior. The technique can at most tell you where an individual butterfly starts and where it ends up, with perhaps the occasional good-luck interception in between. It can't—as a grizzly's radio collar can—track the nuances of individual wanderings, which can reveal significant patterns in an animal's hourly and daily amble through its surroundings. And if you want to parse the secrets of a species' behavior, you need to see it both in panorama and in miniature. What the species does, after all, ultimately rests on what the individual can do.

But how do you follow the travels of one two-inch butterfly? Manageable though the butterflies are when you net them, try shadowing an individual in the wild for more than ten seconds, let alone a whole day or week, and you'll appreciate the difficulty. Apollo is no speed freak, but when active it constantly crosses paths with other identical-looking individuals, plummets into spiky labyrinths of dense alpine vegetation, and occasionally heads away in a beeline, vanishing into the light before it's a hundred feet away. The slightly darker females are even more elusive than the males, more likely to hug the ground beneath the plant cover.

Clearly a radio collar would do the trick. An individual Apollo, however, weighs only about a hundredth of an ounce; you might as well outfit it with the pyramid of Cheops as with a conventional collar. But Roland, working with Graham McKinnon and Chris Backhouse, engineers at the Alberta Microelectronic Center in Edmonton, has come up with an ingenious solution: a super-light-

The super-lightweight, nearly invisible radar transmitter is about a thousandth the weight of the butterfly—about the equivalent of a wristwatch to a human. The tag doesn't seem to interfere at all with the insect's behavior. In tests it has stayed in place and functional for at least two weeks.

weight, nearly invisible radar transmitter that's about a thousandth the weight of the butterfly — about the equivalent of a wristwatch to a human. The tag doesn't seem to interfere at all with the insect's behavior; in tests it has stayed in place and functional for at least two weeks.

And it supplies a giant missing research link. For the first time, field-workers can scope out the potentially revealing secrets of an Apollo butterfly's day. Ecologists now have an easy-to-manage model system that will let them test the mettle of a multipronged top-to-bottom ecological study — beginning with individual behavior, correlating that with the movements of the group, then seeing what happens to a whole population over multiple generations as its habitats shrink, expand, or change. If, as Roland thinks it will, such a study reveals significant secrets of how the species meets environmental challenges, that would justify the far more expensive, longer-term projects it would take to investigate bigger, longer-lived, wider-ranging, and endangered animals — like grizzlies.

The tag looks like an unusually frail strand of human hair, with a pinpoint-size diode attached to the middle of the three-inch-long superfine aluminum wire strand that serves as an antenna. Drop one on the floor and it's gone forever. McKinnon and Backhouse assemble the tags from off-the-shelf components — the diode, for example, can be ordered from Hewlett-Packard, and the cost of the parts is only about $8. But the labor of wiring them together is highly specialized and finical, so they end up costing $30 each.

The technology the tag implements is also ingenious — a relatively recent invention called harmonic radar, commonly used in those bulky antishoplifting tags riveted to every sweater and T-shirt in the mall. The system's been available for some years, and Roland credits the idea of tracking insects to colleague Henrik Wallin. "Henrik showed me some tracking equipment he was using on beetles," Roland recalls. James Riley in England had the same idea and developed a relatively powerful stationary tracking system to follow the movements of bees. But being relatively burly, bees can handle heavier probes. "I started wondering if we might get something really small for butterflies," Roland says. "I approached Graham and Chris, and we started working on it in 1993."

Above: Professor Jens Roland,
University of Alberta, researches
Apollo butterflies in alpine mead-
ows near Banff, Canada.

The Alberta team's innovation thus lay in paring the
tags down to a butterfly-friendly weight and tracking them
with a battery-powered, hand-held device that weighs
about five pounds and fits easily in a day pack. It's a standard unit, manufactured in Sweden and originally
designed for search-and-rescue missions trying to find
people buried in avalanches.

The tracking unit sends out a 1.7-watt microwave
pulse at a 917-megahertz frequency, which
bounces off everything it hits over the unit's 150-
foot range. According to Chris Backhouse, the
physical principle is similar to what happens when you
crank up the volume on your stereo. The distortion you
hear comes from harmonics — grating overtones that
vibrate at two to four times the frequency of the original
note. In harmonic radar the same principle is at work, but
with electromagnetic waves. "The energy from the transmitter sets up a resonating frequency in the antenna wire
on the probe," Roland explains, "and the diode acts as a
kind of one-way gate," absorbing the original frequency
and converting it into the higher harmonic frequency,
which then bounces back to the receiver. That means the

tag—powered only by the radiation striking it—returns a signal at 1,834 MHZ, which the tracker is set to pick up. This neatly eliminates the barrage of 917-MHZ noise bouncing back from every rock and tree trunk within range.

Graduate student Sherri Fownes is Roland's acknowledged master butterfly wrangler and an adept at the art of attaching the probes to insects in the field. In the August afternoon sunlight, the operation looks like pantomime, so nearly invisible is the tag. A typical operation begins with Roland snaring a butterfly, a male. He pinions it gently in his two hands, wings flat, while Fownes scrapes a few hairs off its abdomen, using fine forceps. Then she plucks the tag from an envelope. The butterfly doesn't seem to mind—at least, it stays calm and doesn't struggle. With a blade of grass as applicator, Fownes dabs a minuscule drop of rubber cement on both the tag and the bug's abdomen. She's careful not to get glue on the thorax, which might cause the butterfly to entangle itself in the antenna wire. Finally she taps the probe into place, again with a blade of grass. She straightens a kink in the filament and blows on the butterfly gently a few times to dry the cement. Then Roland releases it.

As it flutters off toward the northwest, Roland grabs the charcoal-gray tracker. By this time the butterfly has disappeared into a crowd of other male Apollos fluttering in the sunlight in search of nectar and females. Roland begins arcing the unit around in various directions until a sudden high-pitched chirp announces the tag—just as the sun moves behind a cloud and all the butterflies, deprived of their energy source, sink to the ground.

Roland loses the signal at that point. Apollo butterflies are like rubber-band-driven toy airplanes: they draw their energy from the sun, so when it disappears they sputter to the ground in a torpor, extending their wings as they wait for it to reappear. Their dark dorsal hair and the dusky tint on their wings near the body are designed to absorb light energy efficiently.

As soon as the sky brightens, the butterflies rev up and head aloft once more. Roland, brandishing the tracker, eventually picks up the wired male and soon spies him heading uphill toward the east. The butterfly disappears into the forest at the northeastern edge of the meadow, remains incognito for a few minutes, then reemerges, now heading south. Random motion, a hunt for food, a quest

Apollo butterflies are like rubber-band-driven toy airplanes: they draw their energy from the sun, so when it disappears they sputter to the ground in a torpor, extending their wings as they wait for it to reappear.

for a female, or a purposeful route the key to whose itinerary has yet to be discovered? These are some questions radar tracking may ultimately answer, though Roland emphasizes that the technique is still in its infancy. Before it becomes routinely possible to document an individual Apollo's habits and talents, Roland will have to address certain technical problems. For example, the portable tracker can keep you homed in on your butterfly, but you still have to follow it across rough terrain before it flies out of the unit's 150-foot range. Every so often the unit picks up a false signal—maybe from a resonating crystal in a rock. And it would be useful (though not so healthy) to sit still and track the insect's movements on a stationary radar screen instead of having to risk losing a speeding bug while chasing it over rough ground.

Roland's group is also refining the tags. "We're working on a loop antenna that would be only half as long as the current one," he says. "And we'd ultimately like to use a printed circuit on Mylar in place of a wire." That would make the tags cheaper, still less of a nuisance for the butterflies, simpler to mount, and easier to see when you drop one on the ground.

A couple of days after chasing the male, Roland tags another Apollo—this time a female—in another meadow about a mile to the east. Her movements prove a bit less erratic than the male's. As soon as Roland releases her, the unit shows her heading southeast for about 50 feet, whereupon she executes a quick dogleg to the north and lands. Then, after a few minutes on the ground, she takes off, completes a graceful curve, and heads southwest toward the forest at the meadow's edge, where she speeds beyond the tracker's range.

"We've been seeing more meadow-to-meadow movement in our butterflies than natural historians would have predicted," Roland says. "They're dispersing more easily than we thought they did." But how? The mark-and-recapture studies, he says, seem to suggest that the butterflies achieve their mobility by zinging along the high ridges that snake in and out among the meadows. "But that may be an artifact," he adds, "because we do all of our capturing on the ridge; we don't search in the forest." Radio-tagging individuals will help determine whether, when they pack up for a new meadow, they prefer the ridge route or the forest route. If it's the latter, the method

They aren't aware of it, but in their own way the wired butterflies of Jumpingpound Ridge may be contributing to a deeper understanding of the universal, enigmatic, and fateful dialogue between an individual's behavior and its habitat.

may help explain how the insects manage to get through foreign territory—whether they just bumble along or have some undiscovered navigating technique.

"Each of our techniques for studying them works well on a different scale," Roland explains. "The challenge will be to link those scales." Mark-and-recapture studies give an overview: what's happening to the population in each meadow; how often do marked butterflies make a bold foray through the intervening woods and reappear in a nearby meadow; what's the longest foray an individual is likely to make? (So far in Roland's study the distance champion is a male that eventually made its way from the meadow where it was first tagged to another well over a mile—and three intervening meadows—away.)

"Our radar tracking has shown us that males follow two types of movement," says Roland. "There's a very local patrolling behavior—that's presumably to encounter recently emerged females. But sometimes they also make much longer movements, anywhere from 800 to 1,200 meters. Maybe that happens when they decide their habitat isn't good." Females behave differently, staying closer to the ground and fluttering less. When they do fly, their movements appear more directed, even deliberate, possibly because they have to be methodical in looking for stonecrop plants to lay their eggs on. Females may call the shots in effective migration when they decide to head into the woods for parts unknown, since the males must follow them to reproduce. But is that really how migration takes place? And if it is, what makes the female decide to bolt? Temperature, too high a density of butterflies, some hitherto unnoticed feature of the landscape, or some change in the stonecrop of her home meadow that makes her restless? Radar tracking, Roland thinks, may answer some of these questions as well.

In recent years the tree line in the Canadian Rockies has been rising; alpine meadows have been shrinking, the woods that divide them expanding. The change may be the result of global warming, or of human forestry policy: the suppression of natural fires may prevent the natural resetting of the tree line. Or it may be a periodic effect that ecologists don't entirely understand. Whatever its cause, though, a change of that sort is sure to have implications for the long-term survival of the butterflies—and, by implication, for all species. What's the biggest forest an Apollo can successfully migrate through? If the meadows

The Apollo butterfly is like a self-contained, easily studied test market for the investigation of ecological problems that may also turn out to bedevil longer-lived, wider-ranging, harder-to-handle animals.

continue to shrink, growing ever farther apart, at what point will the butterflies become unable to migrate and therefore vulnerable to extinction if, say, stonecrop vanishes from the meadow where they're stranded?

To get definitive answers to such questions, you need the research equivalent of a zoom lens, homing in on individual behavior (diode tracking), pulling back to monitor the behavior of populations in a system of neighboring meadows (mark and recapture studies), then backing off yet further to see how the species is doing in a whole region. Nusha Keyghobadi, a graduate student in Roland's group, is interested in that larger picture: she's embarked on a DNA study of Apollo butterflies, not only on Jumpingpound Ridge but in a 30- to 40-mile radius around it. She clips off a harmlessly tiny piece of the insect's wing, then analyzes it for microsatellites — short, repeated sequences of apparently nonfunctional DNA of the same type used for genetic fingerprinting in humans. She's built a library of genetic markers that will ultimately enable her to uncover kinship even in widely separated populations, determining how closely related they are, how long ago they separated, maybe even correlating population movements with historical records of environmental crises — a prolonged spell of adverse weather, for example, or a cataclysmic forest fire.

It's a well-established research technique, but one that's never been used in conjunction with the tiny radar tag, and the possibilities for synergy are rich. "If the diodes can give me information on the behavior and movement of individuals," Keyghobadi says, "that would help me interpret my DNA data." If the radar tracking data reveal a large number of individuals coming and going between two meadows, that would confirm microsatellite data suggesting that the two populations were interbreeding.

Apollo butterflies are simple creatures in the sense that most of their behavior seems hard-wired into their brains: they're not given to displays of temper or creative eccentricity. But severely constrained by biology though it is, their behavior is also apparently quite complex, modulated by the butterfly's need to interact in different ways with its habitat. It doesn't just bumble around at boring random in purely Brownian motion. "For example," Roland says, "we're about to publish data that show

Apollo butterflies are simple creatures. But severely constrained by biology though it is, their behavior is also apparently quite complex, modulated by the butterfly's need to interact in different ways with its habitat.

Apollo butterflies tend to make slow, torturous movements across meadows but directional movements through forests." Something, in other words, enables them to speed efficiently through territory where they can't survive and head efficiently toward the sunlit, stonecrop-rich meadows where they thrive.

What enables them to modulate their behavior remains a mystery. But the survival of their species ultimately depends on their ability to behave in the right way at a critical juncture. And our own fate in a sense depends on only a vastly more intricate elaboration of the same ability. They aren't aware of it, but in their own way the wired butterflies of Jumpingpound Ridge may be contributing to a deeper understanding of the universal, enigmatic, and fateful dialogue between an individual's behavior and its habitat.

Above: Researcher tracks a "wired" Apollo butterfly in alpine meadows near Banff, Canada.

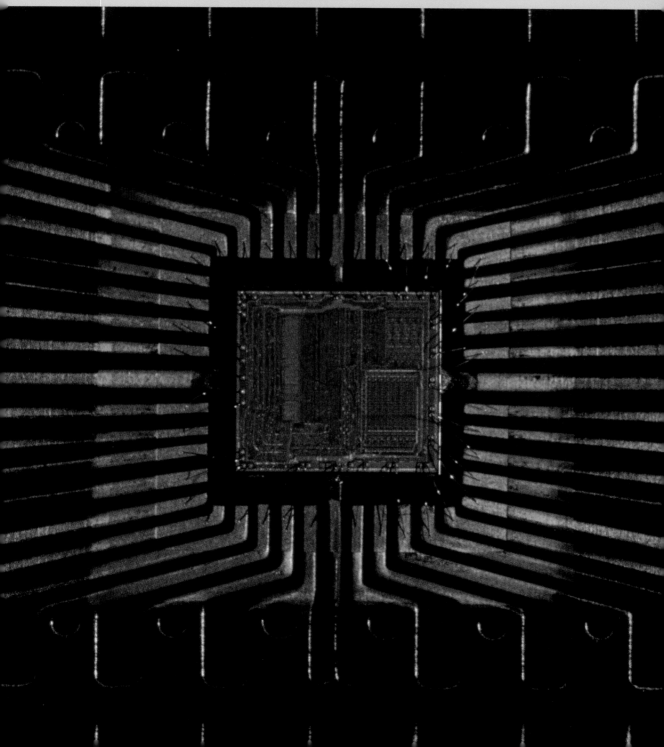

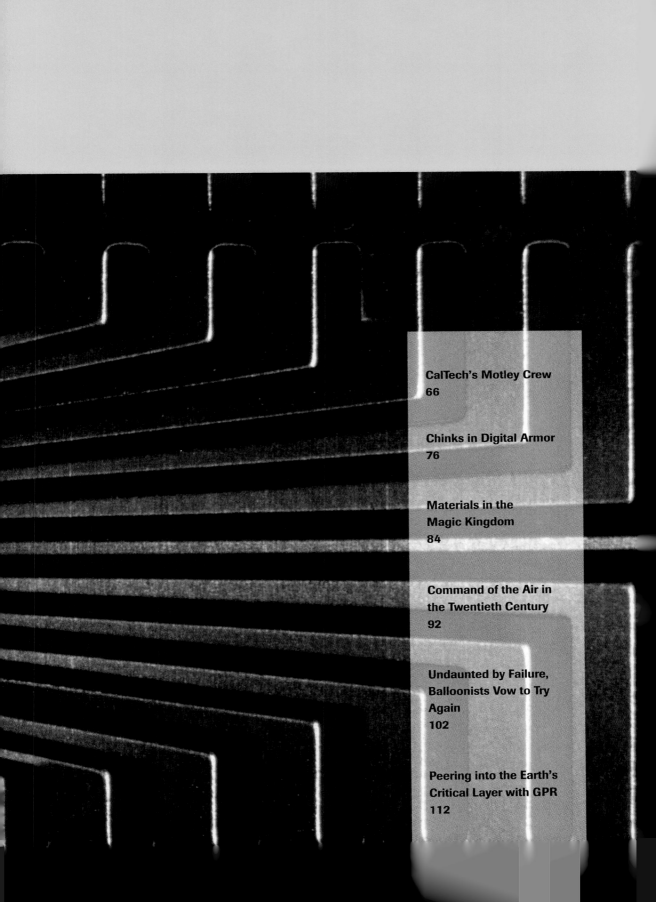

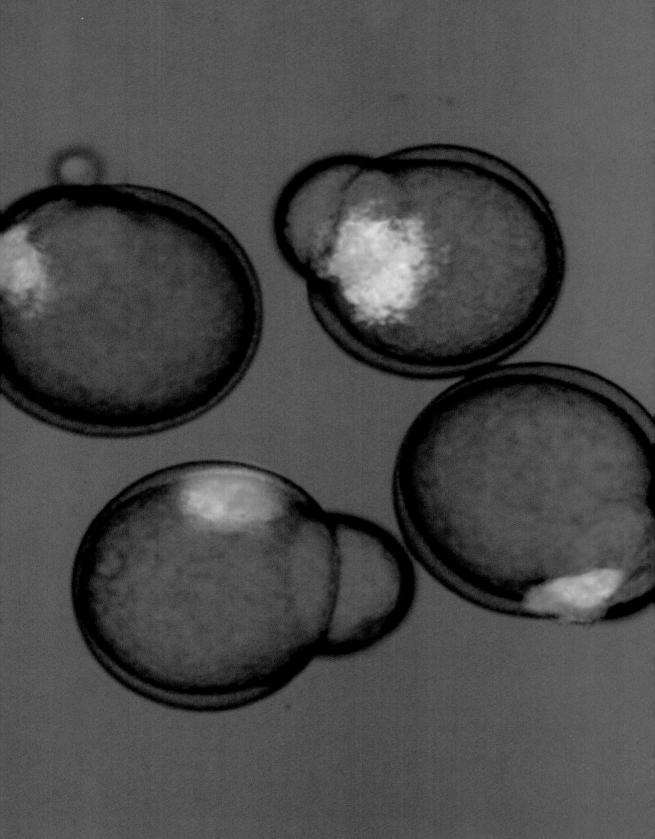

CalTech's Motley Crew

Biological Imaging Center Draws Experts From Range of Fields

DAVID L. WHEELER

P aul Kulesa sits on a laboratory stool and prepares to cut a hole in an eggshell.

Hoping to get a look at a developing chick embryo, he holds one of the 15 dozen fertilized eggs that the laboratory gets each week from a local farm. He is a novice in the laboratory, but he has the patience and precision required for the surgery he is about to perform.

Dr. Kulesa puts a plastic ring on one of the eggs and uses it to draw a circle on the shell with a pencil. Then he takes a scalpel and cuts the shell along the traced line.

He injects India ink under the embryo to make it easier to see, and then, using beeswax, seals a round, clear window in the circular opening. He is ready to make videos of the embryo as it develops.

DOCTORATE IN MATHEMATICS

Dr. Kulesa's doctorate is in mathematics. His unusual background and his experiment are typical of the place where he works, the Biological Imaging Center at the California Institute of Technology.

The center's director, Scott Fraser, says Dr. Kulesa's lack of training as a laboratory biologist is a plus in attempting to get pictures of developing embryos: "Nobody ever trained him that this wouldn't work."

The Biological Imaging Center, which was started in 1991, develops new technologies for seeing inside organisms and tries to apply those technologies to important biological questions. "We want to watch events deep within embryos and brains that haven't been seen before," says Dr. Fraser.

He and the other leaders of the center stir together disparate scientific interests in an informal setting, in the belief that a motley mix of motivated researchers has the

Opposite page: Four fish embryos shortly after groups of cells have been grafted from donor embryos labeled with fluorescent dyes to unlabeled host embryos. Over the next hours and days, the movements and fates of the grafted cells will be followed using light microscopy. This approach allows the interactions between defined groups of cells to be followed in intact embryos as development proceeds.

best chance of rapidly advancing scientific knowledge. Even the laboratory's equipment is set up for use across disciplines. Microscopes that use lasers, for example, are "idiot-proofed" with metal tubes around the paths of the light beams, so biologists not used to working with lasers won't burn their notebooks — or themselves.

Dr. Fraser, who is rarely called "doctor" in his own laboratories, has a laid-back style of leadership and a voice that often seems on the edge of laughter. "I'm more of a heckler than a general," he says.

He describes the center's mission as "science at the lunatic fringe." When its research proposals are reviewed, he likes to see such comments as "This looks impossible, but if it works it will be spectacular."

Dr. Fraser and the other leaders of the center stir together disparate scientific interests in an informal setting, in the belief that a motley mix of motivated researchers has the best chance of rapidly advancing scientific knowledge.

SUSHI AND BEER

The center's annual budget is about $2-million. To maintain the interdisciplinary mix, Dr. Fraser uses sushi and beer to attract new researchers to talks and social hours. He likes to keep the size of the scientific staff at around 30. If it is smaller, he says, the brew of disciplines isn't rich enough. But "if we get too big, then everybody has to wear name badges and it's like walking around a convention."

The interdisciplinary nature of the imaging center is matched in other laboratories scattered around the center's institutional home, the Beckman Institute at Caltech. The institute has no disciplinary departments. One of its key ideas is that if scientists with different backgrounds share equipment, they will end up cooperating in their research as well. "In a normal university setting, people tend to stay in their own departments," says Harry Gray, the institute's director. "They talk about interdisciplinary research, but it's very difficult to do it."

For Dr. Kulesa, the mathematician, the institute's philosophy means he gets a chance to watch as tubes of embryonic neural cells blossom into chick brains. And he is beginning to think about how mathematics might help to answer the central questions of developmental biology.

During development, a single fertilized egg multiplies into billions of cells, sculpted into complex forms. The process is still largely a mystery. When researchers watch development take place, it is as if a house is building itself from a single piece of wood that keeps dividing and taking on different shapes and functions without the help of carpenters.

The technologies that the center uses to watch organismal development include magnetic resonance imaging, which creates pictures of tissue by monitoring the state of protons in the water that pervades it, and advanced forms of microscopy that allow researchers to see more deeply into layers of cells than they could with standard light microscopes.

Two-photon microscopy, for example, combines extremely short, high-intensity infrared laser pulses with fluorescent dye injected into tissue. The dye glows under the laser, beaming an image of the tissue, via cameras and computers, back to scientists. Unlike other forms of laser microscopy, two-photon microscopy can get pictures of tissue for an extended period without burning or bleaching it. The tissue isn't damaged, because the dye reacts to the laser only at the microscope's focal point, not throughout the tissue.

In the past few months, the center's researchers have started to use two-photon microscopy to make time-lapse movies of embryonic cells added to fresh slices of rat brains. Such research might eventually help physicians improve the brain-tissue transplants that are intended to alleviate such afflictions as Parkinson's disease.

IMAGES OF SOFT TISSUE

Magnetic resonance imaging, better known as M.R.I., is frequently used in hospitals to get images of soft tissues that X-rays don't provide. M.R.I. creates three-dimensional data that can be rearranged by computers to offer any perspective that scientists want, such as horizontal cross-sections.

In the past, scientists studying development have had to kill organisms at different stages of development, fix them chemically, slice them up, and look at them under the microscope. With M.R.I., development can be observed from start to finish without hurting the organism. "People have been studying the development of frogs for

M.R.I. creates three-dimensional data that can be rearranged by computers to offer any perspective that scientists want, such as horizontal cross-sections.

Computer Science Faculty

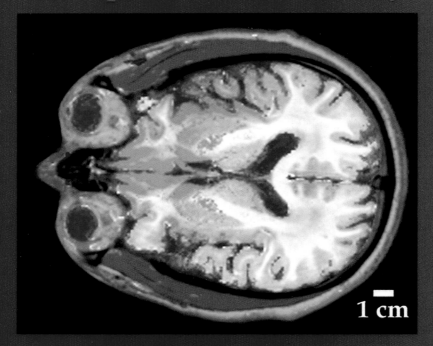

1 cm

Small Primate

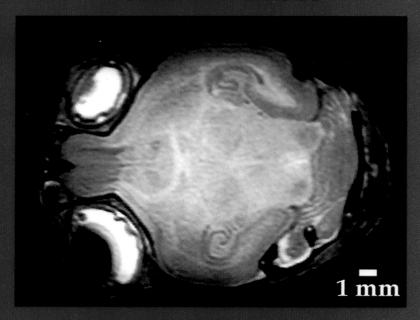

1 mm

200 years," says Russell E. Jacobs, who is in charge of the M.R.I. portion of the center's research. "There are still very important and very basic things that nobody knows. The answers haven't been available, because the animal is opaque."

M.R.I. has changed that, permitting the Caltech scientists to watch, for example, as the brains of rats develop in the womb. "This is the first time we can look at the detailed development of an individual over time — not just the size of the skull or the surface structures, but the inside of the brain," says Michael F. Huerta, an administrator at the National Institute of Mental Health, who works on the "Human Brain Project." The project, which also supports Dr. Jacobs's research, is developing technologies and data-handling methods for neuroscientists.

Eventually, Dr. Jacobs would like to use an M.R.I. microscope to make three-dimensional movies of a monkey's life from conception to senility. Chickens, zebrafish, rats, frogs, and mouse lemurs — tiny primates — already have visited the inch-and-a-half-wide bore of the center's M.R.I. microscope. The apparatus, sitting in a corner of the Beckman Institute's basement, looks like a giant stainless-steel bell. Researchers usually remove their wallets before going near it, so the powerful magnetic field it generates won't erase the coding on their credit cards.

The microscope's images can attain a resolution about one million times that of the conventional M.R.I. apparatus used in hospitals. The Caltech scientists can use the digital movies that the microscope makes to trace the lives of cells as they divide and form ears, jaws, wings, or fins.

FOLLOWING INDIVIDUAL CELLS

The ability of M.R.I. to follow an individual cell is an important advance, says Dr. Fraser. The difference, he says, is like being able to watch individual players in a football game instead of just observing a team moving up and down the field. A stranger to the game can never learn its rules until he can follow the actions of individuals.

"If you are looking at tissue and trying to deduce what the cells are doing, it's at best an educated guess," says Dr. Fraser. Research that has been able to trace single cells, he says, indicates that development is less of a lock-step process than biologists once assumed. The cells

Opposite page: MRI microscopy permits the brains of small primates to be imaged at nearly cellular resolution as shown in the bottom image. This should allow events critical in the development and disease processes to be followed as they take place. For comparison, a high-resolution MRI of a human brain from a clinical imaging magnet permits some of the same structures to be recognized, but only at resolutions 10-20 times worse. (In the human image, there are approximately 1000 times more brain cells in each picture element, making it impossible to follow cellular events.)

Dwarf lemur, cherogaleus medius. These small lemurs offer several advantages for brain imaging studies, including their small size, rapid growth, and reported tendency to develop a senile dementia similar to Alzheimer's disease at only a few years of age.

don't act like soldiers silently obeying a long list of orders from headquarters, but more like members of a commune who talk to each other as they carry out their tasks.

Scientists at the center have labeled cells in the developing retinas of tadpoles with a fluorescent dye and then watched as nerve fibers from the cells reached out to the brain. Such experiments showed that the highly branched tips of the fibers weren't just growing longer. One-third of the branches on the tips were being eliminated and replaced each day, and the pruning and sprouting played an important role as the eye wired itself up to the brain.

The researchers now wonder if that wiring process plays a role in the sensory learning that takes place in mature frogs, monkeys, or humans. Figuring out the rules for the wiring might someday help physicians fix nerve damage, says Dr. Fraser.

STUDYING MULTIPLE SCLEROSIS

The center's researchers don't necessarily seek out medical uses for their work, but they don't shy away from them, either. Eric Ahrens, a physicist there, can't remember much of his undergraduate biology course — chiefly because it started at 8 a.m. He used to specialize in studying how metals at low temperatures conduct electricity. Now he's helping a physician understand an animal version of multiple sclerosis.

Dr. Ahrens and a colleague are studying mice that have been genetically altered so that their nerve cells' insulation breaks down, leading to the same kind of paralysis that happens in humans with multiple sclerosis. He is using his knowledge of spin physics — how nuclei behave in the presence of magnetic fields — to reveal the patterns of water diffusing through nerve cells. Those patterns show when and where extensions from the cells lose their insulating sheaths as the damage from the disease progresses.

One day Dr. Ahrens may be running some equations and the next day crafting a miniature seat belt to hold a mouse immobile in the M.R.I. microscope. He enjoys the variety of work, he says, although "I had an identity crisis when I first came here. I didn't know what journals I should read."

FOCUS ON CHEMISTRY

While some at the center are working on the frontier of M.R.I. physics, others are trying to develop new chem-

Research using two-photon microscopy might eventually help physicians improve the brain tissue transplants that are intended to alleviate such afflictions as Parkinson's disease.

istry. Stains that make it easier for biologists to see particular cells under light microscopes are responsible for many advances in biology. Now the Caltech group is trying to come up with similar stains, known as contrast agents, for M.R.I.

Thomas J. Meade, the chief chemist, joined the center soon after it was started six years ago. Scott Fraser used a scientist's version of a magic trick to get him interested in developmental biology, he recalls. While Dr. Meade watched, Dr. Fraser tilted some laboratory dishes containing frog embryos and left them for 30 minutes — befuddling the usual developmental response of the embryonic cells to the cues of gravity. The next day, he showed the embryos to Dr. Meade again. They had two heads.

"That's chemistry," Dr. Meade thought to himself. "Has to be."

Why was he so sure?

"Everything is chemistry. Who is running the show here? Genes. They're nucleic acids."

"The body is all chemistry," he adds, "if you look at it with the right lens."

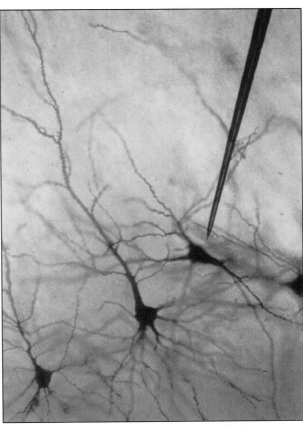

A metal microelectrode of the sort typically used to record brain activity and stained cells in a slice of brain tissue. The electrode is nearly in contact with the cell body of a single neuron. Imaging technique offers an answer to the challenge of following the flow of information through neurons rather than just "eavesdropping" on the activity of the cell as a whole.

'CLINICAL PASSIONS'

After an all-nighter in the laboratory working on some experiments, he has the frenetic energy of someone who is fighting off the attractions of sleep. In his time at the center, he has been awarded 15 patents and has started two companies, one of which is developing a new form of genetic testing. "I have clinical passions," he says. "I have interests in developmental biology, but ultimately, I am a chemist. I make molecules."

To understand the center's work, he says, visitors have to understand how magnetic resonance imaging works, since the technology is central to the center's mission of peeking inside organisms.

In his office is a diagram of a water molecule. He

points to a proton. Like the rest of the molecule, it is in the magnetic field of an M.R.I. microscope. The proton, which acts like a tiny magnet itself, is usually aligned with the M.R.I. microscope's magnetic field. When researchers "excite" the proton with radio-frequency electromagnetic waves, however, it moves out of alignment.

Then the waves are shut off, and Dr. Meade explains what happens to the proton: "This guy wants to go home. Everybody wants to go home. Where's home? Ground state. What's ground state? The lowest energy state."

The time it takes for the protons in water molecules to get back to their original state, or go home, is called their relaxation time. Variations in protons' relaxation times throughout the body, created by variations in the electromagnetic environment of the body's tissues, create the contrasts that make an M.R.I. image possible.

Dr. Meade and other scientists have created contrast agents, which can be injected into cells without harming them. The contrast agents cause the cells to light up in an M.R.I. image by speeding up the relaxation time of nearby protons. Dr. Meade has started to devise other contrast agents that could serve as reporters, relaying news of particular biological activities. One of them, for example, could be hooked up to any gene in a cell and would tip off scientists about when a cell is using that gene.

Such innovations keep flowing from the center, Dr. Fraser says, because of the passions of individual researchers, not because he cracks the whip. Even so, his influence is obvious. "Cleanliness is next to Fraserliness," says a sign in one room—no missing the trash can with a failed experiment, or doing "anything messy in rooms that have microscopes or computers."

The center's researchers often work in binges. "The stage of the embryo that you care about," says Dr. Fraser, "may happen at 2 in the morning or 4 in the morning or at noon."

On this evening, a walk through the center's laboratories along an L-shaped corridor reveals that the interdisciplinary chatter has died down. Only a few solitary souls are working, in silence.

Scott Fraser has to head out early. His wife, also a scientist, is giving an evening lecture, so it's his night to pick up the kids.

Once he was a fertilized egg. Now he walks, talks, and writes articles for *Science*. Maybe someday he can explain how he got from there to here.

Stains that make it easier for biologists to see particular cells under light microscopes are responsible for many advances in biology.

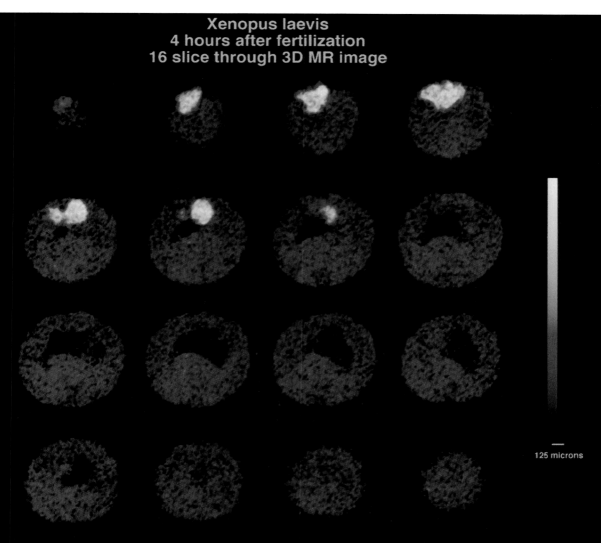

Xenopus laevis
4 hours after fertilization
16 slice through 3D MR image

125 microns

Biological Imaging Center
Beckman Institute
fornia Institute of Technology

This early embryo consists of 256 cells. The eight
great-granddaughter cells of the originally labeled
cell are apparent in the first two rows of slices.

*MRI microscope image of a living early frog embryo, showing a group of
cells labelled with a cell-autonomous MRI contrast agent. The brightly
labeled cells can be followed over time as the embryo develops, allowing
direct assays of the cell movements and cell lineage relationships that drive
embryonic development.*

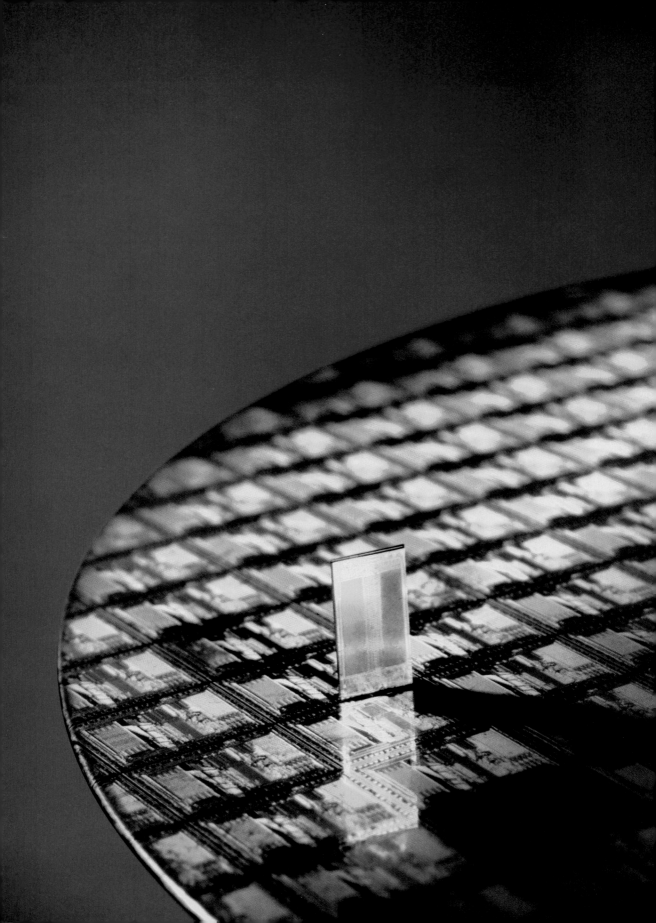

Chinks in Digital Armor

Exploiting faults to break smart-card cryptosystems.

IVARS PETERSON

T he days of a thick wallet bulging with coins, bills, and assorted plastic cards may be numbered. Instead, a single card—a computer in your wallet—could serve as electronic cash, driver's license, credit card, and personal identifier.

So-called smart cards, which incorporate circuitry for processing information and keeping records, are already widely used in Europe and elsewhere for automatically paying tolls, making telephone calls, authorizing access to pay-TV or restricted facilities, carrying medical data, and performing bank transactions.

In the future, many of these functions may be integrated into a single unit. Personal computers could come equipped with smart-card readers to handle transactions over the Internet.

For such a system of electronic commerce to work effectively, however, providers and users must have absolute assurance that any recorded information is safe from prying eyes, that the desired transactions are legitimate, and that both parties to a transaction are who they say they are.

To provide an appropriate degree of security and authentication, smart cards typically incorporate additional circuitry for encrypting digital information. Following a mathematical formula, the embedded cryptosystem scrambles the bits—1s and 0s—representing data, messages, or signatures into gibberish unintelligible to an eavesdropper.

Now, security experts have revealed that smart cards protected by current cryptographic schemes are potentially vulnerable to a novel type of attack. It's possible to force a card into making an error in the calculations used in the encryption process and from the result to obtain

Above and opposite page: Close-up views of a computer chip.

clues needed to break the cryptosystem and trick the card into leaking its secrets.

"Our attack is basically a creative use of a device's miscalculations, or faults," says computer scientist Dan Boneh of Bellcore in Morristown, N.J. Boneh is a member of the team that first identified the problem last fall in a specific type of smart-card cryptosystem.

Other researchers quickly confirmed the theoretical results described by Boneh and his colleagues and extended them to cover additional cryptographic schemes. Then, Ross J. Anderson of the University of Cambridge in England and Markus G. Kuhn of Purdue University in West Lafayette, Ind., demonstrated how such attacks could be mounted in practice against smart cards now in use.

For such a system of electronic commerce to work effectively, providers and users must have absolute assurance that any recorded information is safe from prying eyes, that the desired transactions are legitimate, and that both parties to a transaction are who they say they are. ▼

"This is a new and exciting field of research and one that secure system designers would be prudent to follow closely," Anderson says.

A smart card resembles a standard credit card, but it includes, wedged within the plastic, a memory for storing sets of instructions and recording data and a microprocessor for performing calculations and other bit manipulations according to the embedded instructions. In addition, some types of smart cards have a microwave antenna for transmitting and receiving messages.

Cards that rely on cryptography for security usually have an additional processor and extra memory to provide a secret environment for handling the calculations necessary to encrypt and decrypt digital information and to provide digital signatures.

The most commonly used form of smart-card encryption requires a key—typically a string of random numbers, often binary—shared by both sender and recipient. Numbers selected from the key are used in a series of mathematical operations to scramble the digits representing information stored or transmitted by the card.

One widely used example of such a cryptosystem is the Data Encryption Standard (DES), which in its simplest form requires keys that are 56 bits long and involves 16 rounds of scrambling during encryption. Deciphering the information means going through the same operations in reverse order, using the same key.

Relatively easy to implement, a shared-key scheme has the disadvantage that both the card and the reading system must have access to the same key in order to understand each other.

An alternative method, known as public-key cryptography, requires the use of a pair of complementary keys instead of a single, shared key. One key, which is openly available, is used to encrypt information; the other key, known only to the intended recipient (or encoded in the smart card), is used to decipher the message.

In other words, what the public key does, the secret key can undo. Moreover, the secret key can't be easily deduced from the public key.

The most popular type of public-key encryption, invented by Ronald L. Rivest of the Massachusetts Institute of Technology, Adi Shamir of the Weizmann Institute of Science in Rehovot, Israel, and Leonard M. Adleman of the University of Southern California in Los Angeles, is known as the RSA cryptosystem.

In the RSA scheme, the secret key consists of two prime numbers that are multiplied together to create the lengthier public key. Its security rests on the observation that it's easy to multiply two large prime numbers to obtain a larger number as the answer. The reverse process of factoring a large number to determine its prime-number components presents a formidable computational challenge (SN: 5/7/94, p. 292).

Designers and manufacturers generally describe their smart cards as resistant to tampering. They maintain that it is virtually impossible to take a smart-card chip apart and read the individual bits and bytes of the instructions built into and stored on the chip.

Smart-card cryptosystems, however, are potentially vulnerable to attacks that exploit certain features of how the systems operate. For example, public-key cryptosystems often take slightly different amounts of time to decrypt different messages.

Computer chips.

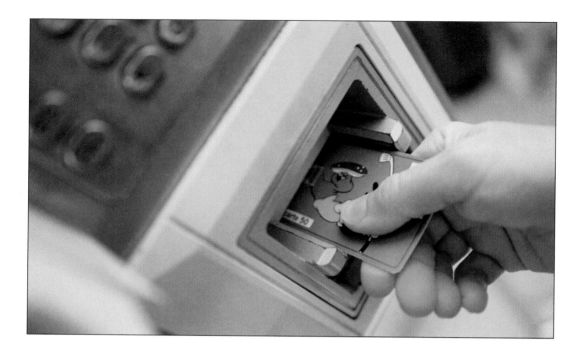

In 1995, Paul C. Kocher, a cryptography consultant in Stanford, Calif., described how secret keys can be found by surreptitiously measuring the duration of many such operations (SN: 12/16/95, p. 406).

Last year, computer scientist Richard J. Lipton of Princeton University made the crucial observation that once a device performs a faulty computation, it may leak information that can be used in breaking a cryptosystem. Such a fault could arise from something as simple as the switch of a bit from 0 to 1 or 1 to 0 at a random position in a secret key.

Working with Bellcore's Boneh and Richard DeMillo, Lipton showed in principle how random bit flips could be exploited to deduce the secret key in the RSA cryptographic scheme when used in a smart card.

The idea is to cause a random bit flip by zapping the card with a pulse of radiation or by suddenly changing the voltage or rate at which the card's chip normally operates. Mathematically inclined criminals could then compare the faulty values generated by the device against the correct values and thus derive the secret RSA key.

Because the method doesn't rely on actually factoring a large number to break the code, it can be equally effective against RSA keys of any length. Making the num-

Smart cards, which incorporate circuitry for processing information and keeping records, are already widely used in Europe and elsewhere for automatically paying tolls, making telephone calls, authorizing access to pay-TV or restricted facilities, carrying medical data, and performing bank transactions.

The smart card has many everyday applications — from banking to making phone calls to charging purchases over the telephone.

bers longer is not enough to protect against such an attack.

"What is significant about the Bellcore attack is that an error introduced at nearly any stage of computation can produce a favorable result for the opponent," says Burton S. Kaliski Jr. of RSA Data Security in Redwood City, Calif.

"The security of RSA and other algorithms has not been questioned, only the security of particular implementations against one form of physical attack," he adds. "The attack can...be prevented by simple modifications to the cryptographic processing."

At the same time, it's dangerous to assume that the secret information stored in "tamperproof" smart cards can't be discovered by an adversary. Such devices must not only conceal the unit's inner circuitry but also effectively detect faults in processing, Boneh says.

Moreover, because all computers make errors from time to time, "our methods work even against machines that we cannot actively tamper with," Lipton says.

Within weeks of Bellcore's announcement that the new smart-card security is vulnerable, Shamir and Eli Biham of the Israel Institute of Technology (Technion) in Haifa found a way to modify the new approach to attack shared-key cryptosystems such as DES, which is used extensively in the financial world to protect electronic transactions.

The result, says Shamir, represents a major assault on nearly all cryptosystems proposed so far.

Theoretical studies indicate that an intruder could unravel DES' 56-bit secret key by analyzing fewer than 200 faulty encrypted messages and comparing them to a single flawless message. As in the case of the RSA system, making the keys longer doesn't help to ward off the attack.

More recently, Shamir and Biham have demonstrated that a fault-based attack can also be used to break a completely unknown cryptosystem, making it possible to extract the secret key stored in a tamperproof cryptographic device even when nothing is known about the structure or operation of the cryptosystem.

A single card—a computer in your wallet—could serve as electronic cash, driver's license, credit card, and personal identifier. ▼

The results obtained by Shamir and Biham were all based on theory, and it isn't clear how applicable they would be to smart cards in actual use. Anderson and others point out that changing a single bit in a secret key, for example, would normally be detected by conventional error-checking methods built into the system.

"Although their attack is very elegant, it is not practical against many fielded systems," Anderson says. An electric pulse or jolt of radiation is more likely to cause the chip to crash than to lead to a faulty encrypted message.

Nonetheless, it is possible to mount a practical attack by causing a fault not in the secret key, but in the instructions of the program that orchestrates the calculations, Anderson says. Using this approach, it's possible to break DES with access to fewer than 10 encrypted messages.

To date, no one has reported a successful fault-based attack on an actual cryptographic device or smart card. However, such attacks are certainly feasible, Anderson contends.

Anderson's own studies have revealed that smart cards are not always as tamper-resistant as their manufacturers claim, and criminals have already taken advantage of such weaknesses. In the last few years, for example, organized gangs in Europe have acquired the capability of cloning the smart cards used for access to pay-TV.

"This raises the obvious risk that banking systems could be next," Anderson says. Indeed, the technology required to implement an·attack based on causing a smart card to decode instructions incorrectly isn't much more complicated than that used to pirate TV signals.

Anderson and Kuhn delayed publishing their findings on breaking tamper-resistant processors until last November in order to give developers of banking systems time to adopt some countermeasures. The report appears in the proceedings of the second workshop on electronic commerce, held in Oakland, Calif.

Manufacturers of smart cards have been aware for some time of the importance of protecting against physical intrusions involving abrupt temperature changes, voltage spikes, and radiation bursts. Many devices already have circuitry to detect such abnormalities.

Moreover, simple procedures such as repeating calculations and checking to make sure the same answer comes out each time can provide additional safeguards, though they often slow smart-card operation unacceptably. Bellcore and other organizations have developed alternative strategies to circumvent the problem.

System developers could also learn from efforts in weapons and space research to develop chip-based circuitry that can survive electromagnetic pulses and other environmental hazards, says Jean-Jacques Quisquater of the Catholic University of Louvain in Belgium.

In spite of these security concerns, the popularity of smart cards for a variety of applications continues to grow. Just as people don't hesitate to write checks even though checks are easy to forge or continue to give credit card numbers over the telephone without worrying about being overheard, they readily use smart cards because of the convenience they offer.

Meanwhile, the cat-and-mouse game between cryptographers and security experts on the one side and technologically literate spies and criminals on the other goes on.

To date, no one has reported a successful fault-based attack on an actual cryptographic device or smart card.

Materials in the Magic Kingdom

When it comes to science, Disney doesn't use a Mickey Mouse approach.

CORINNA WU

For many children and adults alike, a trip to one of Walt Disney's four theme parks is like a pilgrimage to Mecca—it's an excursion they feel they have to make at least once and that they anticipate with excitement and reverence. While there, visitors are immersed in a surreal world where the inhabitants range from human to humanoid and historical characters mingle freely with fictional personalities. Events that would be impossible in real life take place regularly within the parks' boundaries.

In Disney World's Hall of Presidents, for example, Audio-Animatronic figures representing 40 U.S. chief executives, living and dead, convene on one stage to impart words of wisdom to the audience. Abraham Lincoln calls roll, and Bill Clinton delivers a speech.

Seeing John F. Kennedy share a stage with George Washington can strike the visitor as fascinating or creepy. Either way, the Disney "Imagineers" have successfully created an illusion. Doing that takes some ingenuity, not just in the mechanisms that imitate facial expressions and gestures, but in the design of materials as well.

At the American Chemical Society meeting in Orlando, Fla., last August, Disney research scientist Kathleen Nelson discussed some of the materials problems facing the theme parks and their approaches to solving them. Nelson is one of a cadre of Disney scientists who dabble in projects ranging from formulating polymers to mimic human skin to making biodegradable casings for fireworks.

Chemistry and materials work takes up less than a tenth of the company's research and development efforts, says Ben Schwegler of Walt Disney Imagineering in Glendale, Calif., but "it's important and highly visible."

In other words, it helps put the magic in the Magic Kingdom.

Disney has successfully collaborated with fireworks manufacturers to develop starch-based casings that break down into carbon dioxide, water, and other harmless molecules.

Bright fireworks explode in a dark night sky over the illuminated tower of Sleeping Beauty Castle at Disneyland.

Unlike some other theme parks, Disney has enough special materials needs to justify its own research. The theme parks operated by Busch Entertainment in St. Louis, Mo., leave materials research to the contractors hired to build rides and attractions, says spokesman Fred Jacobs. Busch does do some research focusing on marine life and zoology, however. Universal Studios Florida in Orlando will not discuss any of its technical projects.

Disney keeps most of the research it conducts with universities, companies, and other organizations (SN: 7/29/95, p. 72) under wraps, too. In general, collaborators are forbidden to discuss their affiliation with Mickey Mouse and Co., Schwegler says. Disney worries that organizations claiming an association with the company will undermine its ability to sell movie merchandising tie-ins. "Companies pay us millions of dollars for the right to use the Disney name," explains Schwegler. "We're trying to protect their investment."

Since there are four Disney parks in different parts of the world, Disney scientists must take into account how different climates affect the polymer.

The Disney "Imagineers" have successfully created an illusion. Doing that takes some ingenuity, not just in the mechanisms that imitate facial expressions and gestures, but in the design of materials as well.

Though Disney scientists may develop formulas for polymers and paints, they don't make the actual substances themselves. Instead, specialty manufacturers mix polymers and paint to Disney's specifications.

One of Disney's unique materials problems is the development of skin for the Audio-Animatronic figures. No commercially available polymer has the combination of properties that fits all of Disney's needs, Schwegler says. For a start, the polymer must be durable yet flexible. When Abraham Lincoln gives the same speech dozens of times a day, the repeated bending and stretching can cause tears and cracks in his skin.

Any material, no matter how tough, is bound to fail after many repetitions of a movement. Therefore, the polymer must also be easy to repair. "The real cost isn't the injection or the molding process," Schwegler says. It's in the labor required after the figure has been cast.

The polymer has to have not only the malleability of real skin but also the texture. Artists apply theatrical

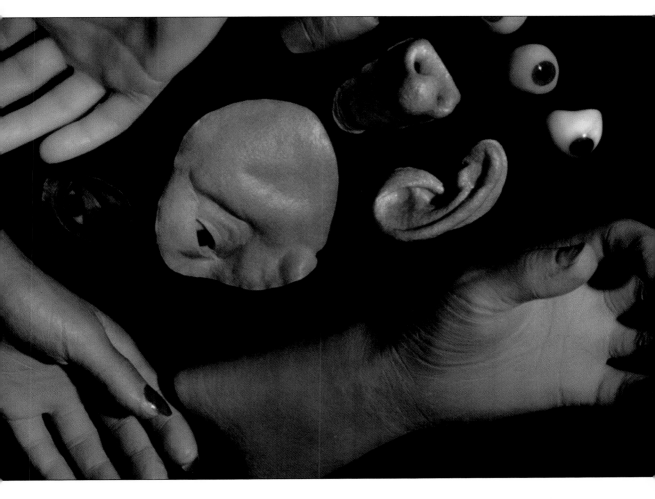

makeup to the figures as if they were human actors. In addition, head and facial hair is planted directly into the polymer, so it must be dense enough to grip the hair tightly. "We never paint on a beard," Schwegler notes.

Since there are four Disney parks in different parts of the world, Disney scientists must take into account how different climates affect the polymer. "The humidity problems in Florida are different from the desiccation in California," Schwegler says. Freezing winters in Paris and Tokyo add other complications. Large temperature swings can make materials expand and contract, causing them to wear out from fatigue. Each set of conditions requires a slightly different material, Schwegler says.

Though Disney will not reveal the formulation of the polymer, polyurethane or rubber is usually used when scientists want something to look like human skin, says E.

Polymer, polyurethane or rubber is usually used when scientists want something to look like human skin. The polymer has to have not only the malleability of real skin but also the texture.

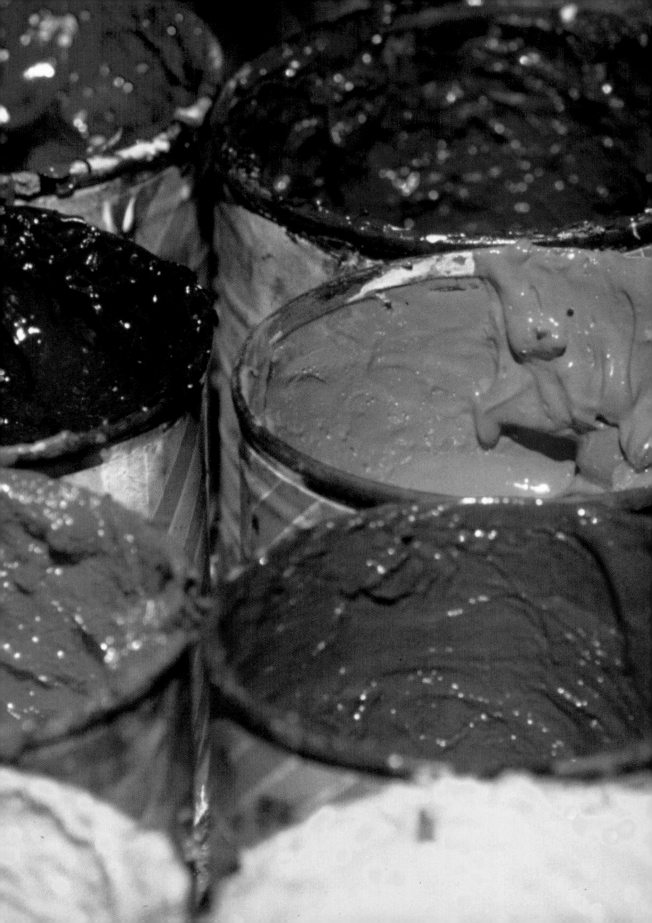

Bruce Nauman, a chemical engineer at Rensselaer Polytechnic Institute in Troy, N.Y. Custom-made polyurethanes are easier to make than harder plastics. "They're made by blending two different oligomers, or prepolymers, in different proportions," he explains. "Then you cast them in the shape you want."

For more common industrial applications, companies are usually better off to redesign a plastic part so they can avoid using a custom polymer, Nauman says. "For a given application, it's quite an art to choose which polymer is best."

Disney often can't rely on commercially available products because the special effects designers rarely use materials as the manufacturer intended, Schwegler says. Take paints, for example. "We dilute them and coat them too thick and too thin. We don't use the right type of brushes. We don't use the recommended applications of spray paint." The Disney scientists modify existing paints to fit their particular needs.

Some Disney attractions require especially reliable paint for outdoor use that falls under the category of architectural coatings. Repainting an attraction like Cinderella Castle, even if it's only done every 15 years, means shutting it down, losing revenue, and, ultimately, disappointing visitors, Schwegler says.

The research also involves keeping up with paint formulas that change — in response to new environmental and safety regulations, for example. "Manufacturers change their formulations frequently without saying anything to their customers," Schwegler says. "For people who are able to follow the manufacturer's recommendations, they never see the difference. But because we don't, problems frequently arise."

When most visitors think about safety, they focus on roller coaster rides like Magic Mountain. But Disney also has to pay attention to less obvious dangers. All material at "kid level" — fake leaves, landscaping, even the lava in the Energy Pavilion at Epcot Center — is nontoxic. "You never know what's going to go in a kid's mouth," says Schwegler. The lava isn't very tasty, he says, but it won't make anyone sick. Some of the special effects in the parks are "literally stuff you could make in your kitchen."

Disney's materials scientists also tackle challenges

Though Disney scientists may develop formulas for polymers and paints, they don't make the actual substances themselves. Instead, specialty manufacturers mix polymers and paint to Disney's specifications.

Large temperature swings can make materials expand and contract, causing them to wear out from fatigue. Each set of conditions requires a slightly different material.

posed by the nightly fireworks displays. In most areas where Disney sets off fireworks, maintenance crews simply go around and pick up the polystyrene shell casings left after the show. They'd prefer to use biodegradable casings, however, in case the debris falls into water or other inaccessible places.

Some types of plastics that are called biodegradable break into smaller pieces without undergoing any fundamental chemical change. "We had many manufacturers come to us, wanting us to test their products," Schwegler says, but these materials don't fit Disney's criteria for biodegradability.

Disney has successfully collaborated with fireworks manufacturers to develop starch-based casings that break down into carbon dioxide, water, and other harmless molecules. The company does not use those casings yet because safety and "business issues" have yet to be resolved, Schwegler says.

The ideal fireworks shell casing would leave no residue at all but would "vaporize like a magician's flash paper in the sky," says polymer chemist Gary Zeller of Zeller International in Downsville, N.Y. Zeller has sent Disney some information on a biodegradable casing he is developing for military applications. The plastic contains enzymes and microbes to speed up its degradation. "The shell turns into mush in 30 days," Zeller says.

Like most companies, Disney is rather tight-lipped about much of its research, but unlike other companies, Disney says, its silence is not just to keep competitors at bay. "When you're at Disney Land, you're on a stage set," Schwegler says. For Disney to reveal its secrets is "like when you go to a magic show and the magician shows you how to do every trick."

Thanks to the scientists quietly working behind the scenes, however, all people see is the illusion.

Some of the special effects in the parks are "literally stuff you could make in your kitchen."

All material at "kid level"—fake leaves, landscaping, even the lava in the Energy Pavilion at Epcot Center—is non-toxic.

Command of the Air in the Twenty-first Century

BRIAN J. NICHELSON

Since the film *Top Gun* was released in 1986, jet fighter aircraft have been more glamorous and more visible than ever. The Navy's F-14 and F/A-18 and the Air Force's F-15 and F-16 aircraft are sleek, fast, and lethal. The intense live televised coverage of these and other aircraft during the Gulf War (Operation Desert Storm) in 1991 heightened their appeal to a broad public.

The world is changing, though, and soon American fighter aircraft—mostly based on 1960's and 1970's technology—will no longer be adequate for the tasks facing them. Fighter aircraft around the world, including those the United States might face in a future conflict, are becoming more capable. Recently developed or upgraded aircraft include the MiG-29, the Eurofighter 2000, the Saab Gripen, the Dassault Rafale, and the Mitsubishi F-2. The proliferation of deadly missiles, both surface-to-air and air-to-air, is another growing threat. Moreover, advancing electronic capabilities around the world mean that better detection, intelligence, and jamming systems will also oppose U.S. air forces.

The Pentagon has been tracking the changing nature of these threats and has been funding research and design competitions with the goal of producing new weapons and aircraft that will ensure the superiority of U.S. forces. One such project, the F-22, is already flying and will soon be produced in numbers. Another, the Joint Strike Fighter, is now on the drawing board as a complement to the F-22 in a tactical role.

The F-22 is a fighter pilot's dream: fast, agile, highly survivable, and easy to fly. It is designed to fly for sustained periods at supersonic speeds (a capability called "supercruise") without being detected by the enemy (its "stealth" features include a radar signature between the

Developing the F-22 has advanced the capabilities of the U.S. aerospace industry.

Opposite page: Lockheed Martin/Boeing's F-22A Raptor.

size of a bird and a bee). These capabilities are reflected in the appearance of the aircraft: the sleek outline, sharply swept wings, canted vertical tails, and a cockpit positioned above and ahead of the fuselage.

The F-22 appeals strongly to military planners because it will require less maintenance and deployment support than today's fighters. Current estimates are that it will take half the maintenance personnel to keep an F-22 in the air, about half the materiel to support it when deployed on an exercise or actual operation, and about $500 million less per squadron to support it over a twenty-year period.

Development of the F-22 began in 1986, when the Air Force awarded a contract to an industry team that included Lockheed, Boeing, and General Dynamics. The prototype plane, called the YF-22, was assembled in 1990, and it won a selection competition against a competitor aircraft in April, 1991. The first F-22 is scheduled to become operational in the year 2004. The manufacturing team has changed since the start of the project (mainly due to mergers) and is now made up of Boeing and Lockheed Martin. If the Air Force gets its way, the F-22 will be in production until 2012, long enough to make 438 planes. Recent studies, however, show that the total cost of the F-22 program may go as high as $80 billion, so the Air Force may have to scale back its plans.

The F-22 is a fighter pilot's dream: fast, agile, highly survivable, and easy to fly.

MATERIALS

A new generation of materials and manufacturing processes have gone into the frame and skin of the F-22. Some are composite materials that are light but strong; others are standard materials that have been processed in a new way. Engineers conducted more than thirty thousand tests to develop acceptable design parameters and to test the integrity of the materials used in the F-22. About 40 percent of the plane's weight is titanium, about 23 percent is made of various composite materials, and about 15 percent is aluminum. The remainder of the plane consists of miscellaneous materials.

Titanium forgings and castings are used throughout the main structure of the aircraft. One large titanium forging weighs 6,560 pounds (2,976 kilograms) before being machined to its final shape, which weighs just 392 pounds (179 kilograms). It is used as a bulkhead and carries some of the highest loads in the structure. Castings made with a new procedure called "hot isostatic pressing" are also used throughout the frame, and in some cases titanium pieces are welded together to construct larger assemblies.

The external skin and many interior pieces are made of graphite-bismaleimide composites, and thermoplastics and epoxy composites are used as needed in such places as engine inlets, landing gear doors, and access panels. A new technique called resin transfer molding was used to make wing spars, frames, and stiffeners. In this technique, fibers are placed in a form, matrix is injected, and the form is then heated in a press until the part is cured. This technology produces parts with complicated shapes to very close tolerances, thus eliminating the need for further machining.

ENGINES

The Pratt & Whitney engine to be used on the F-22 is in keeping with the rest of the plane — it is innovative, powerful, and low-maintenance. The F-22 will have two of these F119 engines, each of which produces 35,000 pounds of thrust. Maintenance time and support equipment will be drastically reduced, compared to earlier engines, and this will help make the F-22 much less expensive to operate in the long run. The exhaust nozzles swivel up and down to give the pilot increased control, especially at unusual attitudes. Thrust vectoring, as this is known, is an important feature in combat and allows the plane to do such things as fly with its nose in an extremely high position, which may be useful during evasive maneuvers or when locking onto a target. The engine also injects cool air into the exhaust stream to reduce the thermal signature, in keeping with the stealth requirement.

The F-22 appeals strongly to military planners because it will require less maintenance and deployment support than today's fighters.

AVIONICS

The F-22's avionics (short for aviation electronics) are the most advanced in the world. They are fully integrated, meaning that different features work together, and are also highly automated, relieving the pilot of much of the workload with which today's fighter pilots must deal. The

The F-22 is designed to fly for sustained periods at supersonic speeds (a capability called "supercruise") without being detected by the enemy (its "stealth" features include a radar signature between the size of a bird and a bee).

main features of the F-22's avionics include three kinds of sensors, an emission control system, graphic displays that show the F-22 and all other aircraft and missiles around it, and an intra-flight data link (IFDL) that allows one plane's computers to share data with others during a mission.

The sensors on the F-22 include the main radar, which detects other planes and missiles; the radar warning receiver, which tells the pilot when another radar is aimed at the F-22; and the communications/navigation/identification system. The emission control system helps maintain the required level of stealth. The pilot sets it to the desired setting, and the computer takes over. If the emission control is set to a low level, the active radar (which sends out signals that could give away the position of the F-22) is turned on only intermittently, and the passive detectors collect data to keep the computers updated. Whether the emission levels are set high or low, all data collected are processed together, aircraft are analyzed by the "identification-friend-or-foe" (IFF) system to see which side they are on, and the information is displayed on a cockpit screen. The IFDL lets the pilot coordinate an attack by sharing data with other F-22's. This means that each pilot can see data from the other planes in the flight, including which targets each one is locked onto, how many missiles each plane is carrying, and how much fuel each has left.

Most of the combat information the pilot needs is displayed on one of three screens. The first, the Situation Display, gives the pilot a "bird's-eye" view of the environment. The pilot's own plane is shown on the screen with navigation data, the location of wingmen and other friendly aircraft, the emission status, and range data. Unfriendly and unknown aircraft are displayed in red and yellow, respectively, along with aircraft type, altitude, speed, distance, and heading. In a combat situation, the pilot will rely on the second display, the Attack Display. It expands on the information from the Situation Display and also shows when the missiles from the F-22 and the hostile aircraft will be in range of each other. This is where the F-22's stealth and speed are crucial: The F-22 can see the other aircraft before being detected, so it can shoot first and then get away quickly. When all conditions are met, the Attack Display flashes the message SHOOT at the bottom of the screen. The third display is the

Defensive Display. This display uses data from the sensors to show the enemy's defensive activity, to indicate when missiles have been launched toward the plane from the ground or the air, and to list the plane's inventory of defensive chaff and flares.

MUNITIONS

The munitions load carried by the F-22 varies with the intended mission, and the plane is capable of carrying a large and diverse load of weapons. Perhaps the "standard" load, at least for air-to-air combat, is a 20-millimeter M61 gatling gun with 480 rounds, two AIM-120 missiles (also known as AMRAAM, for Advanced Medium Range Air-to-Air Missile), and two AIM-9 Sidewinder missiles. The exact mix of these missiles may vary, depending on the mission and expected threat. Additionally, two JDAM-1000 weapons may be substituted for some of the missiles when required. JDAM, or Joint Direct Attack Munition, is a guidance kit that attaches to a bomb, in this case a 1,000-pound (454-kilogram) bomb. The JDAM is accurate to within 36 feet (11 meters), and a new version will reduce that to 9 feet (2.75 meters). These weapons will be mounted inside internal weapons bays — one in the center of the fuselage and one on each side — in order to maintain the stealth configuration. When stealth is not as important, additional munitions and extra fuel tanks may be suspended beneath the wings and fuselage. These configurations would be used when ferrying the aircraft over long distances or when extra combat range is required.

In addition to the above-mentioned weapons, the F-22 will carry smaller, more accurate bombs that the Air Force is now trying to develop. The advantages of these small "smart" bombs are that they will fit inside the F-22's internal bays to maintain stealth, while allowing just one plane to strike more targets with greater accuracy and less unintended, or collateral, damage. The Air Force would like to be able to take something like the JDAM and put it on a much smaller bomb, maybe as small as 250 pounds (113 kilograms). To do so will require some major changes and more miniaturization in the JDAM. Another munition being considered is a 50-pound (23-kilogram) warhead with a 6-inch (15-centimeter) diameter that can hit a target with a 30-foot (9-meter) circular error probable (CEP) and penetrate 6 feet (1.8 meters) of concrete. In

Development of the F-22 began in 1986, when the Air Force awarded a contract to an industry team that included Lockheed, Boeing, and General Dynamics.

addition, new warheads are being designed to explode only after they have penetrated the inside of the building, which creates more damage with a smaller charge.

Other weapons now under development continue the trend for smaller, smarter, more accurate strikes. Some weapons may soon incorporate Global Positioning System (GPS) guidance to increase their accuracy. The Wind Corrected Munitions Dispenser (WCMD) will accurately deliver small warheads from high altitudes. One version will attack armored vehicles, and another will be designed to shut down radar sites, power supplies, and other electronic equipment. The Low-Cost Autonomous Attack System (LOCAAS) is a 20-inch-long (51-centimeter-long) winged bomb carrying an explosive charge behind a copper plate. It will locate and identify the target and fire the charge in a way that shapes the copper plate into one of three patterns. If it sees a heavily armored tank, it will fire a long stream of molten copper to penetrate the armor; if it sees a lightly armored vehicle, it will fire a copper slug; and if it sees an unarmored truck, it will fire a spray of molten copper fragments. Also in the experimental stages is the hypersonic missile. Designed to fly at Mach 6 (six times the speed of sound), it would outfly defensive weapons and have enough momentum to penetrate deep underground bunkers. Researchers expect it to be accurate to within 10 feet (3 meters).

ROLES

The primary role of the F-22 is air superiority — being able to find, shoot at, and kill the enemy. It will be able to do this because of its stealth capabilities, its "supercruise" speed, and advanced electronics. Other roles are being considered for the F-22, partly to take into account its many features and emerging weaponry and partly to help justify its huge cost. Some of these roles, if adopted, may require additional equipment or new configurations of weapons, fuel tanks, and so on.

Because of its stealth and speed, the F-22 will be able to get close to enemy aircraft while they are still taking off. In this "raid disruption" role, the F-22 would destroy the enemy aircraft before they have even organized. Likewise, it will be able to get close enough to destroy aircraft that are carrying cruise missiles. With improved versions of the Sidewinder and AMRAAM missiles, it could also shoot down the cruise missiles after they are launched.

The primary role of the F-22 is air superiority — being able to find, shoot at, and kill the enemy.

In an intelligence role, the F-22's avionics would collect electronic data from the battlefront to be used as targeting data for Tomahawk missiles and other systems. It would also be able to detect and destroy radar sites and other ground defensive systems. finally, the F-22 could safely penetrate deep into enemy territory in order to intercept and relay electronic intelligence signals, such as battle orders, targeting data, and headquarters communiqués.

JOINT STRIKE FIGHTER

While the central mission of the F-22 is air superiority, the military also needs strike fighters that can hit surface targets. Like the F-22's predecessors, the current strike fighters will soon need to be replaced in order to keep pace with the new threats facing them. To fill that need, several manufacturers are now designing the Joint Strike Fighter (JSF), scheduled to enter production in 2007.

The concept underlying the JSF is that of an affordable family of tactical fighters that the Air Force, Navy, and Marines can all use. The plane's cost would be held down by a large production run (almost three thousand), since so many services will use it, and by the fact that between 70 and 90 percent of the parts would be common to each aircraft in the family.

The JSF will be a single-seat, single-engine aircraft (to keep the cost down), intended to replace the Air Force's F-16, the Navy's F/A-18, and the Marine Corps' AV-8B aircraft. Although not all design features are settled, it will be smaller and lighter than the F-22 and probably will incorporate stealth technology, the new small smart bombs, and possibly even voice commands from the pilot. Top speed is envisioned at approximately Mach 1.2 to 1.4, with a range of 500 to 700 nautical miles. With the proper configuration it would also be able to fly an air superiority role. The engines may have thrust vectoring in more than one axis (rather than just up and down), a feature that could prove to provide enough control that the vertical tails could be greatly reduced or eliminated to minimize the plane's radar signature.

The Pentagon is considering, and the aircraft industry is now researching, such concepts as unmanned, tailless, all-wing, supersonic aircraft that would perform the most dangerous missions such as air defense suppression and tactical reconnaissance. Previously, such vehicles have existed only in science fiction; they may soon become reality.

Undaunted by Failure, Balloonists Vow to Try Again

MALCOLM W. BROWNE

With another season of failures behind them but still fired by passionate faith in the possibility of flying nonstop around the world, balloonists are betting that many small improvements in technology will add up to victory in the next few years.

Like the creation of sailboats competing for the America's Cup or Formula-1 race cars battling for Grand Prix championships, the building of long-duration balloons has become a serious engineering enterprise costing more each year. Three balloon teams that tried in vain this month to circle the world spent a total of more than $4 million, and as more teams enter the race in the future, the price of admission will go up steadily.

The goal is to fly as long and as far as possible, but although that goal is simple to state, it can be reached only through a labyrinth of engineering problems, trade-offs and uncertainties, made all the more difficult by the human equation. Before the opening of next winter's season for round-the-world balloon efforts, engineers, craftsmen and meteorologists will recalculate ratios of lift to size, fuel requirements, rates of heat transfer and many other factors affecting balloon flight duration. The calculations will guide them in making construction changes that must be both "elegant and affordable," as one balloon maker expressed it.

But even the most dedicated balloonists have had doubts about whether it is possible even in principle to fly a manned balloon around the world.

Richard Branson, the captain and main sponsor of the Virgin Global Challenger, recalled his doubts in an interview after his unsuccessful flight this month.

"As I was sitting in the capsule while our balloon was plunging uncontrolled toward the earth," he said,

Above: Standing next to his fuel tanks and cabin, millionaire adventurer Steve Fossett, 52, begins his quest to become the first person to fly nonstop around the globe in a hot air balloon. Left: Steve Fossett lifts off from a snow-covered Busch Stadium, in his balloon "Solo Spirit."

"the thought crossed my mind that maybe a round-the-world flight really is impossible. But we stopped our descent in time to avoid a crash, and I've come back to my conviction that circumnavigation is possible. I'd put money on someone doing it 24 months from today."

Mr. Branson, chairman of Virgin Atlantic Airways and many other companies, believes that progress in balloon technology spurred by round-the-world efforts will lead to long-distance balloon tourism for non-balloonists.

"I can see a day," he said, "once we absolutely button up this technology, when there will be fantastic travel voyages for people willing to pay for the marvels you can see only from balloons. I'm already picturing a brochure for such voyages—a brochure I dream of printing five years from now."

The goal is to fly as long and as far as possible, but although that goal is simple to state, it can be reached only through a labyrinth of engineering problems, trade-offs and uncertainties, made all the more difficult by the human equation. ▼

One problem that has come to light is the need for much greater care in checking balloons and all their vital systems before launching. Two of the three balloons that competed this year were brought down soon after launching because of trivial errors in flight preparation that could have been easily corrected.

In one case, experts at Cameron Balloons Ltd. in Bristol, England, discovered last week why the Swiss balloon Breitling Orbiter was forced to land in the Mediterranean Sea on Jan. 12, a few hours after it was launched. The pilots, Dr. Bertrand Piccard and Wim Verstraeten, faced suffocation soon after launching when their pressurized crew gondola became awash in ankle-deep kerosene gushing from a hose.

"The leak was the result of damage a hose clip sustained during the launch," said Don A. Cameron, president of the company. "That clip cost 69 pence—less than one U.S. dollar—but it cost a million-dollar balloon a sporting chance at the big goal."

Mr. Cameron's company is the world's leading manufacturer of long-duration balloons, including two of the three balloons that competed this year: the Breitling

Orbiter and Steve Fossett's Solo Spirit, which got halfway around the world before running low on fuel and landing in India on Jan. 20. Mr. Cameron said damage to the Breitling Orbiter kerosene line, which fueled burners supplying hot air for lift, might have been avoided by running the line outside the crew gondola. Company experts hope to cure this and countless other possible pitfalls before they build their next balloon for the Swiss Breitling team, which plans another flight next year.

A different oversight led to the premature landing of the Virgin Global Challenger on Jan. 7 a few hours after takeoff from Morocco.

Per Lindstrand, a member of the balloon's crew and president of Lindstrand Balloons Ltd. of Oswestry, England, said that before launching someone simply forgot to take off the safety catches securing six large fuel tanks mounted on the outside of the balloon capsule. "After we were up," Mr. Lindstrand said, "we got an emergency message from the ground that the safety catches had been accidentally left on. That meant we couldn't release any of the tanks from inside the pressurized capsule if we needed to jettison them."

It was essential to release the safety catches, which meant that someone had to climb outside the capsule. But since the balloon was at 30,000 feet, the balloon had to descend before anyone could open the gondola hatch and crawl out. Mr. Lindstrand waited until the cool air of evening brought the balloon down to 10,000 feet, but at that point a rotating current of air rising from the Atlas Mountains swept the balloon violently up and down, releasing precious helium and threatening to hurl it into the ground. After the crew had thrown everything movable out of the gondola to recover lift, one of the balloonists, Alex Ritchie, crawled to a perilous perch on the top of the capsule and unfastened the tanks. They were released just in time to halt the balloon's crash dive. But the loss of fuel, helium and supplies doomed the round-the-world mission to failure and the crew decided to land.

Mr. Lindstrand attributed the oversight to overwork and lack of sleep for the ground crew as it prepared the balloon for flight.

Mr. Fossett's Solo Spirit ended its record-breaking flight short of its goal for much more serious engineering reasons.

By the time he reached India, his supply of propane fuel had been exhausted much more rapidly than antici-

If a way could be found to keep a balloon from cooling and heating, its duration would be nearly unlimited.

High-altitude balloons launched without crews but carrying scientific payloads weighing up to a ton have made very long flights, including one that circled the Antarctic continent four times.

Swiss Bertrand Piccard and Belgian Wim Verstraeten took off from a snow-covered Alpine meadow in a bid to become the first to circle the world in a balloon.

pated, and his ground crew in Chicago calculated that he could not continue more than three more days — too little to get him across the Pacific and beyond, to the longitude of his starting point at St. Louis.

"The solution to this unexpected consumption rate," Mr. Cameron said, "might seem to be to carry more propane the next time. However, that gets you into a vicious cycle. Propane is a highly compressed gas carried in heavy steel cylinders. To carry more of it you need a bigger balloon with more lift. But a bigger balloon burns propane faster, so you need more propane. And so it goes."

Mr. Cameron believes that part of the solution may be improved "heat management," an important consideration for all Rozier balloons.

Even the most dedicated balloonists have had doubts about whether it is possible even in principle to fly a manned balloon around the world. ▼

All three balloons that competed this month were of the Rozier type, named for their inventor, Jean François Pilâtre de Rozier, who, with the marquis François Laurent d'Arlandes, made the world's first manned flight on Nov. 21, 1783, over Paris. The balloon built for that flight by the Montgolfier brothers was lifted by hot air generated from burning rags, straw and garbage.

Later, de Rozier designed, built and tested a new kind of balloon that derived most of its lift from hydrogen gas but got extra lift from a burner that heated the gas. The system worked, but the highly inflammable hydrogen caught fire during de Rozier's last flight, and the French aristocrat became the world's first air crash fatality.

During the last five years, manufacturers of long-distance competition balloons have concentrated their efforts on the Rozier principle. A disadvantage of gas balloons lacking supplementary heating is that during the day, sunlight warms them, making the gas inside less dense and therefore more buoyant. A warmed gas balloon rises, its gas expands as atmospheric pressure falls, and at some point, the balloon reaches its capacity and is forced to release lifting gas.

But when the sun sets, the gas inside the balloon cools and loses buoyancy, causing the balloon to descend. To correct this, since the balloon has lost some of its helium or hydrogen, the pilot must throw out ballast, usually in the form of metal shot or sand. Before long, this day-and-night cycle exhausts the balloon's lifting gas and its supply of ballast, and it must land.

A Rozier balloon, however, needs very little ballast. When its lifting gas cools at night, the pilot need not drop ballast, but instead can light his burners fueled with propane or kerosene, and the heat warms air in a cell just below the balloon's main helium cell.

But sunlight still warms a balloon's helium during the day, causing undesirable ascent, and at night, Roziers still lose enough heat to make them descend. If a way could be found to keep a balloon from cooling and heating, its duration would be nearly unlimited. This ideal may never be reached, but balloon makers believe it can be approached.

Most balloon makers cover the outside of long-duration balloons with highly reflective plastic film, which slows the flow of heat in both directions. But besides this, Mr. Cameron's company now builds an insulating layer of air between the inner balloon wall (made of finely woven nylon fabric bonded to a gas-tight plastic film) and an outer balloon skin made of aluminized Mylar film.

Both Mr. Fossett's balloon and the Breitling Orbiter incorporated this Cameron innovation, but it was not enough to give them the necessary endurance to fly around the world. Mr. Fossett's Solo Spirit, brilliantly though it performed, ran out of propane even with the Cameron thermal insulation system in place. Mr. Cameron said that extensive design changes would probably help, including a possible increase in the thickness of the air layer between the inner and outer balloon skins.

Mr. Lindstrand, head of the competing balloon manufacturing company that made the Virgin Global Challenger, believes the Cameron double-wall air insulation system is ineffective. "You have only to see that Steve Fossett failed to get farther than India to realize that the Cameron system doesn't do what it's supposed to do," he said.

The disagreement is expected to persist.

Another set of engineering problems with which competitors are grappling concerns the selection of a balloon's ideal cruising altitude.

In general, the steadiest and speediest winds are the jet streams sweeping through the upper troposphere and

The steadiest and speediest winds are the jet streams sweeping through the upper troposphere and stratosphere. Balloonists try to exploit these winds because their speeds, up to 200 miles an hour, can whisk balloons over great distances before they run low on fuel and ballast.

stratosphere. Balloonists try to exploit these winds because their speeds, up to 200 miles an hour, can whisk balloons over great distances before they run low on fuel and ballast.

But for a balloon to cruise at 20,000 feet or higher, its crew ordinarily needs a pressurized capsule, and even when capsules are built of light aircraft alloys or fiber-reinforced resins, they must be heavy enough to withstand high internal pressure.

Steve Fossett had planned his flight and conditioned his body to cruise at about 18,000 feet in his unpressurized capsule. Balloonists everywhere were amazed that he survived the ordeal.

In the case of the Dymocks Flyer, a huge balloon two Americans and an Australian hope to launch from Australia next December, the strength of the capsule will be critical. Their balloon, made mostly of plastic sheeting similar to that of sandwich bags, is designed to cruise above 100,000 feet in the stratosphere, where jet streams are best. Its capsule is more similar to a space vehicle than a conventional balloon gondola.

Similar high-altitude balloons launched without crews but carrying scientific payloads weighing up to a ton have made very long flights, including one that circled the Antarctic continent four times. But these gigantic balloons, most of them by Raven Industries Inc., in Sioux Falls, S.D., have rarely carried humans.

Another disadvantage is that the Dymocks Flyer crew will have to cruise with the same life-support systems used by astronauts; a loss of capsule pressure at 100,000 feet would quickly kill a crew not wearing spacesuits.

No Rozier balloon could fly that high because there would be insufficient oxygen to allow propane fuel to burn.

"The biggest factor affecting the size of a balloon," Mr. Cameron said, "is the height you want it to reach. The height you can reach for a given weight depends on the volume of the balloon, so you must make it big to fly high. However, the bigger the balloon, the more solar heat it is exposed to during the day and the more heat escapes at night. Keeping the heat flow in both directions to a minimum is essential, but it presents engineering problems that are easier to solve for smaller balloons."

Computer-aided design changes and mathematical models of balloon performance help in engineering, but can be verified only by experiment.

"Flying a newly built long-distance balloon is like trying out a military weapon," Mr. Cameron said. "You can't really test weapons in peacetime. But when they get into action you can use the experience to build the next generation. We're building 20th-generation Roziers now, and the process continues."

Balloon makers lament that their financial support can never equal that spent by National Aeronautics and Space Administration and the aerospace industry on the design and testing of new ideas. But by most standards, the leading balloon makers are amply financed.

Above: Richard Branson and his crew.

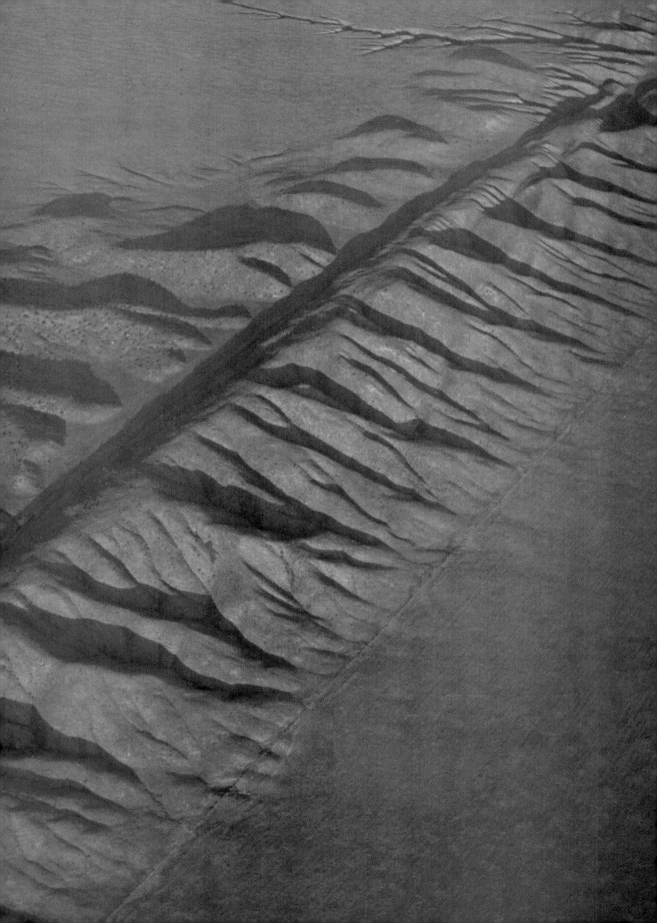

Peering into the Earth's Critical Layer with GPR

Engineering and Environmental Tales from the Underground

ALVIN K. BENSON

round-penetrating radar (GPR) is an active remote-sensing technique developed in the 1960's as a result of research on electromagnetic pulses generated by nuclear blasts. Atmospheric nuclear testing in the 1950's demonstrated that sharp electromagnetic pulses could penetrate the Earth's surface, and this concept led to GPR. GPR technology allows researchers to see below, through, or into otherwise impenetrable objects, and it is having a profound impact on enhancing our knowledge of the shallow subsurface, in particular the upper two meters of the Earth's underground, the most critical layer to human civilization. Most of our food and drinking water, foundations for our buildings and engineering structures, and waste disposal and storage are provided by this layer.

In many geological settings, GPR is a reliable, rapid, nondestructive, and economical method for mapping shallow subsurface soils and sediments, assessing hydrogeologic conditions, and locating subsurface geological hazards. Planning and remedial measures based upon these data can then be implemented to help protect human life and produce minimal threat to the environment. GPR methods have numerous applications in the engineering and environmental sciences, including mapping the following subsurface targets: pipes, cables, barrels, scrap metal, fuel tanks, waste containers, depth to water table, groundwater contamination, land mines, bedrock contours, fault structures, masonry structures and bridge piers, sinkholes, thickness of coal seams, depth of topsoil, layers of soil, tunnels, cavities under pavement, and caves.

A.K. Benson (on left) and two students collecting GPR data. Ground penetrating radar (GPR) system showing the radar antenna (red fiberglass box in center foreground) and the pulse transmitter and recorder unit (upper left in photo) connected to the vehicle battery, which supplies the power to operate the system. Opposite page: San Andreas Fault, California.

PRINCIPLES OF GROUND-PENETRATING RADAR

The GPR technique is similar in principle to seismic reflection and sonar techniques. Pulse-mode GPR systems radiate into the ground short pulses of high-frequency electromagnetic energy (10-1,000 million cycles per second) from a transmitting antenna. Radar surveys are done by towing the antenna by hand or behind a vehicle over the area being investigated. In most surveys, the antenna is in contact with the ground surface, but airborne and space-borne radars work well above ground.

Site in the Wasatch fault zone, Provo, Utah, where a fault with vertical offset of 3.2 meters was mapped using GPR.

Propagation of the radar signal depends on the frequency-dependent electrical properties of the ground. The two most important variables of the targets and the surrounding subsurface materials are (1) the electrical conductivity, or the ability of a material to conduct electrical current; and (2) the dielectric properties, or the capacity of a material to become polarized or store a charge when an external electric field is applied to it. Electrical conductivity of the soil or rock materials along the propagation paths introduces significant absorptive losses which limit the depth of penetration into earth formations. When the radiated energy encounters an inhomogeneity in the dielectric properties of the subsurface, part of the incident energy is reflected back to the radar antenna and part is transmitted into and possibly through the inhomogeneity.

The electrical properties of geological materials are governed primarily by the water content, dissolved minerals, and expansive clay and heavy mineral content. Reflected signals are amplified, transformed to the audio-frequency range, recorded, processed, and displayed. From the recorded display, subsurface features such as soil/soil, soil/rock, and unsaturated/saturated interfaces can be identified. In addition, the presence of hydrocarbons floating on the water table, the geometry of contaminant plumes, and the location of buried cables, pipes, drums, and tanks can be detected.

The GPR data are presented as a two-dimensional depth profile along a scanned traverse line in which the vertical axis is two-way travel time measured in nanoseconds. The recorded GPR data show soil layers and other subsurface features much as they would appear to an observer looking at the wall of a vertical trench below the GPR traverse. If the propagation velocity of the electromagnetic pulse is known, the depth to the reflector can be determined. For low-loss media (low to medium attenuation of electromagnetic energy), the propagation velocity is inversely proportional to the square root of the dielectric constant of the material. Thus, in an otherwise uniform low-loss medium of known or estimated dielectric constant, the depth to the reflector can be approximated from the recorded GPR travel times.

The penetration capabilities of GPR are site-specific and depend upon the frequency spectrum of the source excitation signal and the antenna radiation efficiency, as well as the electrical properties of the subsurface materials. Attenuation losses are caused by (a) conversion of the radiated energy to heat through electrical conduction losses; (b) dielectric relaxation losses in water; and/or (c) chemical diffusion in clay minerals. The effect of signal scattering by small-scale heterogeneities can also increase attenuation with increasing frequency. Materials with high conductivity, such as clayey soils, will rapidly reduce the depth of penetration.

The radar frequency selected for a particular study is chosen to provide an acceptable compromise between deeper penetration and higher resolution. High-frequency radar signals produce greater resolution but are more limited in depth of penetration. Ideally, the resolution is equal to a quarter of a wavelength, but in reality, due to waveform variations and velocity uncertainties, it is typically equal to one-third to one-half of the wavelength of the radar pulse.

ENVIRONMENTAL AND ENGINEERING APPLICATIONS

GPR is a very useful geophysical method for use in environmental and engineering studies. GPR surveys can be used to study contaminants in groundwater, subsurface faulting, and underground cavities (natural or human-made), all of which pose potentially dangerous geological hazards. Geophysical exploration is a nondestructive, cost-effective way to help locate and characterize these hazards, and at many sites, GPR is one of the better techniques for this search into the shallow subsurface.

The ability to see through structural materials with a

Ground-penetrating radar (GPR) is an active remote-sensing technique developed in the 1960's as a result of research on electromagnetic pulses generated by nuclear blasts.

noninvasive reflection technique is having increasing influence on engineering and environmental studies. For example, GPR surveys have located voids in concrete and earth dams, detected sinkholes under highways and airports, mapped reinforcing materials in concrete and underground utilities, determined depth to bedrock under building projects, and located buried waste drums and leaking underground storage tanks. GPR has revolutionized engineering studies of sinkhole-prone regions, such as central Florida. Even when the radar cannot reach the bottom of the sinkhole, near-surface indicators of ground subsidence show up, making it possible to locate the next possible collapse. Management and maintenance of hydraulic engineering structures, such as water-retaining dikes and ship locks in canals, are monitored with GPR. Since these structures cannot be taken temporarily out of use, the GPR method provides a way for quality assessment while leaving them unaffected during application. Tunnel investigations for structural integrity are performed with GPR surveys, and GPR technology was employed to help with a detailed structural analysis of the New York State Capitol building as part of a renovation feasibility study in 1993-1994. GPR is also being used to detect road pavement flaws before they become obvious potholes so that repairs can be made before expensive road and vehicle damage occurs.

GPR is an excellent method for locating subsurface pipes of different kinds of material, such as plastic, metal, concrete, or clay. Applications include finding sewer lines, natural gas lines, and buried telephone and television cables prior to construction activities. In addition, GPR surveys are used to map all kinds of subsurface metal objects, including fifty-five-gallon drums at hazardous waste sites, scrap metal in landfills, and underground fuel tanks. Many lives have been saved by using GPR technology to locate ordnance, including unexploded bombs, land mines, arms caches, and buried ammunition at gunnery ranges. Locating some of these objects can avoid the potential environmental hazards and other problems that would result from digging or drilling directly into subsurface containers, utilities, and explosive devices. As long as the contents of the burial site have dielectric contrasts with the surrounding material, they will be highly reflective and quite apparent on GPR records. Also, since many of these objects typically lie in

The GPR technique is similar in principle to seismic reflection and sonar techniques.

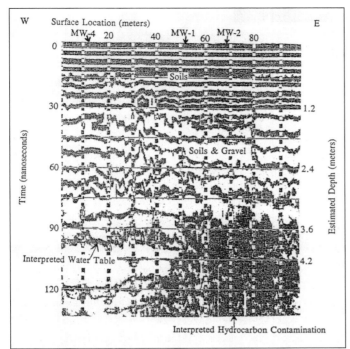

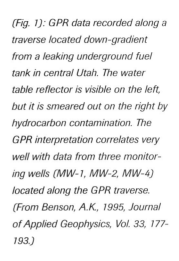

(Fig. 1): GPR data recorded along a traverse located down-gradient from a leaking underground fuel tank in central Utah. The water table reflector is visible on the left, but it is smeared out on the right by hydrocarbon contamination. The GPR interpretation correlates very well with data from three monitoring wells (MW-1, MW-2, MW-4) located along the GPR traverse. (From Benson, A.K., 1995, Journal of Applied Geophysics, Vol. 33, 177-193.)

Fig. 1

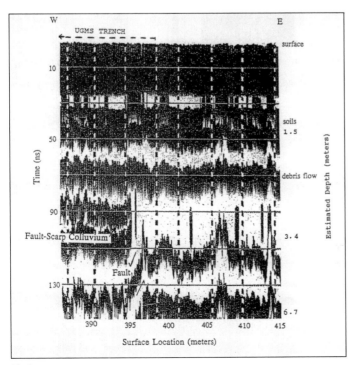

Fig.2

(Fig. 2): GPR profile of a shallow fault in the Wasatch fault zone, Provo, Utah. The main fault is clearly visible, with an estimated vertical offset of 3.2 meters. Location of a trench opened by the Utah Geological and Mineral Survey (UGMS) is shown. The GPR interpretation correlates very well with the trench data. (From Benson, A.K., 1995, Journal of Applied Geophysics, Vol. 33, 177-193.)

areas where the soil layers have been disturbed by digging, even if the materials are not reflective or if they are
covered with an overburden of conductive clay that
inhibits the radar penetration, the burial site can still
often be located by identifying the disturbed soil horizons.

GPR surveys can be very helpful and cost-effective
in providing a map of the three-dimensional distribution
of the surficial soils and fill material. Such maps are critical in foundation studies for engineering projects and in
environmental studies involving subsurface pollution.
Geological layering will be detected with GPR, particularly if dielectric contrasts within the materials are high.
The United States Department of Agriculture has mapped
soils in the United States with GPR. By using occasional
soil borings to determine "ground truth" (actual in-situ
conditions) researchers can trace the soil layers for long
distances with GPR, greatly speeding the mapping
process. Depths to bedrock show clearly, especially if the
overburden geology has different dielectric properties
from those of the rock below it.

MAPPING POLLUTED GROUNDWATER

Unpolluted groundwater is becoming an increasingly valuable resource around the world. In some areas,
supplies have been greatly decreased as a result of care-
less management or disposal of hazardous materials.
Hydrogeologists require methods, such as GPR, to map
the soil stratigraphy at sites where contaminants are in
the subsurface.

GPR methods are especially useful in correlating
time-changing horizons, such as the water table, from one
area to another. In addition to locating the water table, GPR
can help characterize subsurface contamination conditions
produced by hazardous materials by (a) locating buried
materials; (b) determining the presence of contaminant
plumes (organic and inorganic), their source(s), and geometry; and (c) assessing the associated groundwater conditions. For example, the presence of hydrocarbons floating
on the water table and of hydrocarbons seeping into the soil
can often be detected on the GPR record. The water table
typically appears as a strong reflection on a GPR record,
and this reflection is often "smeared out" by reflections
associated with pollutants, such as hydrocarbons. Since
hydrocarbons are less conductive than water, wherever they
are present they tend to enhance radar reflections.

GPR surveys can play an important role in defining the subsurface geology and the associated parameters that govern the movement of contaminant plumes. Analysis of these data sets can help produce a more cost-effective program in strategically locating monitoring wells, as well as provide an effective horizontal extension of borehole data. Understanding the hydrogeologic setting is essential in defining potential contaminant migration pathways and assessing the fate of contaminant movement along the pathways. This understanding comes from data, such as GPR surveys, detailing the three-dimensional distribution of the surficial soils and fill material, the geologic strata and structure, and the groundwater conditions, such as hydraulic and chemical properties of the soils and groundwater.

Hazardous subsurface materials need to be located and mapped for site assessment and for some kind of remedial action, often involving excavation and safe disposal of the hazardous materials with minimal damage to the environment. Early use of GPR methods allows problems to be detected and evaluated sooner and a strategic cleanup program to be implemented more quickly. In appropriate geologic settings, GPR has proven to be a reliable, rapid, and economical method for mapping shallow subsurface sediments and assessing hydrogeologic conditions. The thickness of the sediments, the depth to the water table, and the presence of groundwater contamination can be reliably mapped at field sites where reflector geometries are not too complex and where electrical resistivities are typically high and relative dielectric constants are typically low.

UNSEEN FAULTS

Because of its ability to detect changes in conductivity, as well as its sensitivity to water, GPR provides an unparalleled method for detecting underground discontinuities, including joints, fractures, and faults in bedrock. Planning and development in faulted areas, such as southern California and the Wasatch front of central Utah, must compensate for the geological hazards associated with faulting. Many studies show that future ruptures will probably occur along already existing zones of weakness (faulted areas). Although some faults can be detected by surficial geological mapping, others have no visible expression and can be located only by subsurface investigations. GPR data collected at a site in the Wasatch fault zone in east Provo, Utah, in 1989 first demonstrated the reliable detection of shallow concealed faulting in appropriate geologic settings with GPR. Interpretations of the radar data coincide with most features observed in a nearby trench that was opened by the Utah Geological and Mineral Survey (UGMS) after the geophysical work was completed. The net offset and dip of the fault determined from the GPR data correlate very well with the trench data.

GPR technology allows researchers to see below, through, or into otherwise impenetrable objects, and it is having a profound impact on enhancing our knowledge of the shallow subsurface, in particular the upper two meters of the Earth's underground, the most critical layer to human civilization. ▼

GPR methods can be integrated with geotechnical engineering methods, such as drilling and trenching, to obtain a better understanding of potential subsurface geological hazards at a specific site. The characteristics of the subsurface deformation can be analyzed to gain a better understanding of foundation conditions and of the potential for surface rupture at the site, and thereby to plan future site development by establishing and implementing building codes and zoning ordinances, as well as devising remedial measures for mitigating the effects of potential earthquakes in populated areas.

UNDERGROUND CAVITIES

GPR can also be used to locate air-filled cavities and voids, whether natural or human-made. These caverns include mines, tunnels, caves, and lava vents. Determining their location and geometry has diverse engineering and environmental applications, including the safe construction of buildings, roadways, and airports. For air-filled cavities, good contrast exists between the dielectric constants of the host materials (soils and rocks) and the cavities. Consequently, GPR can be successful in outlining underground cavities. Likewise, GPR can be very helpful in locating areas of subsidence associated with underground cavities, such as unmapped mines and tunnels.

For example, GPR provided useful information about location, approximate depths, and lateral extent for two cavities and associated areas of subsidence under U.S. Highway 6 near Eureka, Utah. Eureka is an old mining town dating back to the 1890's; numerous mine shafts and tunnels lie under the town and surrounding areas. Locations of many of the older underground excavations are unknown, since they were never recorded on any maps. In many places the ground is cracked or collapsed from the mining activity, and some mines have become cone-shaped cave-ins.

Two areas of subsidence in the upper strata underneath U.S. Highway 6 were readily observed on GPR data. Directly below each area of subsidence on the GPR data, characteristic hyperbola-shaped patterns indicate the presence of subsurface cavities, which are either human-made cavities, such as a mine shaft or a tunnel, or sinkholes carved out by water in the underlying limestone. Whatever the source of the subsurface cavities and associated subsidence, GPR can often be a successful, cost-effective method for locating these potential hazards. This information is very useful in planning and site development. Early detection of such cavities and the mechanism or mechanisms causing subsidence can result in substantial savings in time and money.

CONCLUSION

GPR is profoundly enhancing our knowledge of the upper two meters of the Earth's subsurface. This layer contains one of the most complex and least understood ecosystems on Earth, and yet it is the most important layer on our planet because human civilization and all life are totally dependent on it. Most of our drinking water percolates through this layer, and this layer is expected both to provide food for the human race into the foreseeable future and to provide storage for all of our wastes. The foundations for most of our housing, roadways, airports, and other engineering constructs are found in this layer. GPR technology provides a tool that allows us to see into this critical layer, learn about it, and help manage it.

Whatever the source of the subsurface cavities and associated subsidence, GPR can often be a successful, cost-effective method for locating potential hazards.

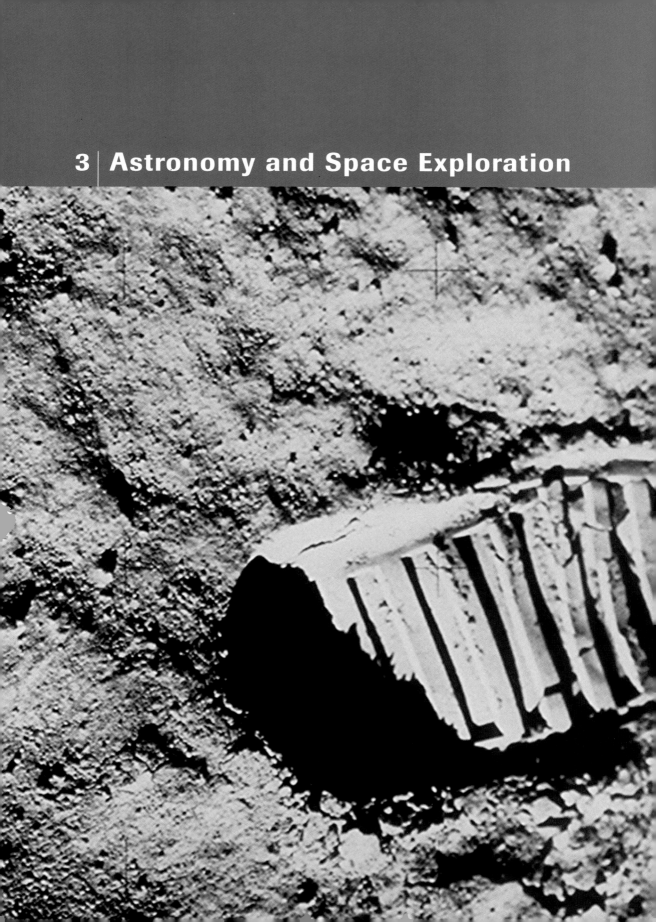

Evidence for Water on the Moon

JOSEPH L. SPRADLEY

The discovery of strong evidence for frozen water at the south pole of the Moon is both hugely surprising and highly significant for the future of lunar studies and manned space exploration. This unlikely discovery was announced at a scientific press conference held in a Pentagon briefing room on December 3, 1996, by a team of military and civilian space scientists working with the Department of Defense's Clementine spacecraft. It was described in the November 29, 1996, issue of the journal *Science* (vol. 274, pp. 1495-1498) under the title "The Clementine Bistatic Radar Experiment," by Stewart Nozette (U.S. Air Force Phillips Laboratory, Arlington, Virginia) and seven other collaborating authors. At the press conference one author, Paul Spudis of the Lunar and Planetary Institute (Houston, Texas), spoke of the possibility of ice: "We are not positive, but we see signals consistent with ice and we think it's there."

Emblem for Clementine mission.

As strange as "lunar ice" might sound, its possibility was suggested as early as 1961 by three scientists at the California Institute of Technology. In the Journal of Geophysical Research (vol. 66, p. 3033), Kenneth Watson, Bruce Murray, and Harrison Brown pointed out that the lunar poles are nearly at right angles to the Sun, never tilting more than 1.6 degrees toward its rays. Thus they theorized that some crater floors near the lunar poles might lie in constant shadow, where vapors from comet collisions could condense and freeze. Such "cold traps" would hover near 40 degrees Kelvin (-233 degrees Celsius), keeping ice so solidly frozen that very little could evaporate into space. Although water would be the most likely condensate, carbon dioxide and other volatile compounds could also be frozen in these polar prisons.

A decade after this suggestion of water ice on the

Opposite page: Mosaic image of the near side of the moon as taken by star trackers on-board the Clementine spacecraft.

Moon, the Apollo lunar missions brought back rock and soil samples that proved to be as dry as dust. Thus the idea that water might outgas from the lunar interior did not seem to hold water. However, the possibility of lunar ice from comets was revived by James Arnold (University of California) in 1979. He estimated that during two billion years, several thousand comet collisions on the Moon could leave up to 100 billion tons of water locked in the form of ice in craters at the lunar poles. Although no large craters exist at the lunar north pole, the south pole is located within an immense impact crater more than 2,500 kilometers (1,553 miles) in diameter with an average depth of 12 kilometers (7.46 miles) as shown by Clementine mapping. This region, called the South Pole-Aitken Basin, is the largest known impact crater in the solar system and contains large zones of permanent shadow.

Oh My Darlin', Clementine

In a cavern, in a canyon,

Excavating for a mine,

Dwelt a miner, forty-niner,

And his daughter Clementine.

The Clementine mission began in 1992 as a project for the Strategic Defense (Star Wars) Initiative by the National Aeronautics and Space Administration (NASA) and the U.S. Department of Defense. It was originally planned as a mission to the near-Earth asteroid Geographos, using new lightweight technology to serve as a platform to test new electronic components and tracking sensors. At the suggestion of Nozette, it was later expanded by two months to include mapping of the Moon as a demonstration of spacecraft and sensor performance before the difficult asteroid flyby. The name Clementine was chosen because the ballad "My Darlin' Clementine" is about the daughter of a miner, and this mission would help determine the mineral content of the Moon and the asteroid. Also like Clementine, it would be "lost and gone forever" after the asteroid flyby.

The Clementine spacecraft was built in just two years at the Naval Research Laboratory in Washington, D.C., as the first example of a new "smaller, faster, cheaper" technology. It was inexpensive by space exploration standards, costing only $55 million, plus $20 million for its Titan II launch missile, with an efficient "mission control" operating out of a small warehouse in Alexandria, Virginia. The spacecraft was designed as an eight-sided prism about 2 meters (6.5 feet) long, using lightweight construction that weighed only 227 kilograms (500 pounds) with a roughly equal mass of liquid fuel. Its thrusting engine was at one end and a high-gain dish antenna on the other end for transmitting data back to Earth. It was powered by a solar array that produced about 240 watts of electricity.

Clementine was launched from California's Vandenberg Air Force Base on January 25, 1994, into a temporary Earth orbit. On February 3 it was injected into a transfer orbit to the Moon, where it was placed in a five-hour lunar orbit on February 19, varying between 400 kilometers and 2,940 kilometers (between 249 and 1,827 miles) from the Moon's surface. After seventy-one days in lunar orbit, its main engine was fired on May 4 to send it to its asteroid target. Three days later tragedy struck when its computer mistakenly allowed its control thrusters to fire for eleven minutes until its steering gas ran out. On May 7 the mission was aborted and Clementine was truly "lost and gone forever" in heliocentric orbit. In spite of this disappointment, the Clementine mission was spectacularly successful in lunar orbit, sending back nearly two million digital images from the Moon at visible and infrared wavelengths, and the surprising evidence for water ice, before aborting.

Oh, my darlin', oh, my darlin',

Oh, my darlin' Clementine!

You are lost and gone forever,

Dreadful sorry, Clementine.

CLEMENTINE'S LUNAR GOLD MINE

The wealth of information collected by Clementine is a resource that will stimulate lunar research for years, and interesting results are already beginning to fill scientific journals. Its lunar mapping instruments included several CCD (charge coupled device) cameras, including one for visible and ultraviolet light, one for near-infrared and one for far-infrared radiation, two star-tracker cameras, and a high-resolution camera that was used in concert with a laser-ranging altimeter. During each of some 350 lunar orbits, Clementine aimed its 1.1-meter (3.6-foot) antenna toward Earth and transmitted some five thousand images stored in its 1.9-gigabyte memory. Reception by NASA's Deep Space Network used 70-meter (230-foot) antennas and image compression techniques to speed transmission. The result was a complete digital map of the Moon and data from eleven wavelength bands to construct a geological map by analyzing color differences in surface rocks to estimate gross mineral content.

Although Clementine was designed primarily for imaging and altitude mapping, the possibility of prospecting for water became evident after the mission started. Early in its lunar run, Nozette proposed using the space-

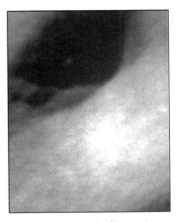

Lunar image taken by Clementine spacecraft with the High Res (HIRES) imager.

craft's high-gain antenna to reflect radio waves with a 13.2-centimeter (5.2-inch) wavelength from the perpetually darkened floors of craters at the lunar poles. If the reflected energy could be detected on Earth, it might provide evidence for patches of ice in these cold traps. This makeshift radar experiment was similar to radar studies of the large moons of Jupiter twenty years before, which revealed their icy surfaces. Such icy surfaces become especially reflective when the angle between the transmitter and the receiver (as seen from the target) nears 0 degrees. Thus radar echoes from icy Europa are thirty times stronger than those from the soil-covered Moon, even though the Moon is slightly larger.

An important first step was to establish that permanently shadowed regions do really exist on the Moon. The chances were good, since the lunar south pole lies 200 kilometers (124 miles) inside the rim of the Aitken Basin and 5 to 8 kilometers (3 to 5 miles) below the highest point of the basin rim. Images from Clementine revealed at least 6,400 and up to 15,500 square kilometers (2,471 to 5,985 square miles) near the south pole of crater floors and valleys untouched by sunlight, an area about the size of the Hawaiian Islands. Several higher points within 30 kilometers (18.6 miles) of the pole are nearly always illuminated. The spacecraft found only about 530 square kilometers (205 square miles) at the north pole in continual shadow. Because of the extensive cold-trap regions at the south pole, it is expected to retain much more trapped ice and other frozen volatiles than at the north pole.

CLEMENTINE'S SEARCH FOR WATER ICE

Because the cold traps at the south pole receive no direct solar illumination and emit very little radiation, they are difficult to observe from Earth. Radar can identify possible frozen volatiles in these regions by reflecting radio waves from them. Under certain conditions, these reflected waves produce a unique radar signature, although such radar observations may not be conclusive, depending on the nature of the surface and the quantity of volatiles present. Radar waves reflect more strongly from frozen volatiles than from silicate rocks because of much lower transmission losses in icy substances. Total internal reflection in ice also preserves the same polarization as that of the transmitted waves, while ordinary reflection reverses the polarization.

Light she was and like a fairy,

And her shoes were

number nine,

Herring boxes without topses,

Sandals were for Clementine.

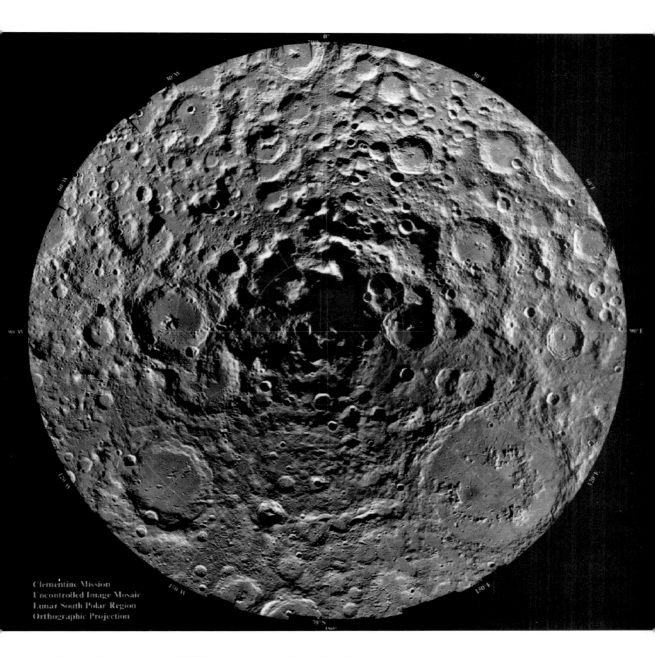

Clementine Mission
Uncontrolled Image Mosaic
Lunar South Polar Region
Orthographic Projection

This mosaic is composed of 1500 Clementine images, taken through a red
filter, of the south polar region of the Moon. The top half of the mosaic
faces Earth. Clementine has revealed what appears to be a major depression
near the lunar south pole (center), evident from the presence of extensive
shadows around the pole. This depression probably is an ancient basin
formed by the impact of an asteroid or comet. A significant portion of the
dark area near the pole may be in permanent shadow, and sufficiently cold
to trap water of cometary origin in the form of ice.

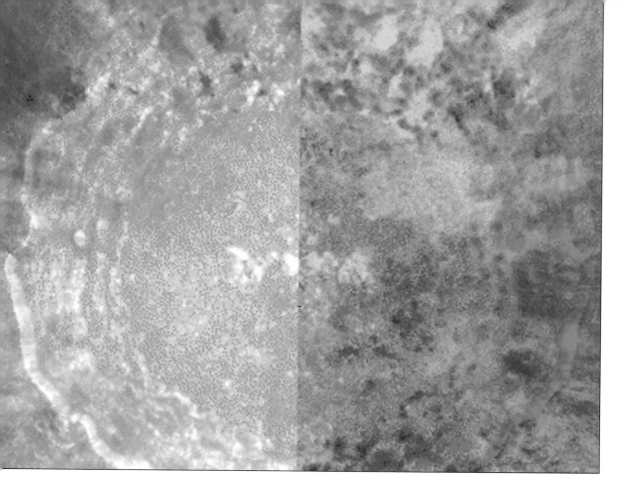

Mosaic of the lunar crater Copernicus produced using images obtained by the Clementine UV/VIS camera. This 95-km crater, is believed to be approximately 800 million years old. The right section of the image is a color composite mosaic of the eastern half of Copernicus. This color mosaic was prepared using images obtained through filters of three different colors chosen to allow small lunar color differences to be mapped in a geologic context.

A unique effect called coherent backscattering may occur as the angle between the transmitter on the spacecraft and the receiver on Earth (as seen from the lunar target) approaches zero. The presence of cracks or inhomogeneities embedded in a low loss material such as ice produces a reflection surge when the reflected waves return along a path close to that of the transmitted waves. This coherent backscattering surge can be caused by double bounce reflection, which also preserves the same polarization as the transmitted waves. Two photons entering the ice with the same phase and reflecting along the same path but in opposite directions will combine coherently after the reflections and amplify the energy returning toward the receiver. This strong reflectivity and high ratio of same polarization to reversed polarization were detected in radar observations of the large moons of Jupiter, the south polar ice cap of Mars, the permanently shadowed polar craters of Mercury, and portions of the Greenland ice sheet.

Radar measurements using a transmitter in orbit can be used as a test for coherent backscattering by measuring the magnitude of reflected waves and their polarization as the angle between the spacecraft and the receiver approaches zero. Clementine's first attempt at this kind of radar astronomy failed in March, 1994, but during a second trial in April one radar track in orbit 234 swept directly over the south pole, and a couple weeks later another track in orbit 301 swept over the north pole. In orbit 234, the radar echo increased and the ratio of same polarization to reversed polarization peaked just as the shadowed areas were within the radar beam and the angle between the transmitter and receiver approached zero. The echo from the next orbit (235) passed about 200 kilometers (124 miles) from the pole and showed no enhancement, nor did a pair of similar scans (301 and 302) over the north pole. Before it was lost forever, Clementine sent back its evidence for water on the Moon.

Data from orbit 234 are not a definitive proof of water ice. Coherent backscattering from low loss media usually produces a narrower peak (less than 0.1 degree) and a larger enhancement of the polarization ratio than the orbit 234 data. Several explanations can be given, including the possibility that the scattering is not from ice deposits. However, orbit 234 data have been averaged over a large area of which less than a third (15,000 square kilometers, or 5,791 square miles) is permanently shadowed. The larger surrounding surface area reduces the polarization ratio (more reflections with reversed polarization), and lunar soil mixed with any ice deposits would further reduce the peak amplitude.

Analysis of the data leads to estimates that south pole ice deposits could be equivalent to about 100 square kilometers (38.6 square miles) of pure ice with a minimum depth of about 1 meter (assuming wavelength scale scatterers) down to 15 meters (49 feet). This would yield at least 100 million cubic meters of ice (100 billion kilograms, or 220 billion pounds). These estimates may be a lower limit, since the viewing geometry does not allow observation of the deepest parts of the shadowed areas. However, if ice deposits do exist, they are likely to be in isolated patches mixed with rocks and dirt. These results are consistent with a 1993 radar sounding from Earth with the 300-meter (984-foot) radio dish at Arecibo, Puerto Rico. Donald Campbell and Nicholas Stacy from Cornell University found high polarization ratios in several craters

Drove she ducklings

to the water

Every morning just at nine,

Hit her foot against a splinter,

Fell into the foaming brine.

Ruby lips above the water,

Blowing bubbles soft and fine.

Alas for me! I was no swimmer,

So I lost my Clementine.

near the south pole using Arecibo's radar system, but their results were too ambiguous to show the existence of ice.

IMPORTANCE OF THE CLEMENTINE EVIDENCE

Permanent layers of ice on the Moon would be even more valuable than gold to planetary scientists. The evidence for water ice on the Moon has important implications for both planetary studies and space exploration. According to Spudis, "For the first time on the Moon, we have a preserved record of the rate of cometary impacts over time. So we can study this deposit and actually understand how the flux of comets in our area of the solar system changed with time." By probing lunar ice layers, scientists believe that they could learn how frequently comets have hit the Moon and what comets are made of. A similar frequency of comet impacts might also apply to the early history of the Earth and shed light on how its oceans were formed.

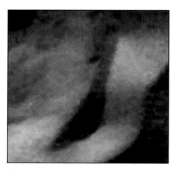

One of many "sample" images taken by the imaging experiments on-board the Clementine space-craft. This lunar image was taken by the Long-Wavelength Infrared (LWIR) imager.

Trapped ice might also support a lunar colony, providing a source of water and oxygen as well as rocket fuel for space exploration. Mountaintops near the lunar south pole are almost perpetually sunlit, offering an ideal place for a solar-powered colony. Spudis suggests, "You might be looking at the most valuable piece of real estate in the solar system." A lunar colony could process ice at such a location and separate water into liquid oxygen and hydrogen like that used to power the space shuttle. "The only difference," says Nozette, "is that this fuel is on the Moon to begin with. We don't have to truck it up from Earth."

Uncertainties about the existence of water on the Moon may soon be resolved. In September, 1997, NASA plans to launch the Lunar Prospector in their Discovery series of space probes. It will carry a neutron spectrometer able to detect hydrogen in any ice below as it passes over the lunar south pole. According to the principal investigator for this mission, William Feldman of Los Alamos Laboratory, this will provide an almost foolproof test for water within 0.01 percent by mass. He claims, "We'll know one month after we arrive whether any ice is there."

*Color ratio image of the Tycho
Crater taken on-board the
Clementine spacecraft.*

How I missed her,

how I missed her,

How I missed my Clementine,

But I kissed her little sister,

And forgot my Clementine.

Giving Birth to Galaxies

After decades of peering ever farther into the dimly lit reaches of space,
and ever deeper into the murky past, astronomers are finally getting a glimpse of galaxies in the making.
But precisely what it is they are seeing at the edge of the universe is open for discussion.

MARCIA BARTUSIAK

Catching a galaxy in the making isn't easy. It requires a great deal of cleverness and years of diligent searching. As a graduate student at the University of California at Berkeley in the mid-1980s, Mark Dickinson did not mind the hard work. He was one of the few astronomers lucky enough to be engaged in mapping the universe's farthest frontier, the region billions of light-years away where galaxies appear to be frozen in their infancy in the distant past. It was a frustrating business, but also rewarding: understanding how galaxies were created is as important to astronomers as deciphering the origin of species is to biologists.

"It could take hours or even several nights at the telescope to obtain just one good candidate," recalls Dickinson. That's because he and his fellow observers were fighting the limits of their instrumentation. Given the time it takes light from a galaxy at the far end of the universe to reach Earth, the farther they peered into the depths of space, the farther they also saw into the past. The trouble was, they couldn't see very much. Galaxies that resided more than a mere couple of billion light-years away were dim, fuzzy, and next to impossible to identify. "There," wrote astronomer Edwin Hubble in 1936, "we measure shadows and search among ghostly errors of measurement for landmarks that are scarcely substantial." Astronomers have tried tracing the evolution of galaxies through those shadowy eons ever since, with little success.

But no longer. The trickle of data that distant-galaxy hunters once collected has now turned into a veritable geyser. Thanks to several key technological break-throughs — the opening of the giant Keck telescope on Hawaii's Mauna Kea in 1992, the improved vision of the Hubble Space Telescope, and advances in telescopic

Understanding how galaxies were created is as important to astronomers as deciphering the origin of species is to biologists.

Opposite page: A spiral galaxy.

detectors—hundreds of young galaxies have now been sighted, with more being found each day. The early cosmos is fast becoming quite familiar. Says Dickinson, who now studies the far universe at the Space Telescope Science Institute, "Since I'm used to scrabbling at the edge, I'm tempted to move on to something more murky."

Astronomers believe that galaxies condensed out of the primordial ocean of hydrogen and helium not all at once but continuously and vigorously, like a toasty fire, over a period of billions of years—through nearly half of the universe's existence. ▼

Thanks to several key technological breakthroughs—the opening of the giant Keck telescope on Hawaii's Mauna Kea in 1992, the improved vision of the Hubble Space Telescope, and advances in telescopic detectors—hundreds of young galaxies have now been sighted, with more being found each day.

"Theorists have so much data now that we're finding it hard to catch up," says University of Washington astrophysicist Craig Hogan. And with the flood of data, old ideas about galaxy formation are toppling. Particularly imperiled is the notion that virtually all galaxies came into existence at the same moment in the distant past, emitting a collective burst of light like some grand fireworks display. Astronomers had once seized on this explanation because it was the simplest. It also seemed to fit the available data: in the 1950s and 1960s, all galaxies as far back as astronomers could see (which wasn't very far) looked pretty much the same as our own. Now, however, astronomers believe that galaxies condensed out of the primordial ocean of hydrogen and helium not all at once but continuously and vigorously, like a toasty fire, over a period of billions of years—through nearly half of the universe's existence. Of course, not everybody agrees about precisely what is going on at the edge of the visible universe. At issue is the exact manner in which the galaxies came to be. Did most of them achieve their full size and identity fairly early, evolving only slightly beyond what they were at birth? Or did they take a walk on the wild side, starting from smaller bits that merged and coalesced gradually, and even at times swapping identities as easily as Imelda Marcos changed shoes.

For theorists such as Hogan, who endured the lean years of scant data, the debate is invigorating. He believes astronomy is now experiencing its third truly great moment this century. The first began in the 1920s when Edwin Hubble, peering through the biggest telescope of the time, the 100-inch reflector atop Mount Wilson in California, recognized that the Milky Way was not alone. After announcing that fact to the world on New Year's Day 1925, Hubble went on to photograph hundreds of distant galaxies, classifying them by shape. About two-thirds of those are spiral galaxies just like ours — a bright central bulge surrounded by a spiraling pinwheel of gas and stars. Many of the other galaxies are denser and egg-shaped, or elliptical, and are largely filled with old stars. Ellipticals, Hubble saw, also tend to huddle together in rich clusters of hundreds and thousands. A smaller portion of galaxies, known as irregulars, are simply loose aggregations of stars immersed in rich pools of gas that do not have any definite shape. Hubble also observed that all the galaxies are moving outward at a speed directly proportional to their distance — an observation that would eventually be explained by the expansion of the very fabric of space-time from the moment of the Big Bang some 9 to 16 billion years ago (the exact age of the universe is still in dispute).

The second revolution culminated in the 1960s, when astronomers probed the heavens at non-visible parts of the electromagnetic spectrum. Radio telescopes, for example, helped astronomers locate quasars, intensely luminous objects billions of light-years distant, which provided the first clues that the early universe was very different indeed from our local, rather humdrum galactic neighborhood. A quasar is thought to be a young galaxy that includes at its center a supermassive black hole formed from the stuff of millions of stars. As additional stray material falls into the black hole, it emits a tremendous light, as bright as a trillion suns. By the time this light reaches us from across the universe, it is very dim — so dim, in fact, that astronomers gazing through optical telescopes had completely overlooked it. Fortunately, most quasars also emit strong electromagnetic waves in the radio part of the spectrum, which makes them stand out when seen through radio telescopes. Only by using these radio emissions as a beacon for pointing their optical telescopes did astronomers finally get a good look at quasars.

At the time, many observers held fast to a specific strategy when it came to studying the early universe. They figured there was a precise era when galaxies were first constructed, when all those islands of new stars "turned on" in

Edwin Hubble, peering through the biggest telescope of the time, the 100-inch reflector atop Mount Wilson in California, recognized that the Milky Way was not alone.

relative unison. It was a time when pockets of gas were gravitationally condensing — that is, forming stars — at tremendous rates, as gas supplies were at their peak. Astronomers therefore were looking for signs of a sudden eruption of light in the distant cosmos. They were searching for primordial galaxies that were making hundreds of stars each year. (The Milky Way now manufactures only about two new stars a year.) For years, they probed the far cosmos but came up empty-handed. They could say only that distant galaxies and clusters looked a bit "bluer," a sign perhaps of heightened star formation. Young and massive stars, flush with energy, tend to put out more blue light.

Others, like Dickinson and his colleagues, had a different game plan. They tracked down particularly active galaxies with loud radio "voices" that could be heard across the universe. Perhaps the booming siren put out by a radio galaxy, they reasoned, was a sign that the galaxy was newly forming. As with quasars, the intense radio beam is believed to be radiating from a spinning black-hole dynamo lurking at the galaxy's center. With the radio signal serving as a guide for pointing an optical telescope to the right position, observers could take a long exposure of the galaxy, since it was too faint to be noticed otherwise. "But we had to look at dozens of candidates to find one that was really distant," notes Dickinson. "It was exciting, but we ended up with only these exotic galaxies. The very same property that drew our attention — the strong radio signal — also made them abnormal." Astronomers weren't sure they could understand the infant universe by studying only its most unusual specimens.

At this point astronomers faced a stark dilemma. After years of searching, the only evidence of bright objects from the early universe they'd found were a quasar here, a radio galaxy there. Perhaps, in retrospect, the fireworks theory was in some part wishful thinking: the very bright explosions of light it predicted were the only thing the telescopes of the day were powerful enough to detect from the early universe.

The new instruments that began to come on-line in the early 1990s gave astronomers another option. For the first time, they were able to look for far more subtle evidence of an alternative scenario — that galaxies were born slowly over many billions of years rather than all at once. To put it another way, astronomers had the means to look

A quasar is thought to be a young galaxy that includes at its center a supermassive black hole formed from the stuff of millions of stars.

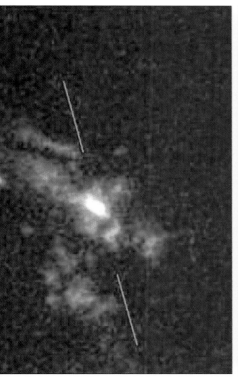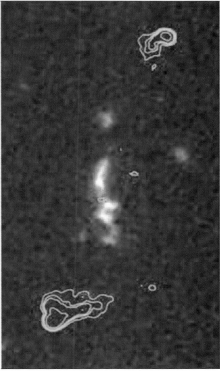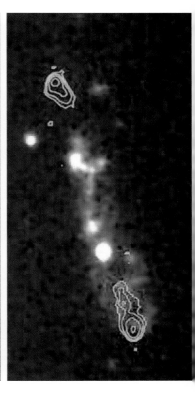

for primordial galaxies under the assumption that these galaxies might look pretty much like those near our Milky Way. "We began to ask, What would an average galaxy, the kind we see around us today, look like some 7 to 10 billion light-years distant?" says Caltech astronomer Charles Steidel. Pretty darn faint, was the answer. But Steidel had an intriguing technique for picking such dim workaday objects out of an already jam-packed nighttime sky.

A newborn galaxy sits at the center of a rich sea of gas (many times richer than the Milky Way's current supply). Even though the millions of new stars in its core emit lots of bright, bluish light, the surrounding gas just "sucks up all those ultraviolet photons," notes Steidel. The most energetic ultraviolet rays never get out of the galaxy. So if you use a spectrograph to break the galaxy's light into its rainbow of separate colors, the resulting spectrum displays a gaping hole—a drop-off—where the high-energy ultraviolet photons should be.

That simple effect gave Steidel and his collaborators a way to start strip-mining the sky for infant galaxies. He knew that as the galaxy's light travels through the cosmos, its waves get stretched with the universe's expansion. The

These Hubble Space Telescope images, combined with radio maps produced by the Very Large Array Radio Interferometer (blue contour lines), show surprisingly varied and intricate structures of gas and stars that suggest the mechanisms powering radio galaxies are more complex than thought previously.

more distant the galaxy, the more its light is shifted to longer and longer wavelengths. Blue light turns redder, while red light waves move into the realm of the infrared. And that means the ultraviolet "gap" shifts as well. "The position of the drop-off in the galaxy's spectrum roughly pegs its distance," explains Steidel. "It's the poor man's way of looking for early galaxies."

The idea was not original with Steidel, but he and his colleagues were among the first to apply it successfully. In 1991, using a telescope in Chile, they found about 20 potential baby galaxies. Each contender had an ultraviolet gap in just about the right position. But that was only a crude screening. To be certain, they needed more precise spectra. "That couldn't be done without the Keck telescope," Steidel says. In 1995 he transferred from MIT to Caltech just so he could be closer to the giant instrument, with its 400-inch segmented mirror that's four times wider than Hubble's once-mighty telescope on Mount Wilson. Within a month of his arrival, Steidel checked out his candidates. Nearly all turned out to be quite distant, residing at a time when the universe was a mere one-fourth its current size and about one-sixth its current age. It took previous galaxy hunters more than a decade to gather such a sample from that era. Since then Steidel has amassed a collection of about 150.

More important, Steidel's galaxies are not exotic. "They're proletarian, run-of-the-mill galaxies," stresses Dickinson, who worked with Steidel on the Keck observing run. Both believe they are seeing the initial cores of elliptical galaxies, as well as the bulges of yet-to-be spirals. (A spiral is thought to acquire its thin disk later, as the surrounding gas cools and settles down around the bulge.) And the population of objects that Steidel is counting in that far sector of the universe just about matches the population of bright galaxies that exists today. This seems to suggest that the major galactic components were in place within a couple of billion years of the Big Bang. That would put the rate of star formation in the average primordial galaxy into the reasonable range of 5 to 100 new stars a year. "That's fast by today's standards," Steidel points out, "but it's not tremendously high."

Some complementary observations support Steidel's picture. For the past ten years, Arthur Wolfe of the University of California at San Diego has been searching for primordial clouds of gas. Wolfe uses quasars as his

As you go farther into the past, more and more of the universe is made up of gas rather than stars and galaxies.

tool. As a quasar's brilliant light shines through the cosmos, some of its rays are absorbed by intervening gas clouds. By studying the absorption patterns—in effect, the shadows of these clouds—he can examine the gas between us and the distant quasar, as if he were inspecting some cosmic core sample billions of light-years in length.

Wolfe found that as you go farther into the past, more and more of the universe is made up of gas rather than stars and galaxies. By the time you arrive at the same era that Steidel observed—four-fifths of the way back to the Big Bang—he sees most of the mass tied up in neutral hydrogen gas. That mass, he found, is "equal to the mass of all the stars in today's universe. And that convinced many people we were seeing the progenitors of galaxies." The Keck telescope is powerful enough to allow Wolfe and his colleagues to observe how these gas clouds move. Even at this early, gaseous stage they appear already to behave like disks the size of the Milky Way, only thicker. "This suggests healthy, big spiral disks are in place," says Wolfe. Which means, he believes, that the biggest galaxies formed fairly quickly and then coasted into the modern era largely intact. Smaller objects, the "galactic fluff" as he calls them, coalesced later. Assembly runs from big to small.

Or is it the other way around? That's what evidence coming from the Hubble Space Telescope suggests. For ten days in December 1995, the Hubble trained its eye on one spot of the sky while it took a series of 342 time-exposure photographs. These images were then combined and computer-enhanced to produce the most deeply penetrating astronomical image ever taken, the Hubble Deep Field. "This picture takes us billions of years back into time, maybe 80 percent of the way to the Big Bang," says Robert Williams, director of the Space Telescope Science Institute. "It's beautiful, yet also profoundly significant. It's an archeological dig that allows us to see some 2,000 galaxies in different stages of development." Over the past year, astronomers around the world have been feeding on its data like hungry piranha.

James Lowenthal and David Koo, among others at the University of California at Santa Cruz, went out to the Keck to examine the Deep Field in detail. They saw many of the same galaxies that Steidel has observed but found them to be far more numerous than those seen today.

Where did they all go? "Either some of these objects have grown so dim that we can't see them today," suggests Lowenthal, "or they've merged." To Koo's eyes, the objects appear rather small and blobby, as though they are smaller gaseous building blocks rather than early galaxies in their own right. Perhaps a galaxy does not condense out of a huge gas cloud, fully formed from the start. Instead it might fit together from smaller structures, like some cosmic-size set of Legos.

Additional evidence for this view comes from another Hubble observation, conducted by astronomers from Arizona State University and the University of Alabama. This group had the space-borne mirror take a set of exposures of a small point of the sky in the Hercules constellation. They uncovered 18 small Lego-like objects, all about 11 billion light-years distant and packed within a region only 2 million light-years across, about the distance between the Milky Way and its nearest spiral companion, the Andromeda galaxy. They believe they have succeeded in catching "sub-galactic clumps" in the act of merging into one or more galaxies. "I don't think that these objects are peculiar," asserts Arizona State astronomer Rogier Windhorst. "I suspect we'll see them all over the sky." They have already found similar structures in another, randomly selected field.

But critics warn that the light being collected from that far era essentially shows the objects in ultraviolet alone, which could be misleading. The compact bodies might simply be pockets of vigorous star formation embedded within hidden full-size galaxies, like bright lights strung over dark Christmas trees. To solve the puzzle, astronomers are trying to observe the motion of these bright objects to determine whether they are truly separate or simply bright parts of larger galaxies.

Should these faraway objects truly be small, it would please theorists no end. They favor a galaxy-forming recipe that calls for tiny units blending into ever-larger assemblies, from dwarfs to giants. Simon White, director of the Max Planck Institute for Astrophysics in Germany, has been trying to perfect just such a recipe for nearly two decades. According to his computer models, the first thing to form are small disks of gas, each about 3,000 light-years wide (just about the size of the objects that Windhorst and company claim they are seeing).

Opposite page: This comparison image of the core of the galaxy M100 shows the dramatic improvement in Hubble Space Telescope's view of the universe. The new image was taken with the second generation Wide Field and Planetary Camera (WFPC-2) which was installed during the STS-61 Hubble Servicing Mission. The galaxy M100 is one of the brightest members of the Virgo Cluster of galaxies. The galaxy is estimated to be tens of millions of light-years away.

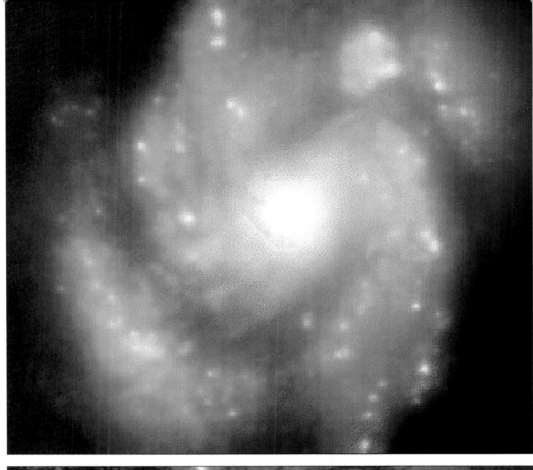

Above: Whirlpool galaxy.

It is believed that galaxies are continually changing. A spiral galaxy, for instance, could later encounter another spiral and merge to form a bulbous, giant elliptical.

These, in turn, join to form a galaxy's central component, its bulge. Some of these bulges might run through their remaining gas very rapidly, in which case, unless they absorb new gas from another source, they turn into dwarf ellipticals. If gas is plentiful, and other conditions are right (they're not crowded up against other objects, for example), they might enwreathe themselves in disks of gas and turn into giant spirals, where new stars continue to form for a longer time — longer than the rapid evolution suggested by Steidel's and Wolfe's observations.

And once they form, do galaxies retain their identity? "No," answers White. "It's my bet that galaxies are continually changing." A spiral galaxy, for instance, could later encounter another spiral and merge to form a bulbous, giant elliptical. Indeed, some nearby ellipticals have been found to contain the vestiges of spiraling disks within them. White envisions a universe of great dynamism; only now are galaxies winding down as they deplete their fuel supplies. We are entering an era of cosmic ennui, as less and less gas becomes available for a galaxy's star-forming needs.

The mystery of galaxy formation would be solved at once if astronomers could follow a particular galaxy through time, which, alas, is impossible. "We can use a telescope as a time machine, but we're either here or there," notes White. "We can't wait around for any individual galaxy to evolve." By adding more "snapshots" to their cosmic album, however, they can forge a link between one epoch and the next. Astronomers are also observing the universe's subsequent stage of development —its "adolescent years," about 5 to 7 billion years ago. So far observations from this cosmic era show ellipticals that seem remarkably old and undisturbed, as though they have stayed much the same for eons. But there are also ragged, strange-looking spirals merging and interacting, and bright dwarf galaxies bursting with star formation, as if they're currently under construction. There is ammunition here for both sides of the galaxy-formation debate.

"I know it sounds as if I'm waffling," says Koo, "but I think both views of galaxy formation are right." Like the proverbial blind men and the elephant, Koo believes that astronomers have been "feeling varied parts of the cosmos." Different astronomical techniques, he points out, will tend to pick out different types of objects. "If you insist on taking the view that galaxies evolved in only one way, then you end up with a dilemma. It reflects our need to simplify, but I believe the universe can accommodate a richness of diversity," he notes.

Ideas may change as swiftly as new data are gathered. Another Hubble Deep Field survey is planned for the southern sky so that astronomers can use an array of giant telescopes coming on-line in Chile, the Southern Hemisphere's astronomical mecca, to do follow-up work. And going deeper into space means peering at longer wavelengths, as the cosmic expansion stretches a galaxy's light beyond the visible spectrum. Advanced infrared telescopes promise to push our cosmic vision even farther into the past.

Already there are hints of new discoveries. Both French and Japanese radio astronomers have detected carbon monoxide molecules in the distant universe, which could possibly be the residue of star bursts in an even earlier era yet to be surveyed. "Like pole-vaulters," says Dickinson, "we keep lifting that bar ever higher."

The mystery of galaxy formation would be solved at once if astronomers could follow a particular galaxy through time, which is impossible.

New Vistas Open for Earthbound Astronomers

MALCOLM W. BROWNE

E ver since the reign of Louis XIV, wine bottles manufactured in Paris by the Compagnie de Saint-Gobain have been green—and so is the glass from which this old French company cast the 100-inch-diameter mirror for America's Hooker telescope on Mount Wilson, Calif.

The quaint wine-bottle color of the 4.5-ton Hooker mirror, which has played a gigantic role since 1917 in humanity's understanding of its place in the universe, reminds its present-day users of the instrument's venerable roots. But the "100 inch," as astronomers affectionately call it, has also become a symbol of a remarkable renaissance in the art of telescope design.

A wave of new techniques based on feedback systems, new materials and mathematics has enabled astronomers not only to build a new generation of far more powerful telescopes but also to rejuvenate older instruments with devices that capture almost every photon of light from distant stars. The Hooker instrument, for example, was consigned to mothballs as a museum piece for eight years, but it has been brought back from the dead as a premier research telescope.

To some extent, astronomy has returned to the ground after three decades in which space-based instruments have often stolen the limelight.

The images and data returned to Earth by the Hubble Space Telescope since its 1993 repair—a comet hitting Jupiter, a storm raging across thousands of miles of Saturn's surface and a nursery where stars are born, for example—have amazed and delighted nonscientists as well as astronomers. And in the last two years, the little Galileo spacecraft has probed the upper atmosphere of Jupiter and sent back pictures that hint of marvels on the giant planet and its moons.

Opposite page: The Keck Observatory, Mauna Kea, Hawaii.

The Cosmic Background Explorer spacecraft of the National Aeronautics and Space Administration revolutionized 20th-century science with its discovery that the microwave echo of the Big Bang is not smooth but speaks of structure even in the earliest epoch of the universe. And a radio antenna dish scheduled for launching this week will work in concert with radio telescopes spread across the United States, Australia and Europe to produce radio images so fine they will be comparable to observing a footprint on the Moon from Earth.

While scores of other spacecraft have also captured attention, new technology and refinements in mathematical analysis have also paved the way for a newly productive era in ground-based astronomy.

The Hooker instrument was consigned to mothballs as a museum piece for eight years, but it has been brought back from the dead as a premier research telescope. ▼

Many of the new ground-based telescopes rival even the Hubble Space Telescope in their clarity of vision, so effectively can their computerized eyes pierce Earth's turbulent atmosphere, which makes stars twinkle and blocks some of the radiation frequencies important to astronomy. On every continent, including Antarctica, new ground-based observatories are springing up to complement the work of space-borne observatories, which, by their nature, are expensive and difficult to operate.

Great though the Hubble Space Telescope has proved to be, it took so long to build that since its inception, new technologies have emerged endowing ground-based telescopes with many of the advantages of those operating in space. These new technologies include powerful computers, new telescope mounts, better observatory designs, feedback systems that squelch the distortive twinkling of stars, interferometers capable of simulating telescopes the size of the entire Earth, special glass mixtures that resist deformation while undergoing temperature changes and much more.

THE QUESTIONS: THE POSSIBILITIES ARE TANTALIZING

The success of observatories like the Keck has led astronomers to forecast the imminent dawning of a golden age of astronomy. Questions that scientists once considered beyond the reach of observation may soon find at least partial answers. Among them are these:

Is there life — or are there at least habitable planets — beyond the solar system?

How much does the universe weigh, and what are the unseen substances that seem to make up much of its mass?

How does the force of gravity relate to the three other known forces of nature: the strong and weak nuclear forces and electromagnetism?

What mechanism created galaxies and large-scale structure in the universe soon after the Big Bang creation event?

What, exactly, are mysterious things like quasars and gamma-ray bursters?

How will the universe end?

Dr. Frederick Chaffee, director of the Keck Observatory in Hawaii, ascribes great importance to the search for extraterrestrial life and habitable planets outside the solar system.

"The human spirit yearns to know whether we are alone," he said, "and the impetus to look for extraterres-

The "100-inch" Hooker telescope at Mt. Wilson, California.

While scores of other space-craft have also captured attention, new technology and refinements in mathematical analysis have also paved the way for a newly productive era in ground-based astronomy.

trial life is not just a product of the media and politicians. For the first time in history, we have the tools to address this great question scientifically."

Big telescopes are expensive. The Keck twins cost $180 million, for example, and that does not include many of the auxiliary instruments that exploit their tremendous light-gathering power.

When asked whether astronomy offers practical benefits to balance its cost, astronomers often reply with a response attributed to the great atomic physicist Enrico Fermi. Fermi was asked during World War II what basic research could do for national defense, and he is supposed to have replied, "It gives us something worth defending."

THE TECHNOLOGY: REJUVENATION FOR AN OLD FRIEND

The new generation of optical telescopes can see much more than their forebears, largely because of two developments.

One is that the cost of making very large light-gathering mirrors has been drastically reduced in recent years, permitting the construction of many telescopes larger than astronomers had once deemed possible. These new mirrors make it possible to detect incredibly dim objects, including galaxies at the very edge of the known universe.

The other development is that the photographic film formerly used to record astronomical images has been largely replaced by much more sensitive charge-coupled devices, similar to television camera chips. Photographic exposures that once took hours or entire nights can now be completed in minutes.

Meanwhile, optical astronomy has been supplemented by radio telescopes with antenna arrays that can act as if they were a single instrument spanning entire continents. The new perspectives on the universe opened up by radio telescopes, astronomers say, is comparable to a gift of color vision to someone who had been colorblind. Radio astronomy is booming.

Other kinds of invisible radiation from the heavens —infrared, ultraviolet, X-rays, gamma rays and neutrino bursts—have also become accessible to astronomers in recent years because of new observatories in space and on the ground. They have revealed black holes, the birth of stars and much more.

No single telescope can answer all the questions astronomers confront, but the newly refurbished Hooker telescope stands as a metaphor for the potential of the new technologies. Through the Hooker's great glass eye, Edwin Hubble discerned in the 1930s that Earth's galaxy is merely one among billions, each made up of tens of billions of stars. He determined that the entire universe is expanding —a fact later explained by the Big Bang theory of creation.

At a recent meeting held at Mount Wilson, Dr. Allan R. Sandage, an eminent Carnegie Institution astronomer who has regularly used the 100-inch since 1949, enumerated the historic discoveries made with it and summarized the new technologies incorporated into the observatory.

"The observations made here by Edwin Hubble led to the Big Bang theory of creation and the closest approach of theology to science — or vice versa," Dr. Sandage said. "The technologies that are revitalizing this observatory and reshaping observational astronomy will exert an enormous influence on science far into the 21st century."

Though the 100-inch telescope was deemed obsolete in 1985, new inventions and the determined efforts of a group of private benefactors saved the Hooker from oblivion, reopening the historic telescope four years ago.

Dr. Robert Jastrow, director of the Mount Wilson Institute that now operates the Hooker Telescope, and his deputy, Dr. Sallie Baliunas, say that astronomers are on the verge of a period of discovery unequaled since the invention of the telescope nearly four centuries ago.

THE STRATEGIES:
NEW APPROACHES TO CHALLENGES

The artisans who are bringing new telescope mirrors into the world are learning new tricks nearly every day.

One of them is Dr. J. Roger P. Angel of the University of Arizona's Steward Observatory, who recently won a $330,000 MacArthur Fellowship for developing a new method for making huge telescope mirrors.

"Within a few years, it should be technically possible to detect the presence of life on planets orbiting the 200 or so nearest stars," Dr. Angel said. "If we detect it, we may never know what kind of life it is—

The Kitt Peak Observatory, Arizona.

microbial or intelligent or something in between. But it is now within our power to send small instruments into space that will be capable of detecting ozone in the atmospheres of extrasolar planets — a possible indication of life of some kind."

Earthbound telescopes need big mirrors, and about 10 telescopes containing mirrors four meters or more in diameter are currently finished or nearing completion. The newest of these, the 11-meter-diameter Hobby-Eberly Telescope at the University of Texas McDonald Observatory near Fort Davis, Tex., was completed on Dec. 12 at a cost of $13.5 million. The telescope, which contains a mirror made up of 91 hexagonal segments, is the product of a collaboration of the University of Texas, Pennsylvania State University, Stanford University and two German institutions. It is expected to begin operation in August.

The largest telescopes currently operating are the pair known as Keck I and Keck II, each containing a mirror equivalent to 9.82 meters (32.2 feet) in diameter. The telescopes, privately financed by the W.M. Keck Foundation and designed by Dr. Jerry Nelson of the University of California at Lick Observatory, the Keck twins are mounted 13,600 feet high on Mauna Kea in Hawaii, above most of Earth's turbulent atmosphere.

Making the Keck mirrors was a formidable challenge. Dr. Nelson recalls that the job had seemed much simpler when he conceived the design in 1977; the work was completed last October.

"We suffered plenty of slings and arrows," he said, "but I was never really discouraged. We tackled each problem as it came along."

The 36 thin glass segments of each mirror were warped by a special jig prior to grinding so that when polishing was complete and the jigs were removed, the segments snapped back into exactly the right shape. Fine polishing was accomplished by bombarding the glass mirror surfaces with beams of electrically charged atoms.

Mounted in each telescope, the arrays of mirror segments are under automatic computer control that compensates for the gravitational forces tending to make them sag as the telescope moves.

Among the accessories built for the Keck telescopes is the Low Resolution Imaging Spectrograph, which is

The largest telescopes currently operating are the pair known as Keck I and Keck II, each containing a mirror equivalent to 9.82 meters (32.2 feet) in diameter.

capturing images and other data from some of the most distant known objects in the universe.

Powerful computers play pivotal roles in all the new observatories. Computers control the tracking of targets in the sky, direct compensating mechanisms that maintain the proper shapes of lightweight flexible mirrors and analyze the mountains of data the telescopes produce.

The largest telescope of the next century is likely to be the Very Large Telescope, which is under construction on the summit of Cerro Paranal in Chile by a consortium of European nations called the European Southern Observatory. When it is finished in 2000, the instrument will consist of four telescopes, each containing a mirror 8.2 meters (26.9 feet) in diameter. By combining the light from all four behemoths and three smaller telescopes, the teamed instruments will have a light-gathering capacity greater than a single telescope with a mirror 16 meters (more than 52 feet) in diameter. The European telescope will thus be the largest optical telescope ever built.

THE MIRRORS: FINDING WAYS TO PUSH LIMITS

Traditionally, telescope mirrors have been made by casting them as disks, allowing them to cool for months and then grinding away the surface glass, a process that usually takes years. But a team or mirror makers under the direction of Dr. Angel at the University of Arizona has devised a much faster and cheaper method. It has built a huge rotary furnace in which glass chunks are melted in a ceramic mold while the entire assembly rotates. The spinning of this red-hot carousel forces the surface of the swirling melted glass to assume a parabolic shape almost identical to the correct final form. After cooling, only small amounts of glass must be ground away, saving time and money.

The Arizona group has successfully spin-cast several large telescope mirrors, including one 6.5 meters (21.3 feet) in diameter that will replace the segmented mirror used since 1979 in the Multiple Mirror Telescope on Mount Hopkins, Ariz. Dr. Angel's group is preparing to spin-cast two huge mirrors that will be mounted in twin telescopes called the Large Binocular Telescope (or Columbus Project), with a combined light-gathering power equivalent to a mirror 11.8 meters, or 38.7 feet.

One of the biggest boons to telescopes new and old is the advent of the technology known as adaptive optics: computerized systems that measure the distortion, caused

New technologies have emerged endowing ground-based telescopes with many of the advantages of those operating in space.

by inhomogeneities in the atmosphere, in detecting a celestial object from one instant to the next and that send continuous signals to what is called a rubber mirror, a deformable mirror backed by tiny piezoelectric actuator supports that expand or contract over tiny distances when the electrical voltage applied to them is varied. Deformations in the mirror are controlled so they exactly compensate for the deformations as light from a star passes through the atmosphere. By matching deformations with counterdeformations, the twinkling of starlight is canceled, making the stellar image sharp.

One of the accessories of some adaptive optics systems is an artificial star created by a bright laser beam. The beam is aimed at a point in the sky close to the target star or galaxy, and it excites molecules of air (or, at a higher altitude, sodium atoms in the upper atmosphere) so they glow brightly. The distortions undergone by the image of the artificial star as it returns to Earth are continuously measured and used by a computer to drive the deformable mirror in the telescope. The resulting compensation fixes not only the image of the artificial star but the image of the real target star as well.

THE SIGNALS: ELIMINATING THE DISTORTIONS

A new system much admired by astronomers at major observatories was devised by Christopher Shelton, of the TRW Corporation, and has been installed on the Hooker telescope, enabling the old 100-inch to take sharp pictures of the surface details of even tiny objects, like the asteroid Vesta, which lies in the asteroid belt between Mars and Jupiter. Mr. Shelton's system is based on rapid computer analysis of the light from a target after it is passed through an array of microscopic "lenslets."

If a tiny part of the wave front of the light arriving from space escapes deflection by the turbulent atmosphere, it passes straight through a miniature lens and falls on a tiny photodetector behind the lens. But if its path is deflected by twinkling, the light is displaced to one side, and the computerized sensors recognize that it is in the wrong place and send instructions to a deformable mirror to correct the error.

Another way to fix disruptive twinkling is a system called speckle interferometry. A device to amplify the signal being received, called a charge-coupled device, is attached to a large telescope and rapidly takes hundreds or thousands of exposures of the target and stores the images digitally. Later, the images are compared by computer with each other; mathematical analysis enables the removal of the distortions, forming a single sharp image.

An astronomer who frequently uses the system, Dr. Brian D. Mason of Georgia State University, said that of about 9,000 bright stars recently surveyed using the Hooker telescope's new speckle interferometry system, 10 percent have turned out to be binary systems, rather than the single stars astronomers had formerly thought them to be.

THE NEW ERA: CASTING A NET FARTHER AFIELD

Perhaps more than any other emerging technique, the magic of interferometry is transforming astronomy.

Astronomical interferometry is the art of combining light or radio waves collected by two or more instruments from a single celestial target. It is not enough to merely merge the light or radio beams; they must match each other's paths so precisely that their waves match, peak for peak and trough for trough. Only the finest computer-controlled micromanipulators are capable of maintaining a perfect match between two or more light beams coming from large telescopes.

For the foreseeable future, the exploration of space beyond the solar system by human travelers will remain a mere dream. But much of the knowledge sought by scientists about remote planets and the workings of the universe can be gained by earthbound men and women. ▼

But interferometry produces spectacular results. When two telescopes or radio antennas simultaneously gather their separate images of a distant object and combine them through interferometry, the result is equivalent in sharpness to what a single telescope of enormous size could produce. For example, a radio telescope network called the Very Long Baseline Interferometer, which will merge signals from its new antenna in space with antennas on three continents, will yield images equivalent to those of a telescope far larger than the entire Earth.

The technique may one day reveal Earthlike planets orbiting distant stars, but hurdles remain.

One of the most serious problems in the detection of Earthlike extrasolar planets is that the dim starlight reflected by a planet will always be overwhelmed by the dazzling brilliance of the star it orbits. Dr. Angel and his colleagues at the University of Paris have designed a space-based interferometer that could solve the problem.

The instrument would consist of four telescope mirrors, each no more than about one yard in diameter, arrayed along a supporting structure about 75 yards long. The apparatus would be placed in an orbit about the same distance from the Sun as the planet Jupiter.

First galaxy viewed by the Keck telescope.

The structure would have to be designed so that light beams arriving from a brilliant target star would be combined slightly out of phase to cancel the starlight. But the phase adjustment of the telescopes would be such that the dim light from any planets orbiting the star would get through, producing not only images of the planets but the spectra of planetary atmospheres, revealing their composition. The presence of ozone in the spectrum of a planet's atmosphere could be a sign of life.

For the foreseeable future, the exploration of space beyond the solar system by human travelers will remain a mere dream. But much of the knowledge sought by scientists about remote planets and the workings of the universe can be gained by earthbound men and women.

The clues they seek are encoded in the particles of radiation and matter that flow constantly into Earth's neighborhood. As new telescopes and technologies are developed to decipher these clues, the prospects have never seemed brighter for squeezing the truth from some of the great cosmic enigmas.

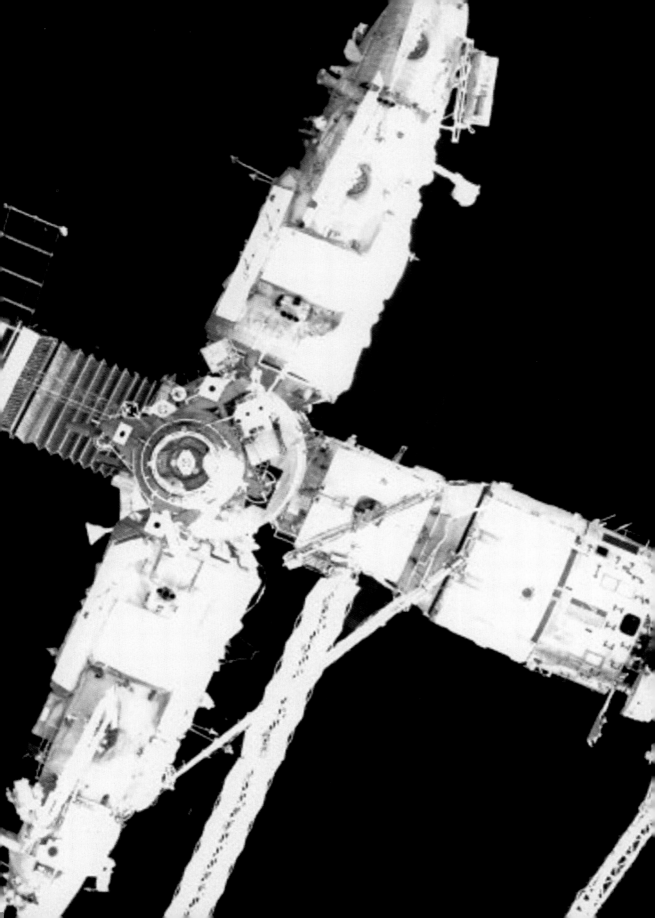

STS-81: A Ticket to Mir

RUSSELL R. TOBIAS

The predawn darkness surrounding the Florida coast turned to daylight with the launching of America's first space shuttle mission of 1997. On board was a crew of six, including Jerry Linenger, who was scheduled to spend four months on the aging Russian Mir space complex.

The on-time launch occurred at 4:27:22.984 eastern standard time, on January 12. The ten-minute window of opportunity had just opened when the giant solid rocket motors attached to *Atlantis* ignited. A flawless countdown preceded the liftoff of STS-81, the eighty-first flight in the space shuttle program. The solid-rocket boosters were successfully separated from the external tank 2 minutes and 25.7 seconds after launch. The three liquid-hydrogen, liquid-oxygen main engines on *Atlantis* continued to fire until the giant fuel tank had exhausted its contents. Cutoff occurred at 8 minutes and 31.8 seconds into the flight, and the external tank was jettisoned. *Atlantis* continued to its planned 214-by-345-mile orbit, where it began its chase of Mir.

At the time of launch, Mir was traveling over the Galapagos Islands about 2,400 miles (3,862 kilometers) southwest of the Kennedy Space Center (KSC). About twenty-five minutes after launch, the Mir crew were notified of *Atlantis*'s launch and were able to view a video uplink of the event. The Mir 22 crew includes Commander Valery Korzun and Flight Engineer Alexander Kaleri, who were launched in a Soyuz vehicle on August 17, 1996. Their spacecraft docked with the Mir two days later. U.S. astronaut John Blaha joined them on September 19, 1996, with the docking of *Atlantis* during the STS-79 mission.

Soon after arriving in orbit, *Atlantis* commander Mike Baker and pilot Brent Jett began a series of maneu-

A flawless countdown preceded the liftoff of STS-81, the eighty-first flight in the space shuttle program.

Opposite page: Mir Space Station in space during rendezvous.

vers to catch the Russian space station. A forty-three-year-old Navy captain, Baker was making his fourth trip into space. He served as pilot of STS-43 (August 2-11, 1991), which deployed the fifth Tracking and Data Relay Satellite (TDRS) and conducted thirty-two physical, material, and life science experiments, mostly relating to the Extended Duration Orbiter and Space Station. Baker was pilot of STS-52 (October 22 to November 1, 1992), which deployed the Italian Laser Geodynamic Satellite (LAGEOS), used to measure movement of the Earth's crust, and operated the U.S. Microgravity Payload 1 (USMP-1). His first flight as mission commander was STS-68 (September 30 to October 11, 1994), which was the second flight of the Space Radar Laboratory (SRL).

Thirty-eight-year-old Navy commander Jett was the pilot of STS-72 (January 11-20, 1996). During the nine-day flight, the crew retrieved the Space Flyer Unit (launched from Japan ten months earlier). They deployed and retrieved the OAST-Flyer, a satellite developed by the National Aeronautics and Space Administration's (NASA's) former Office of Aeronautics and Space Technology, which flew free of the shuttle for about fifty hours. Four experiments on the science platform operated autonomously before the satellite was retrieved by shuttle *Endeavour*'s robot arm. They also conducted two spacewalks (also called extravehicular activities, or EVAs) to demonstrate and evaluate techniques to be used in the assembly of the International Space Station.

Mission specialists Jeff Wisoff, John Grunsfeld, Marsha Ivins, and Jerry Linenger unpacked and activated experiments aboard *Atlantis* and the double Spacehab module. The experiments covered the fields of advanced technology, Earth sciences, fundamental biology, human life sciences, microgravity, and space sciences. Data would supply insight for the planning and development of the International Space Station, Earth-based studies of human and biological processes, and the advancement of commercial technology.

Seven NASA astronauts and two Russian cosmonauts take a break from busy supply-transfer duties on Atlantis' *mid deck halfway through the ten-day STS-81 flight. Left to right at bottom of the frame are Peter J.K. (Jeff) Wisoff, John E. Blaha, Marsha S. Ivins and Aleksandr Y. Kaleri. In the top half of the scene are, from the top left, Brent W. Jett Jr., John M. Grunsfeld, Jerry M. Linenger, Michael A. Baker and Valeri G. Korzun.*

Jeff Wisoff, Mission Specialist 1 (MS 1), was making his third flight as a mission specialist. He was born on August 16, 1958, and received his Ph.D. in applied physics from Stanford University in 1986. He was aboard STS-57 (June 21 to July 1, 1993), which retrieved the European Retrievable Carrier (EURECA) satellite using the shuttle's robot arm (known as the Remote Manipulator System, or RMS). Additionally, this mission featured the first flight of Spacehab, the commercially provided mid-deck augmentation module for conducting microgravity experiments. Wisoff also flew on STS-68.

John Grunsfeld, MS 2, was on his second flight. The thirty-eight-year-old, who received his Ph.D. in physics from the University of Chicago in 1988, was a mission specialist aboard STS-67. The Astro-2 mission (March 2-18, 1995) was the second flight of the Astro observatory, a unique complement of three telescopes to study the far ultraviolet spectra of faint astronomical objects and the polarization of ultraviolet light coming from hot stars and distant galaxies.

Marsha Ivins, MS 3, was making her fourth flight as a mission specialist. On her first flight, STS-32 (January 9-20, 1990), crew members on board the orbiter *Columbia* successfully deployed a Syncom satellite and retrieved the 21,400-pound (9,707-kilogram) Long Duration Exposure Facility (LDEF). Ivins was a mission specialist on the STS-46 flight (July 31-August 8, 1992), during which crew members deployed the European Retrievable Carrier (EURECA) satellite and conducted the first Tethered Satellite System (TSS) test flight. She also flew on STS-62 (March 4-18, 1994), a fourteen-day mission for the U.S. Microgravity Payload 2 (USMP0-2) and Office of Aeronautics and Space Technology 2 (OAST-2) payloads. These payloads studied the effects of microgravity on materials and spaceflight technologies.

Navy captain Jerry Linenger, MS 4, was making his second flight. He was to replace John Blaha on Mir for a four-month stay with the Mir crew. Linenger, a forty-two-year-old medical doctor, held a Ph.D. in epidemiology from the University of North Carolina. Linenger flew on STS-64 (September 9-20, 1994) aboard the space shuttle *Discovery*. Mission highlights included the first use of lasers for environmental research, deployment and retrieval of a solar science satellite, robotic processing of

Data from STS-81 would supply insight for the planning and development of the International Space Station, Earth-based studies of human and biological processes, and the advancement of commercial technology.

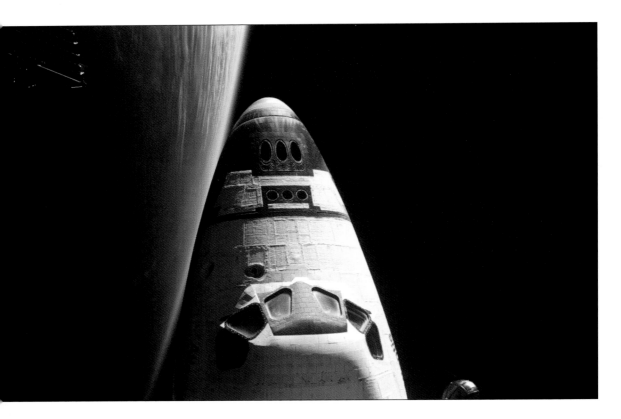

A view from Mir of Atlantis' nose over the Earth's limb.

semiconductors, use of an RMS-attached boom for jet thruster research, and the first untethered spacewalk in ten years, which was conducted to test a self-rescue jetpack.

Three days of maneuvering with the shuttle's small rocket engines brought *Atlantis* within 8 miles (13 kilometers) of Mir. Baker then inched the orbiter toward Mir's docking port. The fifth linkup with Mir occurred 210 miles (338 kilometers) above the Earth southeast of Moscow at 10:55 p.m. eastern time on January 14. Two hours after docking, the hatches between *Atlantis* and Mir were opened, and Baker and Mir 22 commander Valery Korzun shared a hug to mark the start of five days of joint operations between the two crews. During the docked phase of the mission, nearly three tons of food, water, and supplies were to be transferred between the two spacecraft.

After an informal welcoming ceremony in the Mir's core module, the crew members conducted a safety briefing and went right to work, hauling top-priority resupply items into the Russian station. The nine crew members were upbeat as they began their joint work. Blaha said, "We're truly in the space station business."

He completed 118 days as a Mir crew member, which began with his arrival on the Russian station on September 19 as part of *Atlantis*'s STS-79 crew.

On Thursday, January 16, the nine astronauts and cosmonauts of the *Atlantis*-Mir space complex pressed ahead with the transfer of food, water, and supplies to each other's spacecraft in the second day of joint operations of the STS-81 mission. With both spacecraft in excellent shape, the nine crew members floated back and forth between *Atlantis* and the Mir, hauling bags of water, satchels of logistical supplies, and experiment hardware. The supplies and hardware would be used by cosmonauts and U.S. astronaut Linenger during his four months of scientific research aboard the Mir.

Linenger, who officially became a Mir crew member early Wednesday, spent more than two hours with Blaha, his predecessor on the Russian space station, who helped familiarize Linenger with his new home during a handover period. A handover period would be conducted each night during the docked phase of the mission.

That evening, as the nine astronauts and cosmonauts aboard the *Atlantis*-Mir complex slept, scientists on the ground took advantage of television cameras in *Atlantis*'s payload bay to perform a detailed inspection of Mir's exterior. The television survey is designed to provide designers of the International Space Station and other spacecraft with information on the effects of years of exposure to the low-Earth-orbit environment. Scientists and engineers will use these data to understand the effects of orbital debris, to determine the impact of micrometeoroid and atomic oxygen on the various materials and coatings used on the ten-year-old Russian station, and to choose the best methods of protecting space complexes and vehicles of the future.

On Friday, January 17, more than two days after *Atlantis* and the Mir linked in orbit, astronaut Marsha Ivins worked with pilot Brent Jett and Mir 22 flight engineer Alexander Kaleri to haul more bags of water to the Russian complex and additional logistical supplies for U.S. astronaut Linenger's research aboard Mir. Linenger spent several hours continuing to familiarize himself with his new orbital home. He unpacked experiment hardware and helped astronaut John Blaha transfer biomedical samples and other experiment results back to *Atlantis* for Blaha's trip back to Earth. Commander Baker joined Jett in firing

Data from STS-81 would supply insight for the planning and development of the International Space Station, Earth-based studies of human and biological processes, and the advancement of commercial technology.

Mission highlights included the first use of lasers for environmental research, deployment and retrieval of a solar science satellite, robotic processing of semiconductors, use of an RMS-attached boom for jet thruster research, and the first untethered spacewalk in ten years, which was conducted to test a self-rescue jetpack.

Atlantis's small vernier jet thrusters in an experiment to gather engineering data for the International Space Station. The jet firings were part of a structural dynamics test to collect information on the integrity of the mate between two orbiting space vehicles and the effect of the firings on the Mir's solar arrays. Blaha and Linenger neared the end of their workday by stowing wheat plants grown in the Mir's Greenhouse experiment for their return to Earth. New seeds were planted in the Greenhouse for cultivation and harvesting during Linenger's stay aboard the Mir.

By Saturday, January 18, the astronauts and cosmonauts had transferred more than 1,300 pounds (590 kilograms) of water from *Atlantis* to the Mir to resupply the Russian outpost, along with equipment that would be used by astronaut Linenger. A bioprocessing device and an experiment used to grow cartilage cells during Blaha's stay on Mir were transferred to *Atlantis* for the trip back to Earth. Linenger spent most of the day collecting water samples from Mir for analysis back on Earth, and Blaha continued to exercise on a treadmill on Mir to stay in shape for his return to Earth.

On Sunday, January 19, all of the joint transfer activities were completed. Baker, Jett, Wisoff, Grunsfeld, Ivins, and Blaha said good-bye to Mir 22 commander Valery Korzun, flight engineer Alexander Kaleri, and the newest Mir crew member, astronaut Jerry Linenger. The hatches on the two spacecraft were closed at 7:46 A.M. after completion of a review of all of the items transferred since the two vehicles had docked Tuesday night. Among the transfer items were about 1,600 pounds (725 kilograms) of water for use by the Mir crew over the next few months.

Prior to hatch closure, the astronauts and cosmonauts conducted a formal farewell ceremony in the Mir Core Module after fielding questions from Russian and U.S. reporters in a joint news conference. *Atlantis* and Mir undocked at 9:15 P.M. over central Russia, southeast of Moscow. After *Atlantis* separated from Mir, pilot Brent Jett initiated a two-revolution flyaround of the Russian complex at a distance of about 560 feet (171 meters). At 11:00 P.M., Jett fired maneuvering jets to separate *Atlantis* from Mir for the final time until May, 1997, when the shuttle would return on STS-84 to deliver astronaut Mike Foale to the outpost as Linenger's replacement.

With the undocking complete, the astronauts began

reassembling a treadmill device in *Atlantis*' middeck. The treadmill is designed to reduce or eliminate vibrations from crew exercise which could one day compromise the integrity of microgravity experiments on board the International Space Station. Technical glitches the previous week had resulted in lost data, which prompted engineers to reschedule the experiment. Commander Mike Baker, Blaha, and Jett took turns exercising on the Treadmill Vibration Isolation System before it was disassembled for the remainder of the flight. Payload controllers confirmed they had received valuable data from the experiment on ground computers.

During day 10 of the mission, *Atlantis*'s astronauts readied for their planned return to Earth. Commander Baker and pilot Jett activated one of *Atlantis*'s three hydraulic power units, successfully exercising the shuttle's aerosurfaces. Baker and Jett then fired *Atlantis*'s steering jets in a routine prelanding checkout. One of the steering jets failed, but there were redundant systems and the failed jet did not impact the landing.

The astronauts also tested a medical restraint system in the Spacehab module, placing two crew members in the device. The device may be used on the International Space Station to move an ill or injured astronaut from one module to another. Crew members then began to stow items away in their crew cabin before the scheduled deactivation of Spacehab systems and associated hardware.

On Wednesday, January 22, NASA's first shuttle mission of 1997 came to an end when *Atlantis* landed at Kennedy Space Center. The shuttle touched down on KSC's runway 33 at 9:23 A.M. at the end of a 4.1-million-mile (6.6-million-kilometer) journey. Main gear touchdown occurred at 9:22:44 A.M. eastern standard time at a mission-elapsed time of 10 days, 4 hours, 55 minutes, and 21 seconds. *Atlantis*'s return home was delayed one orbit while the flight control team evaluated dynamic weather in the vicinity of KSC.

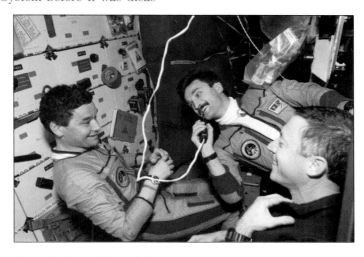

Supplies and equipment transfer are the topic of the day, as Atlantis *and* Mir's *respective commanders have a discussion aboard the orbiter. Left to right are cosmonauts Valeri G. Korzun and Aleksandr Y. Kaleri, commander and flight engineer, respectively, for Mir-22; along with astronaut Michael A. Baker, STS-81 mission commander.*

About an hour after landing, the STS-81 crew moved from *Atlantis* into the Crew Transport Vehicle (CTV). The crew was then transported to the Operations and Checkout Building at KSC, where they were reunited with their families. John Blaha said he was "absolutely stunned" at how heavy he felt when *Atlantis* landed and how wobbly he still felt several hours later. He agreed with NASA to allow himself to be carried off the orbiter. This delighted NASA doctors, who wanted to gauge immediately the effects of long-term weightlessness on the body, including dizziness and weakened bones and muscles. Once the crew was out of *Atlantis*, technicians began removing time-critical payloads from the Spacehab module.

The experiments covered the fields of advanced technology, Earth sciences, fundamental biology, human life sciences, microgravity, and space sciences. Data would supply insight for the planning and development of the International Space Station, Earth-based studies of human and biological processes, and the advancement of commercial technology. ▼

Later, *Atlantis* was towed off the runway and into the Orbiter Processing Facility (OPF) at KSC. Following standard postflight deservicing work, *Atlantis* was prepared for the sixth shuttle-Mir mission on STS-84.

Astronaut Jerry Linenger and his two Russian crewmates aboard the Mir space station were joined on February 12, 1997, by two new Russian crewmates and a German cosmonaut who were launched two days earlier. Mir 23 commander Vasili Tsibliyev and flight engineer Alexander Lazutkin replaced Mir 22 commander Valery Korzun and flight engineer Alexander Kaleri, who returned to Earth in their Soyuz spacecraft on March 2. Joining Korzun and Kaleri for their return to Earth was German researcher Reinhold Ewald, who accompanied Tsibliyev and Lazutkin to Mir for three weeks of research representing DARA, the German Space Agency.

On board Mir, a fire in an oxygen-generating device in the Kvant 1 module broke out on February 25. The fire caused minimal damage but required the five cosmonauts

Blaha, Linenger and Baker greet each other at hatch opening.

and one astronaut to wear protective masks for about thirty-six hours until the Mir space station's systems had cleaned the cabin air.

On March 21, 1997, Jerry Linenger marked one year of continuous U.S. presence in space, begun when astronaut Shannon Lucid was delivered to Mir on March 22, 1996, on *Atlantis*'s STS-76 mission. She was replaced by astronaut John Blaha on STS-79, and he, in turn, was replaced by Linenger.

Conditions on Mir improved in April with the arrival of the Progress M-34 resupply ship. The spaceship was launched on April 6 and docked with Mir two days later. The Mir crew unloaded the supplies and repair equipment and set about fixing one of the Elektron module's electrolysis oxygen generation systems by bypassing a failed filter in the Kvant 2 module. Progress also carried five dozen new lithium perchlorate oxygen candles to bolster Mir's oxygen-generating capabilities.

STS-82:
Astronauts Make a House Call to Hubble

RUSSELL R. TOBIAS

The Hubble Space Telescope got a visit from the space shuttle *Discovery* in February, 1997, for its scheduled update. By the time the astronauts were through with it, Hubble was nearly a new observatory.

Discovery and its crew of seven blasted off from the Kennedy Space Center (KSC) at 3:55:17.017 A.M. eastern standard time on February 11. Astronauts on the STS-82 mission were set to upgrade the scientific capabilities of the National Aeronautics and Space Administration's (NASA's) Hubble Space Telescope (HST) during the ten-day servicing mission by installing two state-of-the-art instruments. They also would perform maintenance to keep HST functioning smoothly until the next scheduled servicing mission in 1999.

The seven-member crew was to conduct at least four spacewalks (also called extravehicular activities, or EVAs) to remove two older instruments and install two new astronomy instruments, as well as other servicing tasks. The two older instruments being replaced were the Goddard High Resolution Spectrometer and the Faint Object Spectrograph. Replacing these instruments would be the Space Telescope Imaging Spectrograph (STIS) and the Near Infrared Camera and Multi-Object Spectrometer (NICMOS). Before the mission, HST's complement of science instruments included two cameras, two spectrographs, and Fine Guidance Sensors.

In addition to installing the new instruments, astronauts were scheduled to replace other existing hardware with upgrades and spares. Hubble was to get a refurbished Fine Guidance Sensor, an optical device that is used on HST to provide pointing information for the spacecraft and is used as a scientific instrument for astrometric science. The Solid State Recorder (SSR) was to

Opposite page: Hubble Space Telescope after capture berthed on Flight Support System (FSS) in Space Shuttle Discovery's *payload bay.*

replace one of HST's older reel-to-reel tape recorders. The SSR provides much more flexibility than a reel-to-reel recorder and can store ten times more data.

One of Hubble's four Reaction Wheel Assemblies (RWAs) was to be replaced with a refurbished spare. The RWAs are part of Hubble's Pointing Control Subsystem. The RWAs use spin momentum to move the telescope into position. The wheels also maintain the spacecraft in a stable position. The wheel axes are oriented so that the telescope can provide scienctific data with only three wheels operating, if required.

Astronauts on the STS-82 mission were set to upgrade the scientific capabilities of the National Aeronautics and Space Administration's (NASA'S) Hubble Space Telescope (HST) during the ten-day servicing mission by installing two state-of-the-art instruments. ▼

The STS-82 crew was commanded by Ken Bowersox, who was making his fourth shuttle flight. Navy commander Bowersox, forty years old, flew his first shuttle assignment as pilot of STS-50 (June 25 to July 9, 1992). It was the first flight of the United States Microgravity Laboratory and the first Extended Duration Orbiter flight. He was pilot on STS-61 (December 2-13, 1993), which was the first HST servicing and repair mission. During the flight, the HST was captured and restored to full capacity through a record five spacewalks by four astronauts. STS-73 (October 20 to November 5, 1995) was his first flight as mission commander and the second flight of the United States Microgravity Laboratory. The mission focused on materials science, biotechnology, combustion science, the physics of fluids, and numerous scientific experiments housed in the pressurized Spacelab module.

Discovery's pilot was Scott Horowitz, who was making his second flight. Thirty-nine-year-old Horowitz, an Air Force lieutenant-colonel, holds a Ph.D. in aerospace engineering. His first flight was as pilot of STS-75 (February 22 to March 9, 1996). Principal payloads on STS-75 were the reflight of the Tethered Satellite System (TSS) and the third flight of the United States Microgravity Payload (USMP-3).

Five mission specialists were assigned to STS-82. Forty-seven-year-old Joe Tanner, Mission Specialist 1, was making his second flight. Tanner flew aboard the space shuttle *Atlantis* on STS-66 (November 3-14, 1994), performing the Atmospheric Laboratory for Applications and Science 3 (ATLAS-3) mission. The mission also carried the CRISTA-SPAS satellite, which was deployed to study the chemical composition of the middle atmosphere and was retrieved later in the mission.

Mission Specialist 2, Steve Hawley, was making his fourth flight into space. The forty-five-year-old astronaut holds a Ph.D. in astronomy and astrophysics. Hawley's first flight was STS 41-D (August 30 to September 5, 1984), the maiden flight of the space shuttle *Discovery*. During the mission the crew successfully activated the OAST-1 solar cell wing experiment, deployed the SBS-D, SYNCOM IV-2, and TELSTAR 3-C satellites, and operated the Continuous Flow Electrophoresis System-III experiment. During the STS 61-C flight (January 12-18, 1986), the crew deployed the SATCOM KU satellite and conducted experiments in astrophysics and materials processing. STS-31 (April 24-29, 1990) deployed the Hubble Space Telescope.

Forty-year-old Greg Harbaugh, Mission Specialist 3, was making his fourth flight. He was a mission specialist aboard the space shuttle *Discovery* on STS-39 (April 28 to May 6, 1991). This unclassified Department of Defense mission involved research for the Strategic Defense Initiative. Harbaugh then served as flight engineer (mission specialist) aboard space shuttle Endeavour on STS-54 (January 13-19, 1993). The mission featured the deployment of the Tracking and Data Relay Satellite-F (TDRS-F), and a 4-hour, 28-minute spacewalk by Harbaugh. From June 27 to July 7, 1995, Harbaugh flew as the flight engineer (mission specialist) on a seven-member (up), eight-member (down) crew on space shuttle mission STS-71. This was the first docking with the Russian space station Mir and involved an exchange of crews. The *Atlantis* space shuttle was modified to carry a docking system compatible with the Russian Mir space station.

Mark Lee, Mission Specialist 4, was making his fourth flight. The forty-four-year-old Air Force colonel first flew as a mission specialist on STS-30 (May 4-8, 1989), aboard the orbiter *Atlantis*. During the mission,

Astronauts on the STS-82 mission were set to perform maintenance to keep HST functioning smoothly until the next scheduled servicing mission in 1999.

crew members successfully deployed the Magellan Venus exploration spacecraft, the first U.S. planetary science mission launched since 1978 and the first planetary probe to be deployed from the shuttle. Magellan arrived at Venus in August, 1990, and mapped more than 95 percent of the surface of Venus. Lee flew as payload commander on STS-47 (September 12-20, 1992), Spacelab-J. In this capacity he had overall crew responsibility for the planning, integration, and on-orbit coordination of payload and space shuttle activities. This cooperative mission between the United States and Japan included forty-four Japanese and U.S. life science and materials processing experiments. Lee also flew on STS-64 (September 9-20, 1994) aboard the space shuttle *Discovery*. Mission highlights included the first use of lasers for environmental research, deployment and retrieval of a solar science satellite, robotic processing of semiconductors, use of the RMS boom for jet thruster research, and the first untethered spacewalk in ten years to test a self-rescue jetpack, during which Lee logged 6 hours and 51 minutes of EVA.

Mission Specialist 5, Steve Smith, was making his second flight at the age of thirty-eight. Smith served as a mission specialist aboard the space shuttle Endeavour on Mission STS-68 (September 30 to October 11, 1994). Smith's responsibilities were split between shuttle systems, Space Radar Lab 2 (SRL-2, the flight's primary payload), and several experiments located in the crew cabin.

Shortly after entering orbit, the crew began their chase to rendezvous with and retrieve the Hubble Space Telescope for its second on-orbit servicing. The 12-ton (12,192-kilogram) telescope was 320 miles (515 kilometers) over Central Africa at the time of launch. It would take *Discovery* two days to make up the 3,200-mile (5,150-kilometer) distance between them.

Discovery's astronauts spent their first full day on orbit preparing for the retrieval of the Hubble Space Telescope by checking out the shuttle's robot arm, surveying the payload bay worksites, and testing the spacesuits that would be used for the four planned spacewalks beginning the following night.

The crew cabin's atmospheric pressure was lowered to reduce the amount of time required to prebreathe oxygen prior to the spacewalks to be conducted by Mark Lee, Steve Smith, Greg Harbaugh, and Joe Tanner. To prepare for the spacewalks, the astronauts assembled on the mid-

Mission highlights included the first use of lasers for environmental research, deployment and retrieval of a solar science satellite, robotic processing of semiconductors, use of the RMS boom for jet thruster research, and the first untethered spacewalk in ten years to test a self-rescue jetpack, during which Lee logged 6 hours and 51 minutes of EVA.

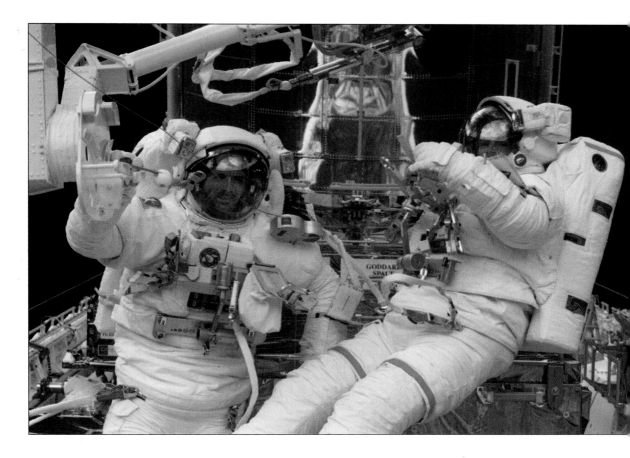

deck to check out all of the tools they would use while servicing the telescope. They successfully tested the spacesuits they would wear while working around and in Hubble in the open cargo bay.

The HST control team shut down the telescope's systems to prepare it for the servicing mission. With its aperture door closed and antennas secure, the HST was ready to be plucked from its orbit for refurbishment.

On Thursday, February 13, *Discovery*'s astronauts successfully retrieved the Hubble, plucking the observatory out of its orbit and berthing it on a special work platform at the rear of the shuttle's cargo bay. Mission specialist Steve Hawley, who first deployed the telescope during the STS-31 mission in 1990, used *Discovery*'s robot arm to grapple Hubble at 3:34 A.M. eastern time as the shuttle and the telescope flew off the west coast of Mexico at an altitude of 370 statute miles (595 kilometers). "You should have seen the expression on Dr. Stevie's face," said Bowersox with the telescope firmly in the grasp of the robot arm. "It looked like he just shook hands with an old friend."

Pausing near the foot-restraint of their in-space cherry-picker device, also called the remote manipulator system (RMS), astronauts Steven L. Smith (left) and Mark C. Lee communicate with and look toward their in-cabin team members during the third spacewalk to perform servicing chores ɩ n the HST.

The retrieval of the 43-foot-long (13-meter-long) telescope culminated a textbook rendezvous executed by Bowersox, who manually guided *Discovery* to within 35 feet (11 meters) of Hubble, enabling Hawley to extend the robot arm for its capture of the astronomical observatory. Less than a half hour later, Hawley lowered Hubble onto the Flight Support System berthing platform in *Discovery*'s cargo bay, where it was latched in place for its servicing. A remote-controlled umbilical was mated to Hubble to provide electrical power for the telescope until it was deployed again a week later.

Hawley then maneuvered the robot arm slowly around the telescope to provide close-up views of Hubble for payload controllers at the Space Telescope Operations Control Center at the Goddard Space Flight Center, who are in charge of Hubble science operations. They reported that the telescope appeared to be in excellent condition, almost seven years into its scientific tour of duty on orbit.

Astronauts Mark Lee and Steve Smith worked throughout Thursday night in the cargo bay of *Discovery*, conducting a spacewalk lasting 6 hours and 42 minutes to upgrade the telescope. The first spacewalk of the second servicing mission of the telescope began at 11:34 P.M. when Lee and Smith switched their spacesuits over to battery power. The spacewalk was slightly delayed to enable ground controllers to assess the unexpected movement of one of Hubble's solar arrays, which slewed from a horizontal to a vertical position as *Discovery*'s airlock was depressurized. The motion was created by an apparent gust of air from the airlock but caused no damage to the array, which was repositioned horizontally.

Once outside, Lee and Smith went right to work, opening the aft shroud doors on Hubble to remove the Goddard High Resolution Spectrograph and the Faint Object Spectrograph. The telephone-booth-sized instruments slid out of their compartments and were replaced by two brand-new instruments, the Space Telescope Imaging Spectrograph and the Near Infrared Camera and Multi-Object Spectrometer. STIS was installed in Hubble shortly before midnight, followed almost two hours later by the NICMOS. Payload controllers then sent commands to check the health of the two instruments, which were declared alive and well and ready for calibration over the next several weeks. The aft shroud doors were finally closed as Lee and Smith stowed the old science gear in

Opposite page: Astronomical image taken by the Hubble Space Telescope.

protective containers for the trip back to Earth. With their work successfully completed, Lee and Smith returned to *Discovery*'s airlock at 6:17 A.M. to wrap up the first of four planned excursions into the shuttle's cargo bay.

The two new instruments will increase Hubble's scientific capabilities. The STIS will take light gathered by the telescope and separate it into spectral components so that the composition, temperature, motion, and other chemical and physical properties of astronomical objects can be measured. NICMOS will allow Hubble to take infrared observations of the universe, giving astronomers the capability to view cosmic objects in nonvisible light.

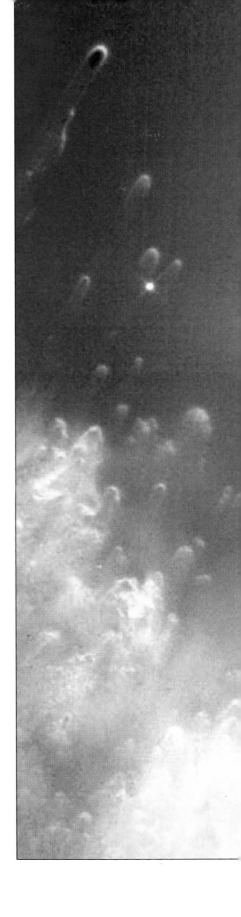

On Saturday, February 15, astronauts Greg Harbaugh and Joe Tanner completed a 7-hour, 27-minute spacewalk in the cargo bay to replace and install several new engineering components in the telescope. Harbaugh and Tanner went right to work, replacing a degraded Fine Guidance Sensor and a failed Engineering and Science Tape Recorder with new spares. Payload controllers verified that the new Fine Guidance Sensor and the new tape recorder were healthy and ready to support the telescope's scientific efforts. The astronauts also installed a new unit known as the Optical Control Electronics Enhancement Kit, which will increase the capability of the new Fine Guidance Sensor.

During the spacewalk, the astronauts and flight controllers took note of cracking and wear incurred by thermal insulation which protects several areas of the telescope. The part of the telescope that is in the direction of travel and always exposed to the Sun had experienced slight cracks and delamination during almost seven years of time on orbit. Flight controllers and Hubble project managers evaluated whether some repair work to certain portions of the telescope's insulation might be performed during the final spacewalks of the flight.

As Harbaugh and Tanner neared the end of their work in the cargo bay, *Discovery*'s small maneuvering jets were fired for about twenty minutes to gently raise Hubble's altitude by about 1.8 nautical miles. The reboost effort by Bowersox and Horowitz was scheduled to be performed again near the end of the final two spacewalks to raise Hubble's altitude by a total of about 5 nautical miles. Harbaugh and Tanner returned to *Discovery*'s airlock at 5:52 A.M.

On Sunday, mission managers decided to add a fifth

spacewalk to the flight to allow flight controllers and the astronauts time to repair tattered thermal insulation on the observatory. The revised plan called for Harbaugh and Tanner to conduct the fourth spacewalk of the flight Sunday night to replace a Solar Array Drive Electronics package and to replace covers on Hubble's magnetometers near the top of the telescope. They would also repair ripped thermal insulation on the light shield of Hubble below the areas where the magnetometers are located. On Monday night, Lee and Smith would venture into the cargo bay again to repair additional thermal insulation, which had degraded on three key equipment bays near the middle of the telescope. Hubble's redeployment was shifted one day, from Tuesday to Wednesday, with *Discovery*'s landing at the Kennedy Space Center still planned for early Friday morning before dawn.

The third spacewalk began at 9:53 P.M. Saturday evening. Lee and Smith removed and replaced a Data Interface Unit, which provides command and data interfaces between Hubble's data management system and other subsystems. They also replaced an old reel-to-reel-style Engineering and Science Tape Recorder with a new digital Solid State Recorder (SSR) that would allow simultaneous recording and playback of data.

The final task for Lee and Smith was the changeout of one of four Reaction Wheel Assembly units that use spin momentum to move the telescope toward a target and maintain it in a stable position. All of the new components were reported to be in excellent condition. *Discovery*'s small maneuvering jets were then fired for about twenty minutes to gently raise Hubble's altitude. Lee and Smith returned to *Discovery*'s airlock at 5:04 A.M.

Harbaugh and Tanner began their second spacewalk and the fourth of the mission by emerging from *Discovery*'s airlock at 10:45 P.M. Sunday night. Their first task was the replacement of a Solar Array Drive Electronics package, which is used to control the positioning of Hubble's solar arrays. Harbaugh and Tanner next ventured to the top of the telescope, where they replaced covers over Hubble's magnetometers, which are used to sense the telescope's position in relation to the Earth through data acquired from the Earth's magnetic field. The spacewalking astronauts then placed thermal blankets of multilayer material over two areas of degraded insulation around the

Following redeployment, the Hubble Space Telescope joined an armada of spacecraft to observe Comet Hale-Bopp. It also took the most detailed global photographs of Mars ever obtained from Earth's vicinity.

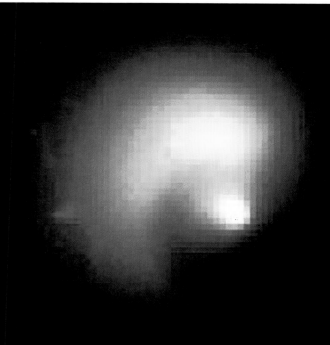

light shield portion of the telescope just below the top of the astronomical observatory. The astronauts had trained for the repair work before the flight in the event that such repairs would be needed.

While Harbaugh and Tanner were finishing their work in the payload bay, pilot Scott Horowitz and payload commander Mark Lee were busy on *Discovery*'s middeck fabricating additional thermal insulation blankets that would be installed on the telescope during a fifth spacewalk planned for later that night. Harbaugh and Tanner returned to *Discovery*'s airlock at 5:19 A.M.

On Tuesday, astronauts Mark Lee and Steve Smith completed a 5-hour, 17-minute spacewalk — the fifth spacewalk — to finish the servicing and refurbishment of the telescope. During their final excursion in *Discovery*'s cargo bay, Lee and Smith attached several thermal insulation blankets to three equipment compartments at the top of the Support Systems Module section of Hubble, which contain key data-processing, electronics, and scientific instrument telemetry packages. Following the completion of that work, Lee and Smith briefly returned to the airlock while flight controllers evaluated a possible glitch with one of four Reaction Wheel Assembly units in Hubble

These NASA Hubble Space Telescope pictures of comet Hale-Bopp show a remarkable "pin-wheel" pattern and a blob of free-flying debris near the nucleus. The bright clump of light along the spiral (seen at right) may be a piece of the comet's icy crust that was ejected into space.

The Hubble Deep Field – one of the deepest images of the universe taken to date with NASA's Hubble Space Telescope.

used to maneuver the telescope for its scientific observations. After determining that further analysis of the Reaction Wheel Assembly would be required, the astronauts were directed to close out their spacewalk and reentered the airlock for the final time at 3:32 A.M. A spare Reaction Wheel Assembly was available aboard *Discovery* for a swapout during an additional spacewalk had it been necessary, but a few hours later, after further analysis, payload controllers reported that the Reaction Wheel Assembly was in excellent shape and operating at the proper speed.

With all of the servicing tasks complete, commander Ken Bowersox and pilot Scott Horowitz fired small maneuvering jets on *Discovery* to complete the reboost of the Hubble Space Telescope, raising its orbit an additional three nautical miles. In all, a total of 33 hours and 11 minutes were logged during the five spacewalks to service and refurbish Hubble, about two hours shy of the time recorded during the five spacewalks for the first servicing mission.

On Wednesday, *Discovery*'s astronauts bid farewell to the Hubble Space Telescope as they placed the orbiting observatory back into its own orbit to continue its investigation of the far reaches of the universe. Mission specialist Steve Hawley again used the shuttle's robot arm to gently release the telescope at 1:41 P.M. At the time of deployment, the shuttle was at an altitude of 334 nautical miles over the southwest coast of Africa. Hubble is now operating at the highest altitude it has ever flown, a 335-by-321-nautical-mile orbit.

Within minutes after Hubble was set free, Bowersox and Horowitz fired jet thrusters to begin *Discovery*'s separation from the telescope. Shortly after deployment, payload controllers reported that the telescope had resumed standard operations and was processing commands from the ground through the Tracking and Data Relay Satellite System.

On Friday, February 21, Bowersox and Horowitz guided the shuttle *Discovery* to a night landing at the Kennedy Space Center in the predawn darkness, setting the orbiter down at 3:32 A.M. eastern time to wrap up the 4.1-million-mile mission. After the first landing opportunity of the day at the Kennedy Space Center was waved off because of low clouds over the Shuttle Landing Facility, the weather cleared and the green light was given to permit the seven astronauts to return home. *Discovery* swooped out of the nighttime darkness and landed at the 3-mile-long landing strip at KSC, which had additional illumination available through the recent installation of fifty-two halogen lights positioned every 200 feet down the centerline of the runway.

During the weeks following redeployment, the Hubble Space Telescope completed its checkout and began returning even better images of the universe. In April, Hubble joined an armada of spacecraft to observe Comet Hale-Bopp. It also took the most detailed global photographs of Mars ever obtained from Earth's vicinity. Taken by Hubble's Wide-Field Planetary Camera 2 on March 10, the images show the planet during the transition between spring and summer in the Northern Hemisphere. In late 1999, the third Hubble servicing mission is scheduled to be flown.

During the weeks following redeployment, the Hubble Space Telescope completed its checkout and began returning even better images of the universe.

A New Generation of Reusable Launch Vehicles: Cheaper, Faster, Safer

BRIAN J. NICHELSON

An American astronaut who once spent several months on the Mir space station asked that a package of M&M candies be included with the next load of supplies from Earth. Assuming that the National Aeronautics and Space Administration (NASA) sent one pound of M&Ms, transporting them to space cost the U.S. taxpayers between $5,000 and $10,000—as does every pound of payload aboard the space shuttle. Its high operating cost is one of the shuttle's drawbacks; it stems partly from the fact that not all components of the shuttle are reusable. The main fuel tank is destroyed when it falls into the ocean, and the two solid rocket boosters must be recovered and refurbished before they can be used again. The intensive work required to prepare a shuttle for its next flight further increases its operating costs. Safety has also been an issue, as became evident after the Challenger tragedy of January, 1986. To many people involved with the space program, these factors argue for a new generation of space vehicle.

Other factors stimulating work on a new space vehicle are the roles in space the Air Force has begun to consider. Traditionally, discussions of military operations in space have been very sensitive and were kept low-key. Yet, the U.S. Space Command has identified four missions: launching and operating spacecraft, providing services and information from space (such as data on weather and navigation), control of space, and the application of military force from space. The Space Command needs a better vehicle than the shuttle to meet the latter two missions.

The U.S. Space Command has identified four missions: launching and operating spacecraft, providing services and information from space (such as data on weather and navigation), control of space, and the application of military force from space. The Space Command needs a better vehicle than the shuttle to meet the latter two missions.

TOWARD AN OPERATIONAL RLV

As a result of these influences, NASA has initiated the Reusable Launch Vehicle (RLV) Technology Program

Opposite page: Lockheed Martin's proposed RLV "VentureStar."

in order to find a cheaper, faster, and safer way to get into space. This program is a joint effort involving NASA, the United States Air Force, and the aerospace industry. It arose from a 1993 study commissioned by Congress called Access to Space. The study concluded that the best option for providing access to space is a fully reusable, all-rocket system, using advanced technologies that are just now maturing. NASA also determined that a single-stage-to-orbit (SSTO) launch system offered the greatest potential savings in terms of reliability, operability, reusability, affordability, and safety. The purpose of the Reusable Launch Vehicle Technology Program is to develop and demonstrate those new technologies as they apply to the next generation of RLVs.

The long-term goal of the RLV Technology Program is to create a vehicle that will lead the world in low-cost space transportation. ▼

The RLV Technology Program involves a great deal of research and experimental work, both on the ground and in flight. The long-term goal is to create a vehicle that will lead the world in low-cost space transportation. NASA would like to see this new vehicle fly dozens of times per year and put payloads into orbit for about $1,000 per pound. Three different experimental vehicles have been or will be used to test the technology: the DC-XA, the X-34, and the X-33. There is a rough sequence to these projects, each building on its predecessor and eventually leading to the full-scale operational RLV.

THE DC-XA

The DC-XA looked much like a spaceship from a 1950's science-fiction movie: a stubby rocket standing on four stick legs. It even flew like spaceships in the old films, lifting off vertically, flying to its destination, rotating to an upright position, then slowly lowering itself to the ground tail-first. Its designers hoped eventually to show a rapid turnaround time between flights—as little as a few hours. The fact that the DC-XA was a single-stage, reusable rocket enhanced its ability to provide useful data to the X-33 program.

Unfortunately, the DC-XA was destroyed after a successful flight on July 31, 1996, when it tipped over and exploded. There are no plans to rebuild it, but the program was not a total loss, since the DC-XA made twelve flights that provided significant data and experience. The ability to land tail-first was an important accomplishment, and it taught NASA and the manufacturer, McDonnell Douglas, a great deal about the safety and reliability of automated control. The complex maneuvers of rotating the vehicle in flight and then lowering it to a landing were accomplished with special automated flight control software that provided control by swiveling the rocket engine nozzles and varying the thrust of its four engines. The DC-XA also provided valuable data about reusability and cost reduction, according to the program manager.

THE X-34

The X-34 project began in March, 1995, as a joint NASA-industry project to create a commercial launcher. By early 1996, however, both corporate partners ended their participation in the project, citing high development costs. A few months later, NASA reformulated the project and contracted with Orbital Sciences Corporation to build the X-34 as a technology testbed demonstrator vehicle.

The "new" X-34 will be a winged, reusable, suborbital test vehicle that will go higher and faster than the DC-XA. NASA will use it to test the viability of a frequent flight schedule (it is being designed to make twenty-five flights per year); flying and landing in crosswinds, rain, and other adverse conditions; and the advanced electronics. The point is that the X-34 will test new technologies that NASA believes are too risky for the larger, more expensive X-33.

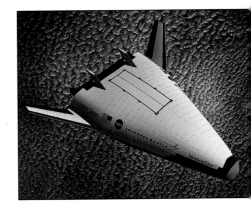

The vehicle will be small: 58 feet (18 meters) long, with a wing span of 28 feet (8.5 meters) and a gross weight of about 45,000 pounds (20,412 kilograms). It will be powered by a simple liquid oxygen/kerosene engine, producing 60,000 pounds of thrust. Plans call for the X-34 to begin flying by October, 1998, and eventually to reach a speed of at least Mach 8, or eight times the speed of sound, and an altitude of 250,000 feet (almost 50 miles, or 80.5 kilometers) in suborbital flights. The X-34 will be dropped from NASA's L-1011 aircraft to begin the flight sequence. Following ignition of the rocket engine, it will accelerate according to a predetermined flight profile. After the engine burn, the X-34 will coast for the remainder of the flight, reenter the atmosphere, and make an aircraft-style landing.

THE X-33

In July, 1996, NASA concluded a competition among Lockheed Martin, McDonnell Douglas, and Rockwell International by selecting Lockheed Martin as its industry partner to build the X-33 under a $900-million, three-year cooperative agreement. NASA hopes the X-33 will show private industry that the technology is safe enough to invest in, prompting industry to build the full-scale RLV (without government funding). NASA will then become industry's customer. The winning design, from Lockheed's Advanced Development Project Office, known as the "Skunk Works," operates on a lifting-body concept in which the body contributes a significant portion of the total lift generated by the vehicle in flight. Other noteworthy innovations include the metallic thermal protection system and the linear aerospike engines.

The delta-shaped body of the X-33 will be 67 feet (20.42 meters) long, and the total span, including two highly canted "wings," will be 68 feet (20.73 meters). When empty, it will weigh 63,000 pounds (28,577 kilograms), but when the required 211,000 pounds (95,710 kilograms) of fuel are added it will weigh well over a quarter of a million pounds (more than 113,400 kilograms). Although the X-33, as a test vehicle, will not go into orbit, it will fly at Mach 15. Because of the lifting body's favorable lift-to-drag ratio at subsonic speeds, its landing speed will be about 165 knots (50 knots slower than the shuttle), thus less demanding on the vehicle and the pilot.

The structure will be made primarily of a graphite-epoxy composite, with titanium control surfaces. These will be covered with a metallic thermal protection system, in contrast to the ceramic insulation used on the shuttle. Tests indicate that the metallic system is lighter and more durable than the ceramic system but does not insulate quite as well. The designers have taken steps to reduce aerodynamic heating by using blunt edges and by keeping the planform loading (hence flight speeds) low. In the hottest areas, protection from 1,700 degrees Fahrenheit (927 degrees Celsius) is provided by honeycomb insulation made of Inconel (a nickel, chromium, iron alloy), while a titanium honeycomb is used in the cooler areas (1,300 degrees Fahrenheit, or 704 degrees Celsius). An additional 4 inches (10 centimeters) of insulation will fill the space between the thermal protection system and the vehicle's structure.

NASA has initiated the Reusable Launch Vehicle (RLV) Technology Program in order to find a cheaper, faster, and safer way to get into space. This program is a joint effort involving NASA, the United States Air Force, and the aerospace industry.

The linear aerospike engine to be used on the X-33 and the operational RLV is a good match for the vehicle because it fits the shape of the vehicle's base, reducing drag, and because it is integral to the vehicle, reducing the installed weight. In operation, the aerospike engine is very similar to a standard rocket engine. In the latter, the exhaust gases enter a bell-shaped nozzle, where the gases expand and flow into the atmosphere. The bell nozzle's shape and diameter can be designed for only one altitude; above or below that design point, the gas stream expands either too little or too much to fit the nozzle correctly, compromising performance and efficiency. The shudder, or rapid swivel, visible in the shuttle's engine nozzles at liftoff, right after ignition, is an indication that the nozzles were not designed for sea-level operation. If the mismatch between the shape of the nozzle and the expansion of the gases is too great, damage can occur.

The aerospike nozzle is just the opposite of the bell nozzle. The gases flow into the atmosphere along the outline of a "plug," or nozzle, which is either conical or linear (like the cross section of a cone extended laterally). Exhaust gases are directed over the nozzle but flow directly into the atmosphere and thus automatically compensate for the altitude. In other words, the output and efficiency of the aerospike stay at a very high level, regardless of altitude.

The ideal spike would taper to a fine point, but this is difficult to incorporate into a vehicle, so the aerospike engines will have a truncated spike. The tradeoff is that the truncated end creates turbulence behind the engine, which in turn creates a loss in performance. To counter this effect, exhaust gas from the gas generator (used to drive turbomachinery which pressurizes fuel) is pumped out the end of the spike. This elongates the wake behind the spike, creating an aerodynamic spike or "aerospike" which is closer to the ideal spike shape, along which the propulsion stream flows.

Although the aerospike engine provides many advantages, the external gas flow also complicates the aerodynamics behind the vehicle; research to understand and improve this type of engine has been conducted since the 1970's. NASA has also begun testing one thrust chamber (the RLV will have fourteen), and with Lockheed they have tested a 5 percent scale model in a supersonic wind tunnel to examine the aerodynamic effects of the engine on the vehicle and vice versa.

The structure will be made primarily of a graphite-epoxy composite, with titanium control surfaces. These will be covered with a metallic thermal protection system, in contrast to the ceramic insulation used on the shuttle.

The engine being developed for the full-scale RLV, the Rocketdyne RS-2200 Linear Aerospike Engine, will be fueled by oxygen and hydrogen in a 6:1 ratio, and each of the RLV's engines will develop 431,000 pounds of thrust at sea level and 495,000 pounds in space. The RLV will use seven engines, with two thrusters each, and a thrust-to-weight ratio of 84. The X-33 will use two Rocketdyne J-2S engines, each of which produces 205,000 pounds of thrust. Because these engines use older technology, however, their thrust-to-weight ratio will be only 35.

Flight testing will begin in March, 1999, and is scheduled to be completed by the end of that year. The flights will originate at Edwards Air Force Base, California, and most will end at Malmstrom Air Force Base, Montana. This route was chosen because of the sparse population between those two points. Once it lands at Malmstrom, the X-33 will be carried back to Edwards on the same Boeing 747 NASA uses to ferry the shuttle. The X-33 will launch vertically, like a rocket, and at the end of its mission will make an unpowered runway landing.

If the X-33 configuration tests well, it may lead to development of the VentureStar, Lockheed Martin's proposal for a full-scale, operational RLV. The VentureStar would first fly in 2003 or 2004, following a $5 billion development program. It will be 127 feet (38.7 meters) long, have a span of 128 feet (39 meters), weigh more than 2 million pounds (907,200 kilograms) at liftoff, and be able to put 30 tons (30,480 kilograms) of payload into orbit one hundred nautical miles above Earth. Its flight profile will be identical to the X-33's.

OTHER EFFORTS

The spaceplane (a popular term for an SSTO vehicle) is gaining momentum, and new efforts are emerging all the time. At a recent Air Force-sponsored conference on the spaceplane, seventeen contractors presented their concepts. Typical of the innovation and imagination shown by these contractors is the plan presented by Pioneer RocketPlane Corporation.

This company is designing a vehicle that will operate on a different principle from any discussed so far. Pioneer believes the growing need for communication satellites will require a system capable of numerous launches with

If the X-33 configuration tests well, it may lead to development of the VentureStar, Lockheed Martin's proposal for a full-scale, operational RLV. The VentureStar would first fly in 2003 or 2004, following a $5 billion development program.

quick turnaround time in order to put a web of satellites into orbit, maintain them, and replace them when necessary. Pioneer's design is a vehicle that will take off from a runway, rocket into space, and return to a runway landing. The company estimates a cost of $2,000 per pound to place a payload in orbit—between 60 and 80 percent less than the shuttle.

Studies have also shown that there may be a market for the spaceplane to deliver cargo between two points on Earth. Pioneer's spaceplane would be able to go from New York to London in less than an hour, and the company estimates it could deliver packages for about $200 per pound.

Pioneer's first step will be to build a prototype vehicle called Pathfinder. About the size of a fighter aircraft, Pathfinder would take off from a runway in a coastal area and fly as an airplane to a rendezvous with an aerial tanker at an altitude of 25,000 to 30,000 feet (7,620 to 9,144 meters). It would be flying on two Pratt & Whitney turbofan engines at this point, and would take on a 130,000-pound (58,968-kilogram) load of liquid oxygen (fuel for the rocket engine) from the tanker. It would then ignite its rocket engine, accelerate to a speed of nearly 8,200 miles (13,196 kilometers) per hour, and climb to an altitude of 80 nautical miles. After releasing its payload (most likely a satellite that would be boosted into the proper orbit by a smaller rocket), it would reenter the atmosphere, restart the turbofans, and make a runway landing.

In yet another direction, a nonprofit consortium was recently formed, with the "strong encouragement" of NASA and the Air Force, to develop an electromagnetic catapult. Called the Maglifter, it would use superconducting magnetic levitation to accelerate RLVs to about 600 miles (966 kilometers) per hour and shoot them out a tube at the top of a 14,000-foot (4,267-meter) mountain. It would dramatically reduce launch costs by either reducing the fuel load or increasing the payload capacity.

4 | Earth and the Environment

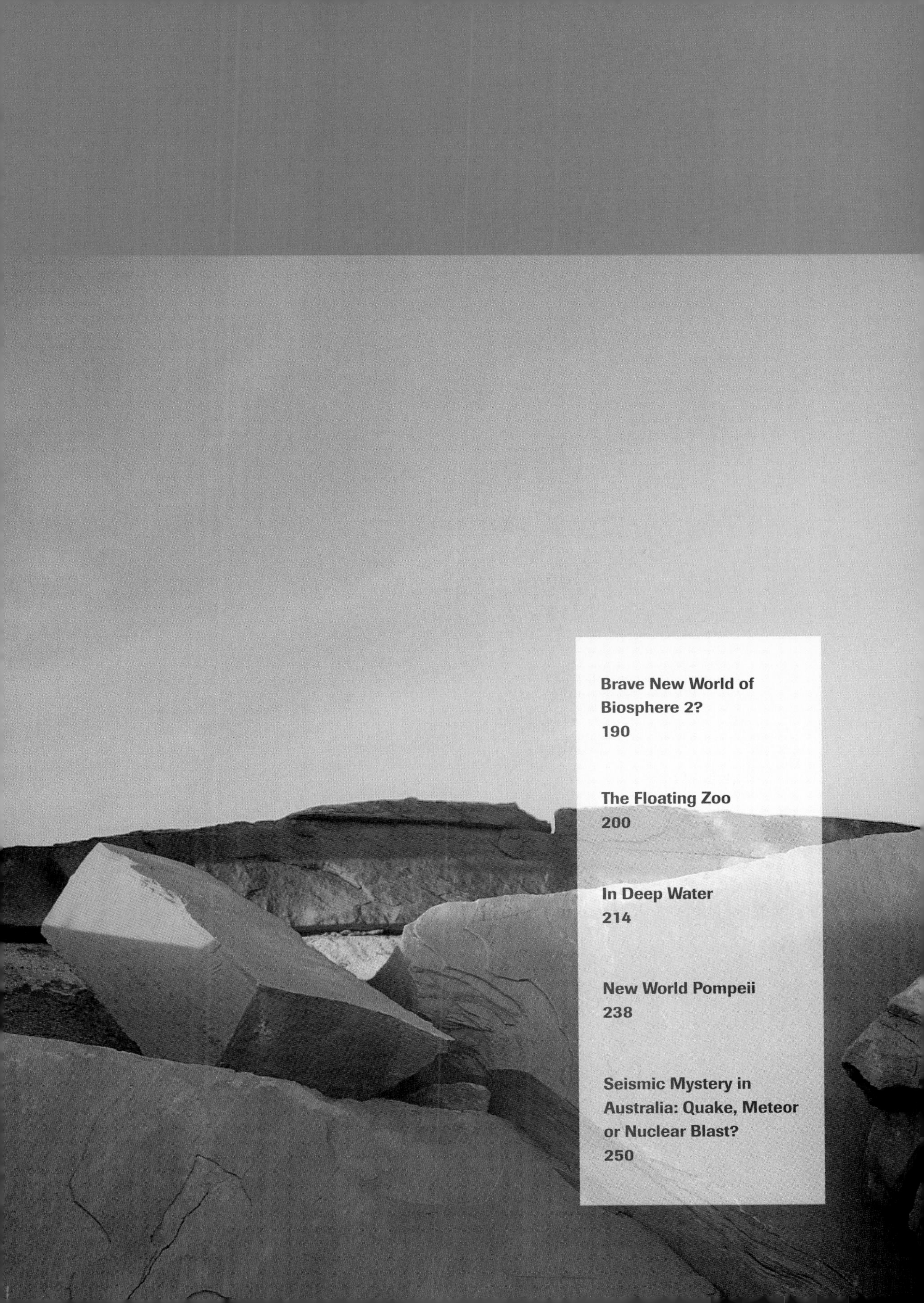

Brave New World of Biosphere 2?

New operators of the desert greenhouse aim to save the planet.

DAN VERGANO

Last month, after 18 years of government service, William Harris abandoned the no-nonsense National Science Foundation for the fringes of science: He took over as director of Biosphere 2. Harris' new boss, Columbia University, began managing the controversial megaterrarium, located in the cactus-filled desert of Arizona, early this year.

Originally conceived as a sealed laboratory for would-be explorers of Mars, Biosphere 2 fell into scientific disrepute when its eight original residents suffered from a lack of oxygen in their artificial atmosphere (see sidebar).

The prestigious university hopes not only to establish a sterling research facility at Biosphere 2 but to experiment with the education of environmental scientists and save the planet into the bargain. "Columbia is going into this with its eyes wide open," says Harris. "The question is whether Biosphere can be converted into a place for real science."

Still, the question remains: Why perform vital research at the site that spawned a thousand late-night television jokes?

"It's a national treasure," says Bruno Marino, a Harvard University researcher who managed the site for much of the last 2 years. Marino took up the reins after Biosphere 2's owner, Texas billionaire Edward P. Bass, banished the original management and decided to make it a facility for environmental science research.

Marino, who still operates an experiment at the site, compares it to the Sphinx. "Its allure is magnetic. It suggests numerous opportunities for research, but it's a difficult riddle to solve."

While the mythological Sphinx tended to kill those who failed to solve the riddle it posed, the only thing

Opposite page: Habitat views at Biosphere 2.

Top: Ocean biome.

Bottom: Rainforest biome.

Opposite page: Desert biome at Biosphere 2.

Biosphere 2's new management has to lose is its reputation. The crew of researchers, educators, and tour guides plans to operate the site as a respected center for environmental science research and education. With a few alterations, they hope this westernmost sprig of the Ivy League will become a center for predicting nature's response to a changing atmosphere.

An intriguing arrangement between the university and Bass allows for long-lasting improvements to the facility. At the end of the contract, the school will either turn in its keys, extend the management operation, or receive outright ownership, says Bass.

For the next 5 years, Columbia agrees to manage Biosphere 2 in much the same manner that other universities run federal laboratories. The deal reportedly pays Columbia $50 million, which it plans to plow back into maintenance and renovations. Simply cooling the greenhouse costs $1 million a year.

"Columbia University's leadership of Biosphere 2 has already proven to be tremendous," says Bass.

In 1991, the first Biospherians stepped into a 3-acre world consisting of living quarters, three agricultural greenhouses, and a photogenic wilderness area that contained a tiny desert, rain forest, savanna, and ocean. They called the facility Biosphere 2, explaining that Biosphere 1 is Earth. The adventurers tried to subsist in a sealed habitat, but true isolation proved impossible.

As a first step in the new vision of Biosphere 2, the living quarters have been opened to the public as a museum. In addition, the 40-foot-high agricultural bays are being sealed off from each other and from the 2-acre wilderness area. "Given an apparatus that was built for some other reason, converting it is difficult," says Wallace Broecker, chief scientist for Biosphere 2 and a researcher at Columbia's Lamont-Doherty Earth Observatory in Palisades, N.Y.

To predict the effect of Earth's rising greenhouse gases, the plans call for keeping one of the agricultural compartments at a temperature and carbon dioxide concentration that reflect local conditions. The remaining bays could be controlled to test the effects of either increased carbon dioxide concentration or increased temperature.

Broecker leans toward the first option. "We know carbon dioxide levels are going to go up."

Science Under Glass

- **November 1986:** Ground broken for construction of Biosphere 2.

- **September 1991:** Early in the month, facility engineers install carbon dioxide scrubbers to remove unexpectedly high concentrations of the gas from the greenhouse. Later, eight Biospherians begin their 2-year tour inside Biosphere 2.

- **October 1991:** A Biospherian leaves the dome to visit the hospital after a thresher accident. She returns with replacement computer parts stowed in a duffel bag.

- **May 1992:** Alarmed by a decrease in oxygen concentrations, John Allen, head of Biosphere 2 and a former leader of a nearby commune, seeks out geochemist Wallace S. Broecker of Columbia University's Lamont-Doherty Earth Observatory for advice. No action was taken.

- **August 1992:** The committee of external advisers recommends hiring scientific director, designing a research plan, and opening data to outside scrutiny.

- **February 1993:** After oxygen concentrations drop to 15 percent of the Biosphere atmosphere, fresh gas is pumped in, violating the original plan. All 11 science advisory committee members resign, citing lack of progress.

Plan view of Biosphere 2.

The first step in either plan is to remove the 2,000 cubic meters of rich soil that sucked oxygen out of the air, drastically weakening earlier Biospherians. At the insistence of the Arizona Department of Agriculture, the dirt — some of which was imported from the Everglades — will be fumigated to kill any nonnative nematodes.

One-third of each agricultural bay will be planted with loblolly pine, redbud, and sweet gum trees, to demonstrate how the forests — and the timber industry — of the Southeast would hold up under increasing concentrations of carbon dioxide. The remaining sections would hold experiments with food crops. "If we look at something on a 10-to 20-year time scale, it will be useful 100 years from now," says Broecker.

In his view, Biosphere 2 offers an unparalleled opportunity to look at the growth of a forest from seed to treetop canopy in an enclosed environment. Short-term studies in the wilderness area, when compared to long-term studies in the agricultural bays, should indicate the reliability of 1- or 2-year experiments.

"It flabbergasted the world when Columbia took over," says Boyd Strain, a botanist at Duke University in Durham, N.C. Strain pioneered the kind of large-scale research on carbon dioxide and trees now proposed in Arizona. He liked the newest plans for Biosphere 2 enough to join its board of external advisers. "I think they're doing the right thing, and they're a good group of people."

Another prominent scientist who endorses Harris and Broecker's plan is ocean physicist Russ Davis of the University of California, San Diego. Davis affirms that the superb engineering controlling the greenhouse makes it possible to carry out realistic, large-scale experiments not possible anywhere else.

"Biosphere gives Columbia a great new tool for dealing with its crusty critics," quips Davis, who occasionally numbers himself among them. After one rancorous meeting held at the site's conference center and hotel, he says, "they stuck me in room 105, and in the middle of the night I woke up with one of their trained scorpions stinging the hell out of me."

With Harris on board, the campus is finally open for scientific business. He completes a team of experts in ocean biochemistry, crop modeling, and forestry hired to manage the various experimental sections.

Eight research projects funded by grants from

Columbia are scheduled to begin next spring. Broecker hopes that these seed money grants of under $20,000 each will attract outside funding, because future projects will have to rely on external dollars. "If you can get funding to do an experiment, we will allocate the space," he says. Some of the scientists from the Carnegie Laboratory at Stanford University, the University of California, Irvine, and the Scripps Institution of Oceanography in San Diego who have received these initial grants plan to study atmospheric methane and nitrous oxide, model plant life cycles, and plot coral growth.

Students labor alongside researchers at Biosphere 2. Columbia calls the 250-acre outpost its western campus and inaugurated the first class of 25 Earth Semester undergraduates this fall. A biologist, earth scientist, and social scientist team-teach classes in an effort to break down barriers among disciplines. The students focus on gaining field experience and thinking holistically about humanity's impact upon the planet.

"It is really well suited to an educational mission, there are so many different ecosystems," says geochemist Debra Colodner, who heads the education program. The students are conducting conventional studies of vegetation, as well as assessing the North Atlantic Free Trade Agreement's (NAFTA's) effects on carbon dioxide emissions from the United States and Mexico. In the next 2 years, Colodner hopes to expand the program to 75 students per semester. "The best thing they'll learn is how hard it is to play God with this 3-acre parcel, let alone the whole Earth."

Since 1991, Biosphere 2 has become one of the biggest tourist attractions in Arizona—it received its millionth guest this September. For $12.95, the visitor still gets a look at the original Biospherians' attempt to create a proto-Mars habitat, "but we are [also] telling people dynamic things are happening on this planet," Harris says.

Columbia hopes to draw the curious into hands-on exhibits about environmental science and current research. A climate change exhibit now on display at the Smithsonian Institution's Museum of Natural History will find a permanent home at the site in 1997. "Our goal is to demystify science for the public," says Harris.

University officials describe their involvement with Biosphere 2 as an attempt to reduce the threat of global

- **April 1994:** Facility owner Edward P. Bass calls in federal marshals to throw out Biosphere 2 officials, accusing them of mismanagement. A few days later, two original Biospherians sabotage the site, smashing windows. They claim to be acting out of safety concerns. The second team emerges.

- **January 1996:** Columbia University begins management of Biosphere 2. Plans are made to convert the facility to a research campus devoted to earth science. Later in the month, comedian Pauly Shore's parody, *Bio-Dome*, reaches theaters.

- **September 1996:** Columbia names William Harris the new director of Biosphere 2, effective Oct. 15.

Biosphere 2 Lung.

climate change. Education, tourism, and research add up to a larger plan, according to Harris. In his view, scientists need to aim their research directly at battling the ill effects of humanity's century-long flirtation with fossil fuels and start educating the public about the dangers of greenhouse gases.

"Lamont-Doherty is like a monastery, removed from the public," says Michael Crow, a vice-provost at Columbia. He envisions decreasing science's distance from the public eye and "putting Biosphere 2 in the driver's seat" of efforts to predict the next century's climate.

The crew of researchers, educators, and tour guides plan to operate the site as a respected center for environmental science research and education. With a few alterations, they hope this westernmost sprig of the Ivy League will become a center for predicting nature's response to a changing atmosphere.

"We believe we've reached a point where human beings have got to take a completely different view about the planet," says Crow. "It's all related to the long-term future of the planet—and I don't mean in just an environmental sense, but in what I would call a stewardship sense. How do you build planetary mangers of the future?"

How indeed? Hubris, the sin of pride, doomed many a challenger of the Sphinx, and some critics wonder whether this key ingredient of tragedy still lingers around Biosphere 2.

At the same time, others contend that a holistic vision, which can only be explored in a complex system, is just what's needed—carbon dioxide concentrations in the air are increasing worldwide, and most scientists consider global warming a reality.

"All I can say is we have great people, and we're working very hard," says Broecker. He's convinced there's something unique about the glass-walled temple of science in the Sonora Desert. The real riddle of Biosphere 2 to him is its existence. "I wander around it sometimes, just bewildered, wondering how it ever happened."

Biosphere 2, located in the desert
in Arizona, is now managed by
Columbia University.

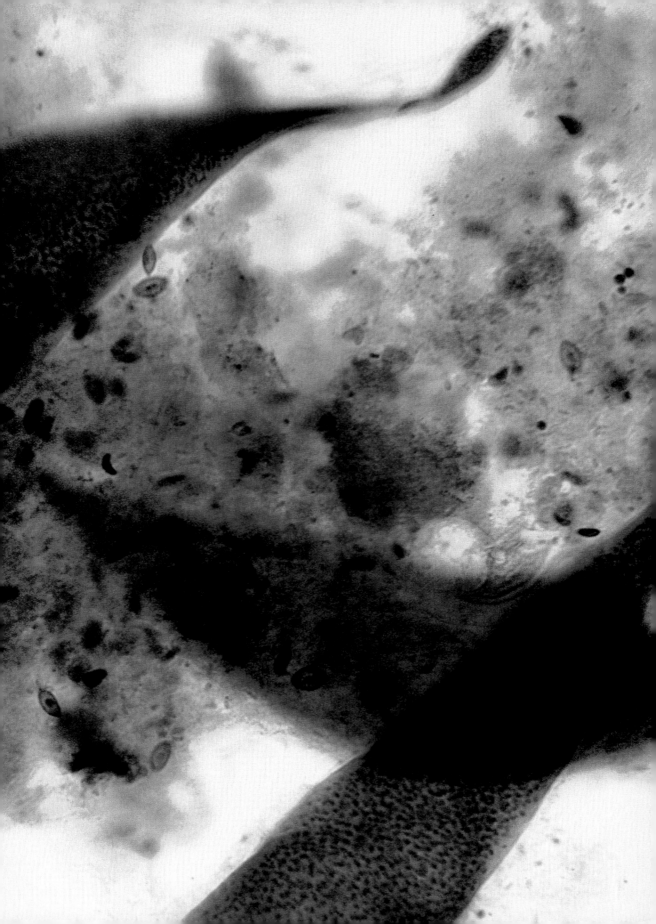

The Floating Zoo

The air teems with viruses, bacteria, fungi, and other microscopic creatures.
They can cross oceans on a gust of wind. Some can cause crop failures, disease, and death.
Some can be used as invisible weapons. And we know next to nothing about them.

KEVIN KRAJICK

I n late 1991 at Lincoln Hospital, a huge red-brick building in New York City, something began killing patients on Ward 8C. First the victims, all of whom were already battling AIDS, came down with a fever and a nasty cough. Antibiotics prescribed by the doctors did nothing. Within weeks patients were eaten alive from inside; holes appeared in their lungs, muscles evaporated. Medical technician Bertha Doctor remembers their eyes, how they looked at her from deep within taut-skinned heads as the victims drowned in pain and fever. Toward the end, as blood filtered into dissolving lungs, the victims' breathing came hard. "They're coughing as much as they can, they're gasping, gasping, and then they stop," says Doctor. The sickness moved from room to room, hall to hall, in a pattern that suggested it was caused by an airborne microbe. Doctor and the rest of the 8C staff were so scared that they secretly gathered in a back room to join hands, cry, and pray. Then they went back to work.

Eventually the sickness was diagnosed and named: Strain W, a new drug-resistant strain of tuberculosis. Science once thought it had conquered this airborne scourge. Now TB is again a global pandemic, taking almost 3 million lives in 1995. Highly contagious forms that ignore antibiotics are becoming more prevalent. TB was implicated in the deaths of 70 people at Lincoln; 90 others (including Doctor) picked up the bacteria before it finished its wanderings.

The Lincoln Hospital outbreak was only one of many recent reminders that the air around us is full of life — life that we know little about and which sometimes views us as prey. A cubic yard of the atmosphere can contain hundreds of thousands of bacteria, viruses, fungal spores, pollen grains, lichens, algae, and protozoa. A good

The air around us is full of life — life that we know little about and which sometimes views us as prey.

Opposite page: Protozoa in water.

sneeze expels over 10 million germs. Certainly it comes as no surprise that diseases like TB, influenza, and chicken pox can spread through the air. But many people may find it shocking to learn how little we know about the airborne habits of the microbes that cause those familiar diseases; we know even less about the habits of the microbes that cause rarer, more lethal, plagues. As if threats from nature were not enough, airborne germ weapons are proliferating—and the Pentagon admits it has been poorly equipped to spot an attack. Aerobiologists, those who study life in the atmosphere, are scrambling to catch up.

Aerobiologists face a fundamental problem: unlike organisms in blood, food, and water, airborne pathogens are still mostly beyond our powers to track. "We greatly underestimate the organisms in the air," says University of Nevada, Las Vegas, microbiologist Linda Stetzenbach. "We can find maybe 10 to 30 percent. There are a lot we don't know anything about."

In recent decades aerobiology has been burdened by its reputation as a charming but somewhat obsolete science. Actually, it is a cornerstone of microbiology. Well over a century ago, in the 1860s, Louis Pasteur proved that food rotted because ubiquitous "organized corpuscles" in the air quickly colonized any organic matter that wasn't sealed off. Decades of experiments through the middle of this century showed that diseases like TB, polio, measles, pneumonic plague, diphtheria, and flu move through the air from host to host. But time and again, drugs and vaccines were so effective in halting the spread of these diseases that aerobiology was pushed to medicine's back burner. If you can fight germs once they reach human bodies, why worry about how they get there?

Biologists and ecologists remained interested in life in the air, even if doctors felt they could safely ignore it. From the 1930s to the 1960s, aircraft- and balloon-mounted instruments found vast armies of seeds and bacteria floating miles above Earth. A Russian rocket sampled the scant air at 40 miles up and found bacteria. In a column of air one square mile in area and 14,000 feet high, researchers calculated that there were 25 million insects. Spores of fungus were found over the Pacific and Atlantic, far from the lands where they started their journeys. The ecology of this air started to make sense. It became apparent that living things routinely go aloft to migrate, to mate, and to find new hosts. Thus in a few

TB is again a global pandemic, taking almost 3 million lives in 1995.

Opposite page: Polio patient Dawn Varma holding her baby for the first time after being in an iron lung since her baby's birth (1959).

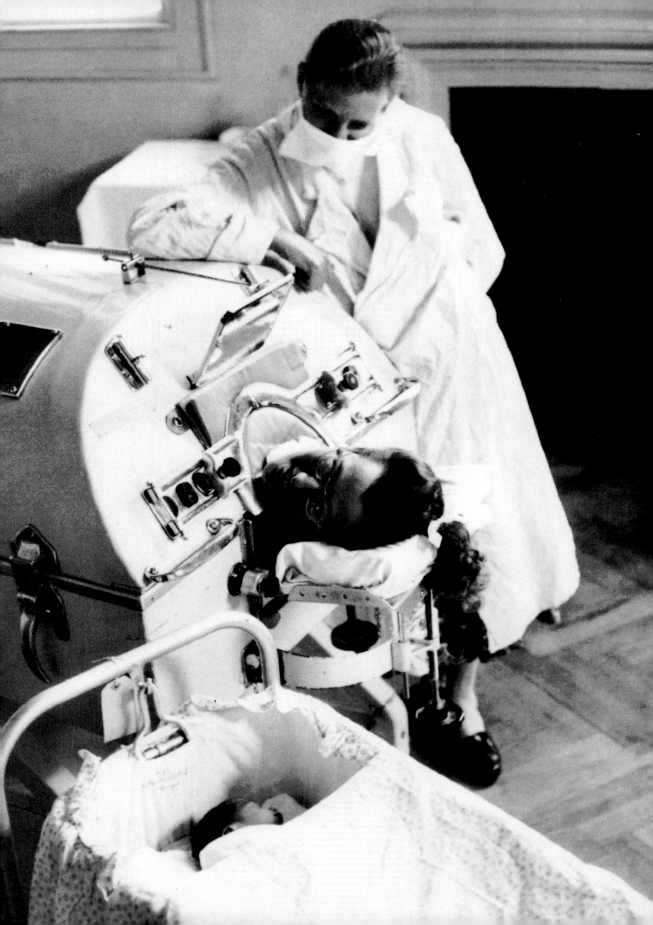

weeks ragweed, plants produce billions of pollen grains, casting them to the winds and to runny noses. The Pallas's wallflower of the Arctic is a particularly exquisite example of airborne engineering: it has evolved seed heads that protrude just above the snow in winter; at this height they can be dislodged by winds, which then sweep them over the crusted surface for miles, even to islands across frozen seas.

While much of this traveling is dedicated to reproduction and finding new land to colonize, much of it, unfortunately, is aimed at infecting land-bound organisms. Like invisible swarms of locusts, fungi can travel from Mexico to Canada, wiping out crops of wheat and corn along the way. Researchers are only beginning to chart the course these spores take. During the day, rising thermals and gusts of wind carry hundreds of thousands of them in each cubic yard, lofting them up to 10,000 feet. At that height, smooth, interstate-like airstreams can carry them along for hundreds of miles at speeds up to 40 miles an hour until rain or other disturbances drive them back to Earth.

Aerobiologists have had good luck studying grains of pollen and fungus spores, in part because they are big and sturdy enough to survive the

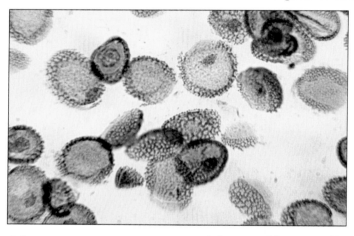

Pollen.

In a few weeks ragweed, plants produce billions of pollen grains, casting them to the winds and to runny noses.

violence of being collected on an airplane-mounted screen, brought to a lab, and counted under a microscope. But detecting microbes in the vastness of the atmosphere is far more difficult — bacteria are 100 to 300 times smaller than fungi; viruses are 100 times smaller yet. Thanks to the endless eddying and mixing of air, huge numbers of microbes may occupy a small space for just a second before scattering, all the while remaining undetected. Instead of trying to spot germs directly, therefore, aerobiologists have until recently tried to vacuum up large volumes of air, blast it into a growth medium, and wait for something to multiply. It's a poor method at best: the microbes are sometimes so battered from their long journeys that they can't reproduce. Those that do manage to grow may take days or weeks to turn up in detectable numbers. And many microorganisms simply refuse to grow unless they are feeding on their particular living target—an apple leaf, say, or a human lung.

As a result of all these factors, estimates of bacteria and virus numbers vary wildly. According to Environmental Protection Agency microbiologist Bruce Lighthart, a cubic meter of air over a single Oregon farm field can harbor anywhere from 900 to 600,000 bacteria depending on the location and time of day. Viruses are the biggest mystery of all. Unlike bacteria, which are content simply to suck up nutrients from a culture dish, viruses must infect a cell before they can reproduce. They have rarely been directly detected in air except in tightly contained lab experiments. But they are certainly around, spreading flu and doing other jobs of which we are unaware. "Maybe we're picking up a hundredth or a thousandth of the viruses," says Lighthart. "I don't know."

Recently aerobiologists have at least begun to get a better catch, thanks to the revolutionary technique known as polymerase chain reaction amplification, or PCR. PCR typically involves using a genetic probe that locks onto snippets of DNA and reproduces them many times over until they are so numerous that they can be easily detected. Last year plant pathologist John Castello of the State University of New York at Syracuse collected cloud and fog particles from the Adirondack Mountains and from treeless islands off the coast of Maine and used PCR to pluck out a plant virus — called tomato mosaic Tobamovirus. He subsequently infected red spruce trees with it, proving that it was alive. Crop plants and timber are the hosts of the hardy Tobamovirus, but Castello found it far from either, offering up the first good evidence that viruses can probably travel on their own, without a host, for many miles.

Chances are the viruses we're most familiar with won't find us on a mountain but inside a home or office. Most of us human hosts spend 80 to 90 percent of our time inside, inhaling, exhaling, and building up concentrations of organisms that would dissipate quickly in the great outdoors. Sneezes and coughs expel germs in mucousy droplets, but most are unwieldy gobs over four-thousandths of an inch across—big enough to fall onto the floor or other surfaces within seconds. If they happen to end up in your nose, they will probably be filtered out

Living things routinely go aloft to migrate, to mate, and to find new hosts.

by protective hairs. But some drops dry and shrink to "droplet nuclei"—measuring two ten-thousandths of an inch across and carrying a few bacteria or hundreds of viruses. These colonies are well-designed for finding a host to infect: they can float for hours or even days on the tiniest currents; the clumped germs help one another maintain critical moisture and temperature. They are small enough to whisk through nasal passages, yet big enough to get jostled out of respiratory-passage air streams by turbulence, gravity, or sudden rehydration and find purchase in the throat or lung.

Mycobacterium tuberculosis is the quintessential airborne germ. It may float alive for hours, protected from dehydration and damaging ultraviolet rays by its waxy coat. But although the bacterium has been studied exhaustively in humans, it has never been isolated from air outside laboratories. Most victims are thought to produce relatively few infectious droplets, and Mycobacterium reproduces so slowly in culture—three to six weeks to become apparent —that other airborne bugs that happen to be sampled with it can crowd it out. So our knowledge of its behavior in air comes in large part from inferences, such as those made from experiments in the 1950s and 1960s in which the air from TB wards was pumped into guinea pig chambers, and from studies of infection rates of humans accidentally exposed to known carriers. Theoretically, it takes only a single TB bacterium to infect a person, but no one knows for sure.

Researchers are now designing a PCR probe to detect TB in air directly, much as Castello has done with tomato mosaic Tobamovirus. They are encouraged by the work of Mark Sawyer, a pediatric infectious-diseases specialist at the University of California at San Diego, who succeeded in detecting chicken pox virus in hospital air. Less encouraging, though, is what Sawyer also discovered: a full day after a patient was discharged he could detect the virus's DNA still drifting around the room—and as far as 50 feet down the hall. Even more disturbing was Sawyer's detection of airborne viral DNA in the rooms of patients with the form of chicken pox that adults suffer from, known as shingles. Unlike the childhood form, shingles creates painful blisters on the skin but does not spread infectious droplets by coughing. Sawyer's results suggest that even scaling skin is a suitable launching pad for the virus.

Epidemics of chicken pox, gastric infections, and TB can rage through hospital wards, apparently through the air, which suggests that institutions are doing a poor job of containing the germs.

Epidemics of chicken pox, gastric infections, and TB can rage through hospital wards, apparently through the air, which suggests that institutions are doing a poor job of containing the germs. Investigations of the Lincoln Hospital TB outbreak have revealed that even in rooms that were equipped with pumps to vent air from the rooms outdoors, air was spewed in the wrong direction, letting germs slip under doors, sidle down corridors, and circle the nurses' station. According to a report by the New York State Department of Health, this was typical. Many hospitals, lulled by declines in serious airborne disease since the sixties, were found with either poor protective systems or none whatsoever. The outbreak at Lincoln, along with others in New Jersey and Florida, brought improvements at many institutions.

Lincoln itself now has a revamped, state-of-the-art TB unit. The surge of fans is constantly audible; they change the air in each room 6 to 12 times an hour. Outside each patient's door is a fist-size air-pressure gauge. Engineers periodically check it by opening the doors and blowing puffs of chalk in to make sure none blows back into the hall. Inside the room, a silvery venting tunnel recessed into the ceiling emits ultraviolet light to destroy bacteria that pass through it. When Celia Alfalla, the director of the TB unit, enters a room, she dons a tight-fitting respirator to keep out germs. If a patient needs to leave his room for tests or X-rays, he pulls a surgical mask over his face to keep germs in. Except for these brief forays, patients are permitted to leave their rooms only if drugs have succeeded in rendering them noncontagious. Alfalla obtains court orders to imprison patients who won't comply, and she is backed up by a surly looking police officer at the entrance to the unit.

HIV virus.

Little about these measures is particularly new — hospitals are simply using them more often now. No one at this point knows what else to do. Despite all the precautions, Alfalla has skin tests every three to six months to check for exposure. "I do get scared every time I get a

Bacteria can travel through sprays created by supermarket vegetable misters, whirlpools in spas, decorative fountains, and hotel showers. One recent study showed that dentists' offices are *Legionella* hot spots, with the bacteria building up inside water-cooling lines for dental drills and shooting out as cavities are filled.

cough or wake up with a night sweat," she says. Bertha Doctor already carries the germ—noncontagious as long as she doesn't show symptoms—and has regular checkups. She has a one-in-ten chance of getting sick, but she has decided to stay on the ward. "We love our patients and we want to see them doing well," she says. "Besides, you go on the bus, TB is there. You go on the street, it's there. You can't not breathe."

Technology has not only failed to curb airborne pathogens; it has inadvertently succeeded in creating new forms. *Legionella* bacteria are a case in point. For millennia, *Legionella*, which lives in ponds and lakes, left humans unmolested. If you drank *Legionella*-laden water, you usually suffered no ill effect. But then we invented giant institutional air conditioners that use reservoirs of water to remove heat, and these reservoirs have proved friendly to these microbes. Powerful vents sweep air over the water and pick up droplets that they carry throughout the buildings; in some systems the reservoirs are put on roofs, and the droplets are then sprayed down onto streets. Suddenly, for the first time, it is possible to *breathe* the bacteria—and in this form *Legionella* can cause the fatal pneumonia known as Legionnaires' disease.

In recent years epidemiologists have discovered that air conditioners are not the only way to spread Legionnaires' disease. The bacteria can travel through sprays created by supermarket vegetable misters,

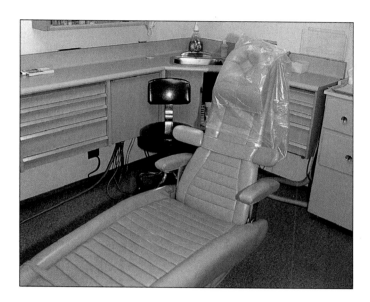

whirlpools in spas, decorative fountains, and hotel showers. PCR and other new methods are showing more clearly how we unwittingly turn everyday appliances into
weapons of germ warfare. One recent study showed that
dentists' offices are *Legionella* hot spots, with the bacteria
building up inside water-cooling lines for dental drills
and shooting out as cavities are filled.

A puzzle about *Legionella* is why it produces such
a range of effects — some people get just a
sniffle (sometimes referred to as Pontiac fever)
and others drop dead. Part of the reason may
be found in amoebas, large single-celled
organisms that live in soil and water — including the
water in cooling systems — and that are sometimes found
floating in the air. Legionella and other kinds of bacteria
are often eaten by amoebas. But according to Tim
Rowbotham, a water microbiologist at Leeds Public
Health Laboratory in England, the devoured bacteria can
turn the tables and feed on the amoebas from the inside
and reproduce. A hapless amoeba may end up carrying as
many as 1,800 bacteria. "If you're unlucky enough to
inhale one of those, you could get quite a dose," he says.

More frightening to many is the emerging evidence
that the once-obscure and now-famous virus Ebola may
also be capable of airborne transmission. One of the
deadliest pathogens on Earth, Ebola spreads mainly
through body fluids, which has limited its periodic ram-

Fungi can travel from Mexico
to Canada, wiping out crops of
wheat and corn along the way.

pages through Africa. But in 1989 and 1990 an outbreak of Ebola may have been spread by air from monkeys in a quarantine facility in Reston, Virginia. This event was popularized in the 1994 best-seller *The Hot Zone*, and became fictional grist for the 1995 movie *Outbreak*. While a fair amount of the accompanying publicity was flashy and dubious, the threat of airborne Ebola is being taken seriously by some experts. In an analysis of recent outbreaks of Ebola in Africa performed by virologist Peter Jahrling, principal scientific adviser to the U.S. Army Medical Research Institute of Infectious Diseases, and his co-workers, the researchers found clusters of deaths —in which victims had no known contact with one another—that made it, in Jahrling's words, "difficult to exclude a component of aerosol transmissibility."

A ccording to military intelligence sources, someone—they won't reveal who—is already experimenting with Ebola as a form of biological warfare.

Meanwhile, further research on monkeys has added more evidence to Ebola's possible airborne danger. When the Reston monkeys contracted Ebola, they came down with an unusual pneumonia not normally associated with the bleeding that is the hallmark of the disease. Researchers injected the Ebola from these monkeys into healthy ones, and they too came down with the pneumonia. It's possible, judging from this evidence, that there is actually a rare separate strain of pneumonia-causing Ebola that prefers to travel by air. In addition, Jahrling has published a long-neglected experiment in which he and his colleagues killed monkeys by putting them into Plexiglas chambers and spraying in small amounts of the germ. According to Jahrling, this shows that while nature may or may not make Ebola airborne, "it's no problem for us to do it. You can make this stuff into a weapon."

This is not just conjecture. According to military intelligence sources, someone—they won't reveal who—is already experimenting with Ebola as a form of biological warfare. This gruesome research is only part of a recent surge of work on bioweapons going on in nations scattered around the world. The official list is classified, but military sources say it includes Iraq, China, Iran, Syria, Egypt, Taiwan, Libya, some countries of the former

Soviet Union, and various terrorist groups. Virtually all biological weapons are designed for air delivery, but they can just as easily be spread by putting a spray tank of anthrax bacteria, say, into the trunk of a New York taxi and politely driving around town. Anthrax in fact is a serious threat, since it's stable in air and easily made; the U.S. Defense Department is sufficiently concerned that it has proposed vaccinating its 2.4 million personnel against the disease—the first program of germ-warfare inoculation the military has ever considered undertaking. Cholera and Venezuelan equine encephalitis (a mosquito-born virus that can paralyze or kill) are also designated as "agents of concern." Animal experiments suggest that diseases with effects similar to Ebola—such as Rift Valley fever, Lassa fever, Bolivian hemorrhagic fever, Marburg virus and Congo-Crimean hemorrhagic fever— can become infectious if made into aerosols. But Army researchers are running vaccine trials for only three of these diseases, and they may have only limited use. Recently the Army made the horrifying discovery that its vaccine for Rift Valley fever—normally transmitted by mosquitoes—doesn't work if the germ is inhaled. A new one has been developed, but it's still being reviewed by the Food and Drug Administration.

According to Brigadier General John Doesburg, head of the Pentagon's Joint Program Office for Biological Defense, the Gulf War made the military realize how poorly prepared it was to detect a bioweapons attack. At the time, the Iraqis were stockpiling thousands of gallons of agents, including anthrax, pneumonic plague, and *Clostridium perfringens* (which leads to gangrene)—and UN inspectors suspect they may still have much of it on hand. The gigantic Desert Storm army fielded only a few outdated biological weapons detectors. "We did not have a substantive low-level air-sampling system," admits Doesburg.

As far as the Army can tell, the Iraqis didn't use bioweapons, but if its experience with chemical weapons is any guide, its soldiers are vulnerable. After years of denial and obfuscation, the Pentagon conceded this summer that some Gulf War veterans' complaints of devastating neurological and intestinal problems could be related to airborne Iraqi sarin and mustard gas; as many as 20,000 soldiers might have been exposed to these substances during the explosion of a chemical-weapons stockpile or other incidents.

Airborne germ weapons are proliferating—and the Pentagon admits it has been poorly equipped to spot an attack.

Doesburg says the Pentagon now has "a very accelerated schedule" of long-term research to develop biological air probes—in 1996 alone it allocated $66 million for this purpose. The military has already come up with an array of gizmos. The first line of defense is a detection

Air currents.

system consisting of a 1,100-pound device that bolts into a Blackhawk helicopter and sweeps a pulsing infrared laser beam as far as 20 miles, analyzing the photons that bounce back from airborne particles. "A man-made cloud looks different from a natural one," says Bruce Jezek, the program director of biodefense at the Chemical and Biological Defense Command at Aberdeen Proving Ground in Maryland. Any cloud that seems unnaturally shaped, he says, will show up on a computer screen. The researchers are working on a second, short-range system to complement this device: an ultraviolet laser that can analyze clouds two miles away, making most biological particles fluoresce. It will, in theory, let its operators know if they are looking at mere smoke and dust or an oncoming cloud of plague.

Then, in development at Aberdeen, there is the Biological Integrated Detection System (BIDS)—a windowless, airtight eight-by-ten-foot Army shelter bolted into the back of a Humvee and crammed with computer screens and other equipment. The shelter, too cramped to stand up in, has a stack that continually sucks air into a device that measures the size of particles. If particle concentrations change suddenly, an alarm goes off; the two operators locked inside the box don masks and switch on another powerful vacuum that quickly distills thousands of gallons of outdoor air into small test tubes of liquid. One operator pulls out some of the tubes and uses a laser to detect the presence of adenosine triphosphate—the molecule that fuels all life. Meanwhile the other operator adds a stain to additional tubes to make any DNA present fluoresce, and counts the glowing cells by running them past an ultraviolet laser. Then the operators put the samples on sticks impregnated with antibodies or other compounds and insert them into analyzer slots that look for reactions indicating the presence of certain bacteria including pneumonic plague, tularemia, and anthrax.

This first generation of BIDS has to be operated by hand, using off-the-shelf equipment found in hospitals or university labs. And to detect bacteria, it takes 25 or 30 minutes. "That's not acceptable," says A. Jeff Mohr, chief of the aerosol and environmental technology branch of the Dugway Proving Ground in Utah. "If you're downwind, you can't get protective gear on." Nor are the detectors terribly reliable. At Dugway, where scientists test devices with simulated outdoor germ attacks using harmless microbes as stand-ins, dust clouds trigger false alarms—an experience that could play havoc on the nerves of soldiers worrying about clouds of deadly germs.

The Army is working on a new generation of detectors, which need 15 to 20 minutes to detect bacteria and boast a false alarm rate of only 5 percent. Mohr hopes to start field tests on the new equipment next month. Even more sensitive detectors are on the drawing board— at Aberdeen, for example, aerobiologist Charles Wick is working on a portable virus detector that will ultimately be able to tease particles through filters made of lipids, shoot them through a laser and give a readout of the quantity and identity of viruses in a matter of minutes. "Pretty neat, huh?" he says. If Wick can make it sensitive to bacteria as well as viruses, such a machine could be useful for civilian life as well. "You would be able to go into a hospital or school and say, 'Your virus count is such and such, and here's what bacteria you have,' and do something about it."

Other scientists agree that such devices would be a great advance, whether in a TB ward or on the battlefield. But airborne life is wildly diverse, and always on the move. We still can't always predict even which way the wind is going to blow. "With aerobiology, as soon as you solve one problem, another comes up," says Mohr. "This is not as precise a science as we'd like."

Aerobiologist Charles Wick is working on a portable virus detector that will ultimately be able to tease particles through filters made of lipids, shoot them through a laser and give a readout of the quantity and identity of viruses in a matter of minutes.

In Deep Water

It can take 1,000 years for a parcel of seawater to circumnavigate the global web of ocean currents.
But the pattern of the currents, researchers are finding, can change much faster than that—
and radically alter Earth's climate in the process.

ROBERT KUNZIG

n our mind's eye we can almost see it whole, the round-the-world journey that seawater takes. We can imagine taking the trip ourselves.

It begins north of Iceland, a hundred miles off the coast of Greenland, say, and on a black winter's night. The west wind has been screaming off the ice cap for days now, driving us to ferocious foaming breakers, sucking every last ounce of heat from us, stealing it for Scandinavia. We are freezing now and spent, and burdened by the only memory we still have of our northward passage through the tropics: a heavy load of salt. It weighs on us now, tempts us to give up, as the harsh cold itself does. Finally comes that night when, so dense and cold we are almost ready to flash into ice, we can no longer resist: we start to sink. Slowly at first, but with gathering speed as more of us join in, and as it becomes clear that there is nothing to catch us—no water below that is denser than we are. We fall freely through the tranquil dark until we hit bottom, more than a mile and a half down.

There we join a pool of other cold, salty water "parcels" that fills the Greenland and Norwegian basins. From time to time the pool overflows the sill of the basins, an undersea ridge that stretches between Greenland and Iceland and Scotland. Then the falling starts again. Now it is not a parachute drop but a headlong rush, downslope and tumbling like a mountain stream, but more powerful even than Niagara: a giant underwater waterfall, cascading into the Atlantic abyss. Falling, we pull shallower water in behind us. From our right flank, as we reach the latitude of Newfoundland, we are joined by a cohort from the Labrador Sea; not quite as dense as we are, this water settles in above us, headed south along the slope of North America. Near Bermuda our ranks are swelled on the left by spinning blobs of warm Mediterranean water, even

*Opposite page: Eddy
currents in the Ionian Sea.*

saltier than we are; they sail like Frisbees out of the Strait of Gibraltar and cross the ocean to join us. Greenland water, Labrador water, Med water—we all fall in together, and gradually we mingle: we are North Atlantic Deep Water now. Mediterranean salt seeps through us like a dye. Though at every step on the road some of us lose heart and turn back north, still our mighty host advances, 80 Amazon Rivers marching along the ocean floor, toward the equator and across it.

Oceanographers call this global journey the thermohaline circulation, because it is driven primarily by heat (in Greek, *therme*) and salt (in Greek, *hals*, which also meant "sea"). The thermohaline circulation is more than a natural curiosity. It spreads solar heat from the tropics to the high latitudes; it is what keeps Europe, for instance, warm and habitable. ▼

All through the South Atlantic our army remains intact, hugging the western slope of the ocean basin. But that reassuring guide ends where South America does, and in the stormy Southern Ocean we are scattered by the great centrifuge, the Mixmaster, the buzz saw—what metaphor can do justice to the Antarctic Circumpolar Current? Sweeping around the frozen continent from west to east, with no land to stop it, it carries now some 800 Amazons of water. It blends the waters of the world, obscuring their regional roots. The fierce winds drag us —ever so briefly—to the surface off Antarctica, where we absorb a blast of cold and quickly sink again. We spread north now into all the oceans, mostly at a depth of half a mile or so, some back into the Atlantic, some into the Indian Ocean, many of us into the Pacific. In that vast and empty basin we drift northward until we reach the equator; there the trade winds part the waters, and tropical heat mixes down into us, buoying us to the surface. It is time to head for home.

Blasting and wending our way through the confusion of Indonesia, with its near-impenetrable wall of islands, we cross the Indian Ocean, collecting salt from the hot shallows of the Arabian Sea. Southward then down the coast of Mozambique, and we are picking up speed, in preparation for our triumphant return—but rounding the Cape of Good Hope is not easy. Again and again we are beaten back. Only by detaching ourselves in spinning eddies from the main current do some of us manage to sneak into the South Atlantic. There we are joined by water that never bothered with Indonesia and Africa but instead took the colder shortcut around South America, through the Drake Passage.

One last obstacle remains for us all—the equator, where this time we must cross the 12-lane highway of east-west surface currents set up by the trade winds. We do it again in eddies, giant ones that spin us north along the Brazilian and Venezuelan coasts before they finally shatter in the Caribbean and in the process dump us into the Gulf Stream at its source off Florida. This is the homestretch, at last; Iceland looms ahead. A millennium has passed since we left.

Oceanographers call this global journey the thermohaline circulation, because it is driven primarily by heat (in Greek, *therme*) and salt (in Greek, *hals*, which also meant "sea"). The thermohaline circulation is more than a natural curiosity. It spreads solar heat from the tropics to the high latitudes; it is what keeps Europe, for instance, warm and habitable. Given its tremendous force and its antiquity—it has been going on for tens of millions of years—one might imagine that nothing short of continental drift could change it. And one might dismiss as preposterous the notion that human beings, of all feeble agencies, could affect it at all. But the evidence suggests otherwise. We might already be on our way to shutting it down, with consequences for our climate we can only dimly foresee.

Wallace Broecker, or Wally to just about everybody —as in *The Glacial World According to Wally*, the title of one of his self-published books—dates from an era when oceanography was young and a boy could ask big questions about the ocean without huge tomes of technical literature tumbling off the shelves to crush him—questions like: What does the seafloor look like? Why is there a Gulf Stream? What causes ice ages? Back in the late 1950s, when Broecker was pursuing his Ph.D. at Columbia's Lamont-Doherty Earth Observatory in Palisades, New York, his adviser urged him to answer that last question in the conclusion to his thesis. "You might say I'm still writing the last chapter," Broecker says.

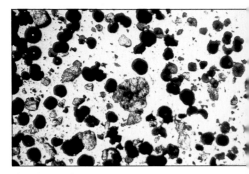

Sand particles.

Above: Beginning of icecap in Greenland.

Broecker is still at Lamont today. He has been studying the thermohaline circulation for decades now, except that he has a different name for it: he calls it the conveyor belt. For an article once, Broecker had an artist draw a picture of the conveyor. It showed a broad band of deep water sweeping down the center of the Atlantic to the Antarctic, spreading into the Indian and Pacific, welling up to the surface there, and returning as an equally broad and unwavering band to the North Atlantic. This image drives some oceanographers crazy because they have spent the past few decades realizing just how complicated the flow of water in the ocean really is. Of course Broecker knows that the conveyor belt image is a crude simplification. But he also knows that, notwithstanding its complexity, the thermohaline circulation does something very simple and important: it transports heat into the North Atlantic and salt out of it. In that sense it is like a conveyor.

Broecker remembers exactly when it was that he first made the connection between the conveyor belt and climate change. It was in 1984, in Switzerland, while he was listening to physicist Hans Oeschger of the University of

Bern. Oeschger was lecturing on the climate record contained in a mile-and-a-quarter-deep ice core extracted from the Greenland ice sheet, which is a relic of the last ice age. By that time there was a well-developed theory of ice ages; it attributed them to cyclical changes in Earth's orbit that change the seasonal distribution of sunlight falling on the Northern Hemisphere. Those cycles—the so-called Milankovitch cycles—seemed to explain why over the past 700,000 years or so, northern ice sheets had repeatedly advanced and retreated, with fits and starts lasting tens to hundreds of thousands of years.

But the Milankovitch theory could not account for what Oeschger was seeing in the core from Dye 3 in southern Greenland: evidence for far more rapid climate fluctuations during the last ice age. One strand of evidence was the ratio of oxygen isotopes in the ice. The heavier isotope, oxygen 18, is less prone to evaporate from the sea surface than light oxygen 16, and more likely to rain or snow out of the atmosphere sooner when it does evaporate. During an ice age, when a lot of water is removed from the ocean and locked up in continental ice sheets, the heavy isotope tends to remain behind in the ocean, and thus marine sediments become enriched with it. Meanwhile the ice in places like Greenland becomes depleted of oxygen 18: the colder the air is, the less likely it is that water vapor containing the heavy isotope will make it to Greenland before precipitating out of the atmosphere. Thus the oxygen isotope ratio in the Greenland ice is a thermometer. It measures how cold the air was over Greenland when the ice was laid down.

Oeschger's second strand of evidence was actual samples of that ancient air—tiny bubbles that became trapped inside the ice when it formed. He and his colleagues had discovered they could analyze the chemical composition of those bubbles by putting a half-inch ice cube in a vacuum chamber and crushing it between beds of needles. In 1982 they had reported that the atmosphere during the last glaciation was different in a very important way from the preindustrial atmosphere, the one that existed right before we started aggressively burning fossil fuels: it contained only about two-thirds as much carbon dioxide. That made sense, since carbon dioxide tends to warm Earth by trapping heat. But it was not easy to see how small fluctuations in Earth's orbit could change the CO_2 level.

A well-developed theory of ice ages; it attributes them to cyclical changes in Earth's orbit that change the seasonal distribution of sunlight falling on the Northern Hemisphere.

And the findings Oeschger reported in 1984 seemed even more distant from the Milankovitch theory. By then he and his colleagues had analyzed one section of the Dye 3 core in great detail, measuring changes over small time intervals. The ice in that section had been deposited 40,000 to 30,000 years ago, during the height of the last

Glacier detail.

ice age. Yet, remarkably, its oxygen isotopes showed that during that period the climate had not been unwaveringly cold. Abrupt fluctuations in the isotope ratio revealed that the mean annual temperature over Greenland had risen as much as 13 degrees Fahrenheit within just a decade or two, then stayed high for a millennium before falling just as rapidly. And when the Swiss researchers popped the air bubbles in the ice, they found something more remarkable still. The carbon dioxide concentration of the ancient atmosphere seemed to have fluctuated in lockstep with air temperatures. In just a thousand years or so it had risen and fallen by as much as a quarter.

The temperature fluctuations had been seen before. Willi Dansgaard, the Danish researcher who had first suggested that ice cores would make good climate records, had found similar oxygen-isotope swings along the whole length of the Dye 3 core. Dansgaard had suggested that these swings might be caused by "shifts between two different quasi-stationary modes of atmospheric circulation." But Oeschger's carbon dioxide measurements seemed to eliminate that possibility. The atmosphere could certainly not change its own carbon dioxide concentration by 25 percent. In his talk that day in Bern, Oeschger hinted that the answer might lie in the ocean, which is a giant reservoir of dissolved carbon dioxide. At that point Broecker's mind leapt into a quasi-stationary mode from which it has yet to emerge. Maybe it was *ocean* circulation that was changing, he thought: "I said, oh my God, if you turned on and off the conveyor, it would do exactly what you want."

Even today no one, including Broecker, can say exactly how changes in the thermohaline circulation might have produced dramatic changes in atmospheric CO_2. And for the moment the question is moot, anyway —because no one, including Oeschger, has been able to detect the rapid CO_2 fluctuations in ice cores from other regions of the world. Although no one doubts that ice age CO_2 levels were far lower than today's, there is considerable doubt that they fluctuated dramatically. The sharp peaks and valleys in the oxygen-isotope record, on the other hand, are definitely real; they have been seen in cores from all over the world. During the last ice age the climate really did lurch back and forth between cold and relatively warm conditions. Broecker calls these lurches Dansgaard-Oeschger events. And his explanation for them, though it was inspired by Oeschger's CO_2 results, has fared better than those results themselves. (Science itself sometimes lurches forward in mysterious ways.) The conveyor belt really does seem to have switched states in the past—and in so doing to have changed the amount of heat it transports to the North Atlantic.

The best-documented case, naturally, is the most recent one. Long ago paleobotanists had discovered that the final retreat of the ice sheets did not go smoothly. It started rapidly and promisingly enough, around 16,000 years ago—but then around 12,500 years ago the temperature plummeted again. For more than a millennium, Europe was plunged back into glacial conditions. The forests that had only lately taken over the landscape gave way again to Arctic shrubs and grasses, including a wildflower, *Dryas octopetala*, that—thanks to its well-preserved remains—ended up giving its name to the whole sorry period: the Younger Dryas.

Broecker proposed that this resurgence of cold had been triggered by a collapse of the conveyor belt. During the coldest parts of the ice age, he says, when sea ice spread south past Iceland, deep water formation was shut off. As the ice began its rapid retreat 16,000 years ago—driven ultimately by the Milankovitch variations in sunlight—warm, salty water again reached the region north of Iceland. There it gave up its heat to the cold west winds, which shipped most of it to Europe. The chilled, salty water sank to the seafloor, thus starting up the conveyor. As the conveyor transported more and more heat to the north, it accelerated the retreat of the ice.

Then something curious happened. In North

The oxygen isotope ratio in the Greenland ice is a thermometer. It measures how cold the air was over Greenland when the ice was laid down.

America, in what is now southern Manitoba, a giant lake of glacial meltwater had formed to the west of the lobe of continental ice that protruded south into the central United States. This body of water—called Lake Agassiz, after the nineteenth-century Swiss-born naturalist Louis Agassiz, who had recognized the reality of ice ages— was larger than all the present Great Lakes combined. At first its water drained down the Mississippi into the Gulf of Mexico. But as the ice sheet retreated north, a new and shorter path to the sea was opened: through the Great Lakes Basin and into the St. Lawrence. Thirty thousand tons a second of freshwater began rushing into the North Atlantic from this new source, right into the northward-bound leg of the conveyor belt. All that freshwater substantially diluted the water in the conveyor—in fact, the seawater was no longer salty enough to sink to the ocean floor by the time it reached Greenland. Without that sinking, the conveyor was shut off. So was the heat the conveyor delivers to the North Atlantic region. The ice advanced again, and *Dryas* flowers began blooming again on the plains of northern Europe.

Just as sediments in the Gulf of Mexico record this diversion of glacial meltwater (their isotope ratio went up during the Younger Dryas), sediments in the Atlantic itself record the throttling of the conveyor. The first evidence of this was uncovered in 1987, not long after Broecker proposed his theory. It came from a broad seafloor elevation called the Bermuda Rise, 400 miles northeast of the island, where mud washes up in thick drifts that make for detailed climate records. Ed Boyle of MIT and Lloyd Keigwin of Woods Hole reported that the Younger Dryas was readily discernible in a sediment core from the Bermuda Rise—or rather, in the shells of microscopic creatures known as foraminifera, some species of which float at the surface while others live in the mud. During warm periods like today, they found, the forams absorb into their shells the distinctive chemical imprint of the North Atlantic Deep Water that washes over them. But during the Younger Dryas, the forams were stamped instead by Antarctic Bottom Water, invading from the south and apparently meeting little resistance. The North Atlantic Deep Water must have been weak then—which is another way of saying the conveyor belt was weak, and possibly had turned off altogether. This result was very gratifying to Wally Broecker.

During the last ice age the climate really did lurch back and forth between cold and relatively warm conditions.

The Lamont archive contains more than 18,000 cores of seafloor mud in various states of desiccation.

Oceanographers soon began finding other records of rapid climate fluctuations. And they began to realize that, just as the Younger Dryas was only the last in a long series of climate swings recorded in the Greenland ice sheet, the North Atlantic Deep Water spigot had been turned on and off, or at least down, many times during the last ice age. During its weak intervals, Antarctic water had advanced right up to the base of Iceland. Judging from the sediments, there was never any peace at all in this 100,000-year north-south war of the water masses; the front surged back and forth constantly, rapidly — on the timescale of centuries, anyway — with each shift in fortunes corresponding to a major shift in the operation of the conveyor.

All these shifts, obviously, could not be blamed on the capricious drainage of Lake Agassiz. Nor does there seem to have been an abundant supply of other giant lakes waiting to be diverted at regular intervals into the North Atlantic. On the other hand, there certainly was an abundant supply of ice.

"Sediment cores suggest..." — the phrase scarcely does justice to the suffering of sedimentologists, and to the painstaking labor that goes into extracting even a single clue to Earth's climate history from a long column of seafloor mud. Extracting the core itself is not the half of it. During the 1950s and 1960s, Lamont scientists were directed to pull up a core every day they were at sea, wherever they might be. Today, as a result, the Lamont archive contains more than 18,000 cores of seafloor mud in various states of desiccation.

Finding the right core for your purposes is one problem, but Gerard Bond has an advantage there; his office adjoins the core archive, and his wife, Rusty Lotti, is the archive's curator. The bigger problem is teasing climate information out of the core once you have it, with nothing to sustain you through the long hours of tedium but faith — faith that in the end, a scattering of sand grains and microscopic shells may vouchsafe to you the reality of a dramatic change in Earth's climate tens of thousands of years ago. A rearrangement of ocean currents and winds, a surging of ice sheets — all this is there in a handful of sand or less, if you know what to make of it. To that end Bond and Lotti have spent the better part of the past five years scalpeling through a few select sediment cores. Bond reckons that he personally has counted 700,000

Glacier Bay, Alaska.

sand grains, one by one under a microscope, sorting them by type. "No geologist in his right mind would ever do anything like this," he says — except, perhaps, a geologist who has strayed into the orbit of Wally Broecker.

Bond came late to the study of marine sediments, or at least recent ones. His career had been devoted to the study of sedimentary rocks on land, mostly half-billion-year-old Cambrian formations in the Canadian Rockies. In the late 1980s, though, he conceived the idea that he could see evidence of Milankovitch cycles in the shifting colors of the strata. As a way of testing that idea, he started looking at recent sediment cores, in which the evidence for Milankovitch cycles was well established. The dried-out cores themselves did not show color variations very well, but fortunately for Bond the researchers who extracted the cores had routinely photographed them while they were fresh and wet, and published those photographs in books — page after page of section after section of mud. Bond cut up an article devoted to one core, called DSDP 609, and pasted the photographs end to end on the wall outside his office. He now had 700,000

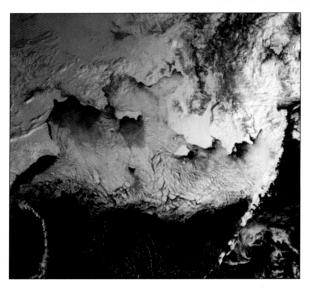

North Pacific Sea ice.

years of climate history running down a 30-foot hallway. Looking at the photographs from an angle, he could readily see the sequence of ice ages and warmer interglacials marching down the hall in a kind of binary code: dark, light, dark, light, dark, light. And when he digitized the photographs and measured the core's color more precisely, he could tell that it varied tremendously on a much more rapid timescale than that of ice age and interglacial.

Bond decided this variability was worth studying and wrote up a proposal to secure the necessary grant. He still thought of the project as little more than a brief detour out of the Cambrian Period. And he did not expect much when, as a courtesy, he sent a copy of the proposal to Broecker, whose professional turf he was proposing to tread on. Broecker was far from resenting the intrusion. "Wally knew all about ice cores and these problems of abrupt climate change — I knew nothing about that at the time," Bond recalls. "He came tearing over to my office.

He saw the gray-scale shifts and he said, 'That's just like the ice-core record.' So that was how I got started. Wally really twisted my arm."

By then Lamont scientists had long since figured out what the light and dark stripes in an Atlantic sediment core represented. The light sediment consisted mostly of calcareous foram shells, deposited in a period of relatively equable climate. The dark sediment, on the other hand, came from far away: it consisted of grains of rock scraped off the land by advancing ice sheets, carried out to sea by icebergs, and deposited on the ocean floor when the icebergs melted. Thick stripes of iceberg debris at a latitude of 50 degrees, where Bond's DSDP 609 came from—the latitude of the south coast of England—obviously must have been deposited in periods that were pretty cold. But until Bond started quantifying the color variations in his core, no one had realized that they indicated much more rapid fluctuations in climate.

With Broecker urging them on, Bond and Lotti and a couple of technicians started dissecting DSDP 609 as no core had been dissected before. They cut samples out of every one of its 800 centimeters—out of every century and a half of climate history. Each thimbleful of mud then went through filtering, to separate out the microscopic shells and grains of rock. Those tiny particles were then spread onto a palm-size tray that had been gridded off into 45 compartments, to facilitate counting, and subjected to several stages of analysis. First one technician would pick over the sample looking for surface-dwelling forams; if they were predominantly of a polar species whose shell coils to the left, it meant that the sea surface over the sediment core had been very cold during that period. Then another technician would go over the same sample to pick out the bottom-dwelling forams, scanning the scattered grains under a binocular microscope and gently lifting out the white, toothlike shells with the moistened tip of a fine paintbrush. It took an hour to do one sample, and after that you might end up with no forams at all; but if you had at least two or three, you could measure their oxygen-isotope and carbon-isotope ratios. Finally Bond himself scanned the sample to sort the rock grains. Those grains could tell him, a sedimentary petrologist with decades of experience, where the icebergs had come from. It would have taken him years to train a technician to do that reliably.

A sedimentary petrologist with decades of experience, could tell from rock grains where the icebergs had come from.

Bow River Valley, Banff, Canada.

One of the first things Bond noticed was that there was something wrong with equating light sediments with forams and dark sediments with ice-rafted rock. There were places in the core that were light and yet foram-free — because they were crammed with grains of white limestone. "It really shocked me," Bond recalls. "You would think that with icebergs coming from all these different sources, there would be a mix of things. And the layers above and below this were the normal mix of quartz and feldspar and very minor amounts of limestone. Then all of a sudden, *boom*, there was this enormous amount of limestone, a huge change in the composition of the grain. There aren't that many places where that kind of stuff can come from."

In fact there was only one place that was plausible, one place on the North Atlantic rim where an advancing ice sheet was likely to have ground over limestone bedrock: the Hudson Strait, at the mouth of Hudson Bay in Labrador. Bond soon learned that the limestone layers were present in cores from the Labrador Sea, too — and being closer to the source, they were much thicker than the ones in DSDP 609. And from Broecker, Bond learned that a German oceanographer, Hartmut Heinrich, had identified the same layers a few years earlier in a core a couple of hundred miles southeast of DSDP 609.

An astonishing vision took shape in Bond's mind: a vision of a giant ice sheet surging through the Hudson Strait, its underside melting and refreezing around shattered bits of limestone, and of a vast armada of icebergs setting sail from the thunderously collapsing edge of that ice sheet. Drifting down the Labrador Sea and out across the North Atlantic on the prevailing current, they gradually melted and dropped limestone on their way. A couple of glaciologists later tried to estimate how much sediment might have been deposited in just one of these "Heinrich events," and they came up with a figure of around a trillion tons. Bond himself estimated how much freshwater the melting icebergs might have shed into the surface layer of the North Atlantic. He put the concentration at 1 part in 30, which is about what you would get by dropping an ice cube into every quart of ocean. That would be more than enough to freeze the conveyor belt.

Heinrich events happened every 7,000 to 10,000 years or so during the last ice age. But as Bond and Lotti tore deeper into DSDP 609 and another core from the eastern Atlantic, they began to see that Heinrich events were just the tip of the iceberg, as it were. Dense layers of dark rock grains between the Heinrich layers indicated that smaller iceberg armadas had been launched more frequently—but not from the Hudson Strait, because the grains were not limestone. After sorting the dark grains, Bond found that 2 of the 15 separate types he'd defined stood out: black volcanic glass from Iceland, whose active volcanoes at the time poked through a thick ice cap; and redstone—quartz and feldspar coated with iron-rich hematite—that seemed to come from the Gulf of St. Lawrence. Judging from the spacing of the dark layers, iceberg fleets had departed from those ports every 1,500 years, and every fifth or sixth one of them had encountered an even larger Heinrich armada from the Hudson Strait. More important, nearly all the iceberg fleets coincided with Dansgaard-Oeschger events, that is, with periods of sharply cooler air over Greenland.

Every 1,500 years, then, the following events occurred in the North Atlantic region: the air over

Every time we burn fossil fuels, especially coal, along with the carbon dioxide we emit sulfur dioxide. If we emit enough sulfur dioxide, thereby worsening the world's acid rain and smog problems, it could help protect us from the worst of global warming.

Greenland, having suddenly warmed nearly to interglacial temperatures, plunged back into deepest cold in the space of a decade. Ice sheets in North America and Iceland, and possibly elsewhere as well, discharged fleets of icebergs that drifted as far south as 45 degrees of latitude. And the formation of deep water in the North Atlantic was stopped or sharply curtailed. "Sediment cores suggest" that the conveyor belt was weakened during the last ice age but never turned off entirely. Water continued to sink in the North Atlantic, but it was apparently not salty enough to sink all the way to the bottom. It settled instead at an intermediate depth, flowing southward, with Antarctic water sloshing northward underneath it.

All these events happened repeatedly in the last ice age—but unfortunately, researchers cannot be sure in what order. When they look up from their sediment or ice cores, they are haunted by the specter of the chicken and the egg. Perhaps the ice sheets, responding to their own internal rhythm of growth and decay, launched their iceberg armadas whenever they got too fat; the melting ice then clamped down on the conveyor; and the weakened conveyor transported less heat to the North Atlantic, thereby cooling the air over Greenland. But then why would at least two different ice sheets decide to purge themselves simultaneously, as Bond discovered? Perhaps instead the air got colder first, which caused all the ice sheets around the North Atlantic to surge into the sea, which turned down the conveyor, which made things colder still. But then what cooled the atmosphere in the first place?

Add to this dilemma another one: geography. When Broecker first started thinking about Dansgaard-Oeschger cycles, and the Younger Dryas in particular, he was looking to explain how temperatures in the North Atlantic region could ever have taken a sudden millennial nosedive. Computer models of Earth's climate, chiefly the one developed by Syukuro Manabe at the Geophysical Fluid Dynamics Laboratory in Princeton, confirmed Broecker's hunch that the conveyor belt could do the job by switching abruptly to a weakened state. They even reproduced the regional extent of the Younger Dryas cooling, which at the time was thought to have been felt primarily in Europe and to a lesser extent in eastern North America. But in the last decade the evidence has changed. The Younger Dryas and the other Dansgaard-Oeschger events are no longer merely North Atlantic curiosities. "No way can I get gigantic cooling everywhere," grumbles Manabe. Yet that is what the evidence points to, and it comes from some unusual places.

Huascaran, Peru, is not the first spot most researchers would think to look for the causes or effects of changes in the North Atlantic. It is a glacier-covered mountain in the Andes, 9 degrees south of the equator and 200 miles north of Lima. The highest of its twin peaks reaches 22,205 feet. Lonnie Thompson of Ohio State University did not make his drilling team climb that high; they stopped just shy of 20,000 feet with their six tons of equipment, at a saddle point between the two peaks, where the ice was more than 700 feet thick.

Thompson is used to skepticism from his scientific colleagues. He has been drilling into mountain glaciers for nearly two decades now, ever since he got bored with drilling in Greenland and Antarctica. Not long after he started, Willi Dansgaard, the polar-drilling pioneer, wrote a letter to him and to his funding agency saying that the technology did not exist to do what Thompson wanted to do. This did not help Thompson's cause. But he knew Dansgaard was right. He had already discovered that on his first expedition, in 1979, to a glacier called Quelccaya in southern Peru.

"We were naive," he recalls. "We thought we could use a helicopter and bring a drill up from Antarctica, and we'd get it up there and drill the core and that would be it. But the elevations we work in, above 19,000 feet, are really out of the range of most helicopters, and when you have a lot of convective activity in the mountains, it makes flight very difficult and dangerous. We'd be flying along at 19,000 feet and the helicopter would just fall. There was no way we could get near the surface." Because the technology did not exist to land a big ice-drill on an Andes peak, Thompson logically concluded that he would have to build a drill light enough to carry up on his back — and the backs of his graduate students and a few dozen porters and mules. If the technology did not exist, he would invent the technology.

Fourteen years after that first failure, Thompson found himself camped on Huascarán with a carbon-fiber drill and 60 solar panels to power its heated, ring-shaped tip through the ice. As each length of ice core was extracted from the borehole, it went into insulated pack-

Today the tropics are the planet's largest source of water vapor; it rises there off the warm sea surface and is carried by winds toward the poles. Along the way it precipitates as rain and snow, and at the same time serves another critical function: it is the most important greenhouse gas, more important even than carbon dioxide.

ing material and then into a walk-in storage cave that Thompson and his crew had dug into the glacier. When the cave was full, the porters were called. Working in the pitch darkness of 3 A.M. — the coldest, and so most desirable, time of day — they hoisted the ice onto their backs and carried it down a 50-foot ladder that sloped across an 80-foot-deep crevasse; then on to the edge of the glacier, where mules waited to take it to the foot of the mountain, where trucks waited to take it to a fish freezer in the town of Huaraz. Some of Thompson's graduate students did not appreciate the beauty of that crevasse, which widened steadily as the expedition wore on ("Sometimes they made career choices when they looked at the ladder," Thompson says), but fortunately porters were plentiful. "We happened to drill this core at the height of the Shining Path guerrilla activities in Peru," says Thompson. "On one side that was a problem, because there was danger. But on the other side, we had a complete hotel to ourselves, so we could set up a laboratory. And we had all the porters we needed." Not that Thomas [sic] himself spent much time in the hotel: he camped out on Huascarán for 45 days, working sunup to sundown in winds that ripped his tents and in air that was half as thick as at sea level.

To what end this amazing effort? When Thompson drilled his cores to bedrock at Huascarán, he got access to a deep past: the ice at the bottom was 20,000 years old. It had survived intact since the last peak of the last glaciation.

The conventional wisdom had been that the ice age had left the tropics largely untouched. The Huascarán cores give that view the lie: the oxygen isotopes in them indicate that at the height of the glaciation the temperature on the mountain was 15 to 22 degrees below what it is today. If you extrapolate that temperature down to sea level, as Thompson did, you find that the surface of the tropical Atlantic, where the snow falling on Huascarán comes from, was at least 9 degrees colder than today. Like the atmosphere at high latitudes, the tropical atmosphere was also much drier in the ice age: the strata from the bottom of the Huascarán cores contain 200 times more dust than falls on the mountain today. That dust was apparently blown in from Venezuela and Colombia, where vast tracts of land that are now savanna were then covered by dune fields.

Most surprising of all, the Younger Dryas shows up clearly in Huascarán ice.

A few years ago, while Broecker was writing the first edition of *The Glacial World According to Wally*, he developed a severe case of writer's block as he approached the last section, in which he had hoped to set forth his grand hypothesis of what had driven all the climate change during the last glaciation. It was more or less the same last chapter he had failed to write for his Ph.D. thesis, only now the facts had gotten considerably more complicated. Broecker found he still did not have a coherent hypothesis. By 1996, though, he was groping toward one. It was inspired by the work of Lonnie Thompson on Huascarán.

That ice core offers the strongest of several strands of evidence that the tropical atmosphere was extremely dry during the ice age — Thompson and Broecker estimate it contained only 80 percent as much water vapor as it does today near the surface, and only 40 percent as much at high altitudes. Today the tropics are the planet's largest source of water vapor; it rises there off the warm

sea surface and is carried by winds toward the poles. Along the way it precipitates as rain and snow, and at the same time serves another critical function: it is the most important greenhouse gas, more important even than carbon dioxide. If the water vapor concentration in the last ice age was substantially lower, then that alone would have cooled the planet substantially.

In Broecker's hypothesis, rapid changes in the water vapor concentration, caused somehow by changes in the conveyor belt, are what produced the millennial global climate swings of the last ice age. The most likely trigger, he says, is still a shot of freshwater to the North Atlantic. Icebergs streaming off the North American ice sheet could weaken the conveyor over the course of centuries; but when the last berg had melted and the atmosphere was in the coldest and driest trough of a Dansgaard-Oeschger cycle, such that not much snow was falling on the northern latitudes, then the North Atlantic would quickly grow salty again, salty enough to sink into the deep off Greenland, and the conveyor would spring back to life. Models such as Manabe's show that the conveyor can rebound rapidly when it stops getting hosed with freshwater. And a hypothesis such as Broecker's explains how a sudden warming of the North Atlantic can propagate rapidly through the atmosphere to the Peruvian Andes and other points south — provided that somehow the resurgent conveyor can pump water vapor back into the tropical atmosphere.

The operative word is *somehow*. The equatorial ocean is a zone of major up-welling currents, which might be expected to influence the amount of water that evaporates from the sea surface, and which might in turn be under the influence of the conveyor. And in the equatorial Pacific off Peru, at least, the up-welling shuts down from time to time, during the phenomenon known as El Niño. That suggests to Broecker that the tropical atmosphere may have discrete states of operation as well, like the conveyor belt, and that it might flip in response to a flip of the conveyor. But he grows a bit exasperated when he is pressed for a more precise link between the two. "The only part of the system that we know about that has multiple states is thermohaline circulation," he says. "Okay? And we know from evidence in sediment that thermohaline circulation did change. Okay? So the working hypothesis has to be that these changes in thermohaline circulation have far-reaching effects. And what I'm trying to tell you is that we don't know what the link is. What you're asking for is the big missing piece of the whole puzzle. I mean, we have every other piece in place, and we're missing a major piece."

Would that it were really only one.

In 1991, when Lonnie Thompson went back to Quelccaya, the Peruvian glacier he had first climbed 12 years earlier, he found that it was melting. There were three lakes downhill from the ice cap that had not been there before. Thompson was disappointed but not surprised. In Venezuela, three glaciers have disappeared altogether since the early 1970s. Three have disappeared from Mount Kenya in Africa as well; since the early 1960s glaciers there have lost two-fifths of their mass. "It's throughout the tropics," says Thompson. "Every glacier that we have any data on shows a very rapid retreat taking place. You have to ask why that might be."

Thompson's hunch is that his vanishing glaciers are an early sign of man-made global warming. Even a slight warming caused by the carbon dioxide we have added to the atmosphere might be enough to evaporate a lot more water off the tropical ocean. The water vapor might then amplify the warming enough to melt the ice. Thompson, unlike Broecker, is inclined to believe that the tropical atmosphere drives the conveyor belt, rather than the other way around.

An experiment that Manabe did a few years ago with his climate model lends some support to that view. Manabe allowed the concentration of carbon dioxide to keep increasing at the rate it is now, about 1 percent per year, until after 140 years its atmospheric concentration had quadrupled. From then on he let it remain constant. As Earth's temperature rose, so did the amount of water vapor in the atmosphere, and winds carried it to high latitudes, where it fell as rain and snow. In Manabe's model world, the rivers of the far north — the Mackenzie, the Ob, the Yenisei — became torrents emptying into the Arctic. From there the water made its way south into the Greenland Sea. By the 200th year of the simulation, the thermohaline circulation had stopped dead.

It is possible that the carbon dioxide concentration will not quadruple over the next century and a half — that Earth's fractious community of nations, with their

If the water vapor concentration in the last ice age was substantially lower, then that alone would have cooled the planet substantially.

In Venezuela, three glaciers
have disappeared altogether
since the early 1970s. Three
have disappeared from Mount
Kenya in Africa as well; since
the early 1960s glaciers there
have lost two-fifths of their
mass.

burgeoning head counts, will agree on the drastic economic and technological changes needed to limit the growth of fossil fuel emissions. If the CO_2 level were only to double, Manabe's model predicts that the conveyor belt would merely weaken for two or three centuries and then restore itself—much as it may have done in the Younger Dryas. There is also a more plausible reason to believe the conveyor belt may survive. Every time we burn fossil fuels, especially coal, along with the carbon dioxide we emit sulfur dioxide, to the extent that we do not scrub it out of the smokestack plume. If we emit enough sulfur dioxide, thereby worsening the world's acid rain and smog problems, it could help protect us from the worst of global warming. Sulfur dioxide is a "parasol" gas—it reflects sunlight back into space—and Manabe's model did not take this effect into account in predicting thermohaline collapse. He thinks it could prevent that dire outcome—particularly if the Chinese burn through their vast deposits of coal without worrying about acid rain.

On the other hand, Manabe's model also did not take into account the possibility that the Greenland ice sheet might melt in a CO_2-warmed world. It is hard to imagine just how the conveyor belt would handle that kind of freshwater jolt to its soft spot. "We cannot eliminate completely the possibility of the 'drop dead' scenario," says Manabe.

What would happen if it did drop dead? Some good might come of either a collapse or a weakening of the conveyor belt. Manabe's model suggests that global warming might be somewhat moderated around the North Atlantic rim, particularly in Europe, by a Younger Dryas-type cooling effect. But the truth is we really do not know how a change in the conveyor belt would affect the world's climate. The only thing we can safely conclude from Manabe's model and from the sediment and ice-core evidence is that a rapid change in the thermohaline circulation is possible now, even when the world is not in the midst of an ice age.

The thermohaline circulation has been around for tens of millions of years at least, but some researchers date it in its present form to just 3 million years ago. That is when the Isthmus of Panama emerged from the sea, connecting North and South America and dividing the Atlantic from the Pacific. In a recent book, paleontologist Steven Stanley of Johns Hopkins proposed that this change was crucial to our own evolution. The establishment of the modern conveyor belt, Stanley argues, paved the way for the ice ages; and as Africa grew cooler and drier and forests gave way to savannas and deserts, our australopithecine ancestors were forced to come down from the trees. Stanley's book is called *Children of the Ice Age*, but it might as well have been called (had the publisher been indifferent to its sales potential) *Children of the Thermohaline Circulation*.

After 3 million years, the children have grown up now, sort of: they have acquired the power to slay their parent. Have they grown up enough to stay their own hand? Wally Broecker is not optimistic. "Little has changed since Roman times," Broecker wrote in the conclusion to one of his own books, *How to Build a Habitable Planet*. "Man fiddles and hopes that somehow the future will take care of itself. It surely will, but mankind may not like the course it takes."

New World Pompeii

Fourteen hundred years ago a Central American volcano erupted, encasing an entire village in ash.
Today that modest village is revealing what no stone temple or gold mask ever could:
the details of ordinary life.

MARY ROACH

Looters have never been a problem at the ruins of Cerén in the lush Zapotitán Valley of El Salvador. It's not that the security is tight or that the site is especially remote. Cerén is just an hour's drive from the capital, San Salvador, through hills of impossibly vivid greens and a sky so blue and pure you think you died and woke up in a Cheer commercial. No, it's more that there isn't, barring wheelbarrows and fancy German tape measures, anything to loot. No jade figurines, no hammered gold. The artifact list from this Mesoamerican ruin reads something like this: corncob, thatch fragment, carbonized bean.

While there is nothing remarkable about a bean, a 1,400-year-old bean is altogether another matter. Under normal conditions, organic matter in the tropics decomposes in a few months. Unless, as with Cerén, something extraordinary takes place to preserve it.

On a summer evening some 14 centuries ago, in the quiet hours between dinner and sleep, an underground storm began brewing close to Cerén. There must have been some sort of warning, a billow of steam or an ominous trebling, because something convinced the Cerén villagers, just a half mile away, to drop what they were doing and run.

It was a wise decision. Within days, their homes had disappeared, buried beneath 16 feet of scalding wet volcanic ash. The eruption did not merely unleash a slow molten ooze. The pressure of the shifting magma blew open the Earth, forming the volcanic cone, Loma Caldera. On the way to the surface, molten rock hit water, creating a blast of steam and hot ash that broadsided Cerén. Loma Caldera's tantrum continued for days. There were 14 separate explosions—some raining hail-size stones of ash, some launching 100-pound "lava bombs" of solidified

Opposite page: Niche vessel found at Cerén site.

magma. Cerén was entombed as its inhabitants left it: dinner dishes unwashed, mice in the corn bins, a duck tethered to a post.

Instead of digging up plastic soda bottles and tinfoil, as he expected, he found Mayan pottery in the style of the Classic Period, A.D. 500 to 800. Carbon dating confirmed that Cerén was indeed an ancient site. ▼

Cerén's villagers—like Pompeii's—left in a hurry, leaving behind the bulk of their possessions. But unlike the unlucky Pompeians, all Cerén's residents seem to have escaped.

And so it remained for some 1,400 years. In 1976, the owners of the land that covered Cerén decided to build a grain silo. In the course of leveling a hillside, a bulldozer operator struck the adobe wall of a Cerén home. The worker called the National Museum in San Salvador, which dispatched an archeologist. On seeing thatched roofing—which normally disintegrates in a decade or so —the archeologist proclaimed the structure to be recent and of no scientific value. Two years and several demolished buildings later, an archeologist and Mesoamerican scholar from the University of Colorado, Payson Sheets, visited the site and began poking around with his trowel. He'd heard that they'd found a number of old pots and a building buried under volcanic ash, which was surprising, since as far as he knew there hadn't been any local eruptions over the past few centuries. So he thought he'd have a look. Instead of digging up plastic soda bottles and tinfoil, as he expected, he found Mayan pottery in the style of the Classic Period, A.D. 500 to 800. Carbon dating confirmed that Cerén was indeed an ancient site. Excavations began the following year.

In 1981 war evicted science. Excavations resumed in 1989, and Sheets returned to Cerén. This is his seventh season at the site.

At the moment, Sheets is sitting in the Cerén dig house, a cinder-block shoe box that serves as lodgings for himself, three graduate students, two artifact conservators, a half dozen lizards, and a thriving community of bloodsucking insects. Above Sheets's head is a hole in the roof where an iguana fell through.

The topic is Pompeii. "The media are forever calling Cerén the New World Pompeii," Sheets says with a sigh. "I don't like that term. At Pompeii, you didn't get good organic preservation." The ash that buried Cerén was fine and moist; the ash that encased Pompeii was dry and came down in pea-size clumps. The two factors that determine quality of preservation, Sheets explains, are the moisture content of the ash and the size of its particles.

Still, there are obvious parallels. Cerén's villagers—like Pompeii's—left in a hurry, leaving behind the bulk of their possessions. But unlike the unlucky Pompeians, all Cerén's residents seem to have escaped. So far, the only human remains at Cerén were teeth found among the remnants of a collapsed roof. (That was a bit puzzling until an Indian worker at the site pointed out that it's a Central American custom to toss lost teeth onto the roof for good luck.) Plant and pottery remains, though, are abundant, and that's what has allowed researchers to piece together a surprisingly detailed portrait of village life in the Classic Period.

Until Cerén, little was known about the Mesoamerican peasant class. Normally villages are aban-

Cerén site.

Site of excavation at Cerén.

Household archeology is the science of dirty dishes and half-eaten corncobs. From finger swipes on the inside of a bowl, we know how the people of Cerén ate, and from remnants of food, we know what they ate.

doned gradually. Those who leave take everything with them, until all that remain to be studied are garbage and a few foundations. Partly for this reason, Mesoamerican archeology has tended to focus on the ruling elite. "The preservation of palaces and pyramids is normally much better than that of the humble dwellings of commoners," says Sheets. "Also, their massive construction makes them much easier to find."

A compounding factor is what Sheets calls the Indiana Jones syndrome. Archeologists have had a tendency to assume that, as Sheets puts it, "it's better to search for fancy jade masks and gold ornaments than to look for the things that were important and available to most of the population."

"With any civilization that's being studied," he says, "if the households of commoners aren't being investigated, you've eliminated the bulk of the population." It would be as if, one day hence, all that was known of United States society in the last decade of the twentieth century had been gleaned from the ruins of mansions and churches. "How can you understand the society if you ignore most of the people?"

Sometime in the 1970s archeologists broadened their focus, giving rise to a subdiscipline called household archeology. "It's like ethnography," says Sheets. "Only we can't interview people, so their possessions have to speak for them." Household archeology is the science of dirty dishes and half-eaten corncobs. From finger swipes on the inside of a bowl, we know how the people of Cerén ate, and from remnants of food, we know what they ate. We know they made twine from agave fibers and, most likely, beer from fermented corn. We know they drew figures on the bathhouse walls. We know how many pots each family owned and where they put them when they didn't feel like cleaning them. From the abundance of stone tools and painted gourds, we know that Cerén villagers probably traded goods with neighboring villages. And by examining the placement of bedrolls and the state of the cooking pots, we know that it was evening when Loma Caldera erupted and disrupted the villagers' lives."

To date, Sheets and his crew have unearthed 11 buildings: several households, a sauna for ritual sweat baths, a public hall, and a structure in which a shaman worked. Twenty more have been located but have yet to be unearthed. The number of buildings leads Sheets to believe that Cerén was a thriving village, with perhaps a couple of hundred inhabitants.

Sheets has used every method short of dowsing to find buried structures. In the early years, he and his crew could be seen wandering the cornfields, banging hammers on steel plates and using a seismograph to time how long it took the shock waves to reach a series of buried seismic receivers. If the waves were passing through dirt or ash, they would arrive simultaneously. If some waves hit, say, an adobe building, those waves would travel faster; the packed clay of adobe bricks conducts sound waves better than relatively less dense ash or dirt. Ground-penetrating radar and electrical resistivity, variations on the same theme, yielded better results and have largely supplanted the seismograph.

Does Sheets plan to dig up every building he finds? How do you decide when enough's enough? Sheets slaps at a mosquito. "You know you're pretty well done when things become routine. Surprises mean you're still learning."

The latest surprise arrived during the unearthing of Structure 10. It contained a deer skull headdress, several

To date, Sheets and his crew have unearthed 11 buildings: several households, a sauna for ritual sweat baths, a public hall, and a structure in which a shaman worked.

religious artifacts, and a large food preparation area, leading Sheets to believe the building was a center for religious ceremonies and feasts.

"There'd been an expectation, fueled by elite-driven archeology, that a small village wouldn't have its own religious center," Sheets says. "It was assumed that for religious things people would travel five kilometers to the pyramids at San Andrés, which was a political and economic hub for Mesoamerican culture. That's clearly not the case."

Another surprise turned up in Household 2. The mystery artifact was a stack of organic layers with traces of red cinnabar paint. Sheets and his colleagues thought it might be a codex, a booklike document made of folded bark or deer hide. Fragments of codices had been found at centers of the Mayan elite, but never among the peasant class. The layers and the earth on which they lay were block-lifted and flown to Washington, D.C., to the Conservation Analytical Laboratory of the Smithsonian Institution (a customs nightmare second only to Sheets's attempt to bring two kilos of fine white volcanic ash through Miami International Airport).

It wasn't a codex. It was a storage vessel fashioned from a gourd. The dish had collapsed as it decomposed, leaving nothing but decorative paint and thin layers of rind. "It's unfortunate," says Sheets. "A written text would have put to rest lingering uncertainties regarding the ethnicity of Cerén residents." Judging from the decorative styles of the ceramics and the division of the households into separate structures for cooking, sleeping, and storage, Sheets believes Cerén's residents to have been either Maya or Lenca, a local group that may have adopted Mayan ways. Others have speculated that they might have been Xinca. Both the Lenca and Xinca groups occupied areas just a few miles outside traditional Mayan centers in present-day Guatemala and El Salvador. Sheets shrugs. "If you think we know nothing of the Lenca—the Xinca? We barely know how to spell their name."

Whoever they were, the Cerén villagers had a good life. "We had no idea people lived so well 14 centuries ago," says Sheets. They ate a nutritious and varied diet, including three varieties of beans, corn, squash, avocados, palm fruits, chilies, nuts, cacao, deer, and dog. They had so much food that they put it away for storage in a

Ground-penetrating radar and electrical resistivity, variations on the same theme, yield better results in locating buried structures, and have largely supplanted the seismograph.

variety of woven and ceramic vessels. And there are signs that they traded cotton, and perhaps pottery, for obsidian from villages some five miles away.

If Loma Caldera erupted today, the mystery artifact —should archeologists one day return to the site—would be a thin tube attached to a handheld gas-powered engine. Closer inspection would reveal a tiny light at the end of the tube. After much head scratching, someone would identify the object as a proctoscope, circa 1985.

"It's for looking into ash holes," says Sheets. We are standing in the tin-roofed building that serves as Cerén's lab, and he isn't making a joke. The moist volcanic ash that settled around Cerén's plants and organic debris packed so firmly that when the plants decomposed, cavities remained in the ash, their walls imprinted with the surface detail of what had once been there. So exact is the mold that one can fill it with dental plaster and, after a day's hardening, dig away the ash to unveil a perfect plaster replica of the plant as it stood at the time the ash fell. Around the houses of the Cerén villagers lie plots of ghostly white plants, phantom corncobs and agaves from beyond the grave.

By affording a sneak preview of an ash hole's configurations, the proctoscope has cut down significantly on dental supply bills. (Sheets went through some 400 pounds of dental plaster one year, provoking deep curiosity at the San Salvador dental supply store.) Not every plant or fallen tree branch need be preserved. Only if the scope reveals something new will the archeologists mix up a batch of plaster.

This afternoon workers have uncovered a row of mystery holes near Structure 3. Sheets fetches the proctoscope, a Fujionon brand that he bought "used, but cleaned." He starts the engine and peers through the eyepiece. His guess is that it's a savila plant, which would be a new species for Cerén. Identifying a plant from the inside out is an estimable talent. To the untrained eye, it looks like a hole in the dirt.

A pair of Salvadoran workers from Cerén's modern-day counterpart, Joya de Cerén, are mixing plaster and water in small plastic bags, shaking them over one shoul-

A clay vessel filled with acorn squash seeds, unearthed at Cerén.

der like bartenders mixing martinis. "Here comes the high-tech part," says Sheets. One of the men bites off a tiny corner of the bag, fashioning a nozzle of the sort used to decorate cakes. He spits out the plastic and proceeds to squirt plaster down the hole.

"These guys came up with the idea of using plastic bags," Sheets says. "We were trying IV bottles, horse syringes. Nothing was working." It's not the first time modern technology has been shamed by the homespun methods of the locals. A glitch in the ground-penetrating radar system, for example, is that interference from the electrical system of the truck that hauls the radar equipment can spoil the data. Sheets and his colleagues tried using oxen and an oxcart belonging to a Joya de Cerén villager instead of a truck. The resulting data were the cleanest anyone could recall seeing. "The geophysicists who'd loaned us the instrument were begging us to bring them back an oxcart and a pair of oxen," says Sheets.

T he sad irony of his work, he notes, is finding that the people of the region were living far better in A.D. 600 than they are today. ▼

Some ancient tools at Cerén also have an edge on their modern counterparts. So impressed is Sheets with the carved obsidian blades found at the site that he's gone into partnership with an eye surgeon to market a surgical version. They are, he says, sharper than surgical steel, or even diamond, blades.

The Cerén villagers were also experienced farmers, as the neatly planted and carefully tended fields surrounding the Cerén homes attest. "It is a clear sign of permanent settlement," says Sheets. "And it shows that they were as skilled in farming as they were in architecture."

Indeed, the residents of ancient Cerén seemed to know more about earthquake-resistant buildings than do the urban planners of San Salvador. They built homes with *bajareque* walls: adobe reinforced with sunflower-like *Tithonia rotundifolia* stalks, or *varas* — Mesoamerica's answer to reinforced concrete. As Cerén structures are unearthed, they're buttressed with laurel stakes, a modern equivalent of the Cerén *varas*, which are inserted into holes left by the decomposed stalks.

When a major earthquake shook El Salvador in

1986, it failed to damage Cerén's structures. "Without the reinforcement," Sheets says, "we'd have been dead in the water." Case in point: the National Museum in San Salvador was severely damaged and eventually condemned. Luckily, the storehouse that contains the major artifacts from Cerén was unharmed.

Brian McKee, an archeology graduate student at the University of Arizona, sits down in a dirt path along which passes a continuous chorus line of men and red wheelbarrows. His task today is to oversee a pair of workers who are at this moment carefully spooning dirt, as though it were a precious metal, from a cloth sack into water. Six unopened sacks lean against the wall. The workers are performing flotation, which isn't as refreshing as it sounds. What floats are bits of bone and plants and seeds, as opposed to dirt, which sinks. It is one of many meticulous tasks at Cerén. For every square meter of the site, archeologists tabulate exactly what is there and in what amounts.

"Flotation is not," allows McKee, "what you'd call the most exciting thing in the world."

Still, from this tedious sifting the researchers have gleaned a botanical surprise: one of the most common Cerén grass species, used by the ancient villagers for thatch, is extinct in the region today. Cerén's ethnobotanist, David Lentz, presently off-site at the New York Botanical Garden, blames the disappearance of the species on the introduction of hardier grasses from Africa. These grasses are better adapted to herbivory than the native grasses of the New World, which has few native ungulates.

"In Africa," says Lentz, "if you want to be a grass, you have to be used to being chewed on. These poor local plants didn't know what hit them. After the cattle and African grasses were introduced, it was sayonara to the local species."

Figuring out how Cerén villagers made their buildings is one problem. Figuring out how to preserve them is another. The biggest threat, says McKee, are the swings in seasonal humidity. In the rainy season the clay adobe absorbs moisture from the air and ground, causing the clay to swell. When the humidity falls, water evaporates from the clay, which shrinks back down. The repeated shrinking and expanding breaks chemical bonds, causing the clay to "spall"—archeology lingo for disintegrating into little bits and flaking off.

The residents of ancient Cerén seemed to know more about earthquake-resistant buildings than do the urban planners of San Salvador. When a major earthquake shook El Salvador in 1986, it failed to damage Cerén's structures.

Plaster agave.

Researchers have gleaned a botanical surprise: one of the most common Cerén grass species, used by the ancient villagers for thatch, is extinct in the region today.

Mayan methods of preservation are helping. In a clearing outside the lab, workers can be seen pounding escobilla stems and leaves on stone mortars. The plant yields a gluey mucoid substance that's mixed with water and sprayed on the adobe, a technique Salvadorans have used for centuries to preserve their homes. The archeologists have found that spraying the adobe during the dry season helps keep the moisture level constant; the escobilla helps hold the clay together.

Salt is the other villain. When water evaporates from clay, it leaves a layer of salt on the surface, much the way sweating leaves one's skin salty. But evaporation also leaves a salt residue just below the clay surface, and this is where the most damage occurs. When water evaporates, the salt crystals below the surface expand, forcing the clay minerals apart and causing more spalling.

To protect against damage from spalling, the escobilla solution is mixed with a small amount of clay, creating a *repello sacrificial* — literally, a sacrificial skin. "So now when spalling happens," says McKee, "it's the new material on top that we lose." (The new clay has a different look and texture, so archeologists can tell the original material from the protective layer.)

For dry, disintegrating materials, such as potsherds or bones, the artifacts conservation team at Cerén creates another form of protective skin. Harriet Beaubien and Ellen Rosenthal, both from the Conservation Analytical Laboratory, saturate the artifacts with a diluted solution of a resin called Acryloid B-72, which penetrates and strengthens the material. This method, however, is a technique of last resort. In general, conservators try to preserve artifacts without using additives. "You never know if the synthetic additives are going to do acid damage," Beaubien explains.

But when it comes to storage materials, synthetic additives are a conservator's salvation. Rosenthal holds up a piece of packing paper. It is so shot through with tiny holes that it looks like a player-piano score.

"Bugs," says Beaubien. "We've got insects that'll eat the sizing off paper. We've got pack rats, mice, and termites that'll motor through boxes in a matter of days. Forget about 'acid-free,' 'cellulose-based,' and 'environmentally friendly.' Give us spun-bonded, nylon-webbed. Give us Ziploc bags and chemically sound inks."

She holds up a Tupperware box, the edges of its lid

whittled by tiny teeth. Then she points to a stack of plastic Continental Airlines snack boxes, each one holding a single artifact carefully placed in a polyethylene mount. "These work better because the mice can't sink their teeth into them. Payson sweet-talked a stewardess into giving him 80 of them." It's a surreal sight, bones and scraps of fiber where you're used to seeing ham sandwiches and cookies.

Sheets is sitting at his desk, a gray metal relic with conspicuously fewer drawer handles than drawers. His seersucker shirt, clean for this morning's powwow with San Salvador bureaucrats, is sweated through and smeared with ash.

The sad irony of his work, he notes, is finding that the people of the region were living far better in A.D. 600 than they are today. Where the residents of Cerén constructed sophisticated buildings with wood-reinforced adobe and elevated roofs that allowed breezes to circulate, the peasants of contemporary El Salvador live in simple clay brick or cinder-block homes. Compared with the houses of Cerén, these homes are hot, inelegant, and unsafe in an earthquake. More people are crowded into smaller rooms, and they own fewer aesthetically pleasing possessions. They live mainly on corn and beans and rarely eat meat or fresh vegetables. Sheets is acutely aware of the contrast every time he visits the home of one of his workers or drives by the squatters' camps that line the roads out of San Salvador. "It's impossible not to notice," he says. "People are living in shacks of cardboard and scraps of plastic."

What keeps bringing him back to Cerén? He leans back in his chair. "You want to know what makes it worthwhile? I'll tell you a story. It was a Sunday in July 1993, the opening of the site museum. Bands were playing. The president was here. At one point I overheard a young girl and her grandmother standing at a photograph of one of the Cerén kitchens. The grandmother was saying, 'That's the kind of kitchen I was raised in, with an earth floor and open walls....' That's the really exciting thing—the elements of continuity between the archeological past and the traditional Salvadoran household of today. But the country is modernizing so rapidly that those traditions are being lost. In doing cultural conservation, we are trying to give that past as good a future as we can."

The moist volcanic ash that settled around Cerén's plants and organic debris packed so firmly that when the plants decomposed, cavities remained in the ash, their walls imprinted with the surface detail of what had once been there. So exact is the mold that one can fill it with dental plaster and, after a day's hardening, dig away the ash to unveil a perfect plaster replica of the plant as it stood at the time the ash fell.

Seismic Mystery in Australia: Quake, Meteor or Nuclear Blast?

WILLIAM J. BROAD

Late on the evening of May 28, 1993, something shattered the calm of the Australian outback and radiated shock waves outward across hundreds of miles of scrub and desert. Around the same time, truck drivers crossing the region and gold prospectors camping nearby saw the dark sky illuminated by bright flashes, and they and other people heard the distant rumble of loud explosions.

The mysterious event might have been lost to history except for the interest of government investigators in Australia and the United States who eventually came to wonder if the upheaval was the work of the Japanese doomsday cult accused of the poison-gas attack on Tokyo subways in 1995 that killed 12 people and hurt thousands.

The fear was that the terrorists had acquired nuclear arms or other weapons of mass destruction and had been testing them that night in the Australian wilds.

The hope was that the upheaval was an earthquake, a mining explosion or even a meteorite strike from space, any natural event.

The evidence was ominous. Investigators discovered that the cult, Aum Shinrikyo, had tried to buy Russian nuclear warheads and had set up an advanced laboratory on a 500,000-acre ranch in Australia near the puzzling upheaval. At the ranch, investigators found that the sect had been mining uranium, a main material for making atomic bombs.

The clues were judged worrisome enough to set in motion a wide scientific investigation that is still going on today.

"Many experts had dismissed the possibility of nukes" in the hands of terrorists before the emergence of Aum Shinrikyo, Dr. Gregory van der Vink, head of the science investigation, said in an interview. "But the group

The Olgas, Northern Territory, Australia.

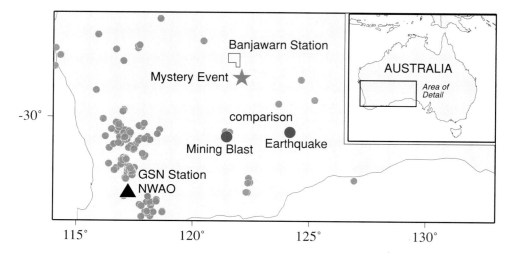

was into biological and chemical weapons and was attempting to acquire nuclear ones. I'm still amazed."

At the request of Senate investigators, the science inquiry was led by the Incorporated Research Institutions for Seismology, or IRIS, where Dr. van der Vink is director of planning. The IRIS consortium is based in Arlington, Va., and financed by the National Science Foundation, a Federal agency. It has more than 80 member institutions at universities in the United States. It also has more than 100 seismometers on all continents, the largest global network of these devices, which pick up faint vibrations traveling through the earth's rocky interior.

One aim of scientists using the IRIS network is to try to distinguish natural disturbances from nuclear explosions, a goal that recently took on new significance as the United Nations called for an end to all explosive testing of nuclear weapons around the globe. Much research, including that by IRIS members, now aims at monitoring such a ban.

Pinning down the nature of the outback incident was seen as an important test of the emerging skills.

The doomsday cult that caused the worry first caught world attention after the Tokyo subway attack of March 20, 1995, which involved the deadly nerve gas sarin, and was the world's first large chemical strike by terrorists. The cult was quickly implicated and is now charged in Japan with planning a virtual civil war meant to be carried out with some of the world's deadliest weapons.

After the Tokyo attack, government investigators

Investigators discovered that the cult, Aum Shinrikyo, had tried to buy Russian nuclear warheads and had set up an advanced laboratory on a 500,000-acre ranch in Australia near the puzzling upheaval. At the ranch, investigators found that the sect had been mining uranium, a main material for making atomic bombs.

around the world raced to learn more about the shadowy group. Aum Shinrikyo, or Supreme Truth, turned out to have accumulated some $1 billion and to have won more than 50,000 converts in at least six countries.

In the United States, the permanent subcommittee on investigations of the Senate Governmental Affairs Committee, at the urging of Senator Sam Nunn, mounted a major investigation of the cult.

Senate investigators found that the group had thousands of disciples in Russia and had bought guns, a military helicopter and other weapons there. The group's construction minister, Kiyohide Hayakawa, the reputed mastermind of the cult's efforts to arm itself, went to Russia 21 times from 1992 to 1995, visiting there a total of 180 days.

Senate investigators say the cult recruited at least two nuclear scientists in Russia. Notebooks later seized from Mr. Hayakawa show he wanted to buy the ultimate munition there. In one entry, he asked, "How much is a nuclear warhead?" and listed several prices.

In Australia, the activities were just as troubling. Cult members arrived in April 1993, a little more than a month before the mystery blast. Mr Hayakawa, apparently fresh from visits to Russia, was among the initial party. After visiting several remote sites, the group bought a 500,000-acre sheep farm in Banjawam, Australia, about 400 miles northeast of Perth. The site has a known uranium deposit.

The cult eventually brought in chemicals, gas masks and respirators, and picks, shovels, mining equipment and a mechanical ditch digger. It also set up a laboratory stocked with computers, glass tubing, glass evaporators, beakers, Bunsen burners, mixing bowls and a rock-crushing machine.

Documents seized from Mr. Hayakawa include some 10 pages written during his visit to Australia in April and May 1993 that refer to the whereabouts of Australian properties rich in uranium, including one reference praising the high quality of the ore.

The disturbance shook the earth on May 28, 1993, at 11:03 P.M. local time, but it was not until after the Tokyo attack of March 1995, that an Australian geologist, Harry Mason, brought the seismic upset to the attention of Australian Federal Police and Senate investigators. He was prompted in part by public disclosures in June 1995 of uranium mining at the cult's ranch.

One aim of scientists using the IRIS network is to try to distinguish natural disturbances from nuclear explosions, a goal that recently took on new significance as the United Nations called for an end to all explosive testing of nuclear weapons around the globe.

Shoko Asahara, leader of the cult Aum Shinrikyo.

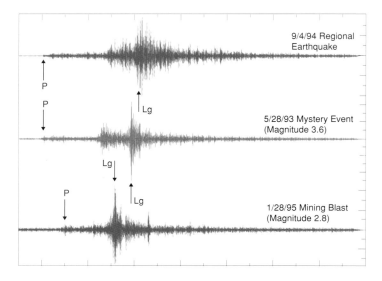

9/4/94 Regional
Earthquake

P

P

Lg

5/28/93 Mystery Event
(Magnitude 3.6)

Lg

P

Lg

1/28/95 Mining Blast
(Magnitude 2.8)

Seismic observatories in Australia tracked the event to a location 28.47 degrees south latitude, 121.73 degrees east longitude, a remote area near the cult's ranch. But uncertainty in the readings was such that the actual site of the disturbance could have been anywhere in 485 square miles of Australian hinterland.

Mr. Mason's 19-page report summarized interviews he had conducted with people who were in the remote area on that clear moonless night. They saw the sky blaze, heard loud explosions and felt the ground shake.

Mr. Mason noted that earthquakes were very rare in the region and that mining explosions were illegal at night. "I currently believe that a nuke is a very real possibility but a meteorite and an earthquake cannot be ruled out either," he wrote Senate investigators in October 1995.

With that information in hand, the investigators contacted IRIS, which was happy to help and had a number of seismometers in Australia. Though the most sensitive unit was inoperative at the time of the blast, another in the town of Narrogin, near Perth and some 400 miles from the disturbance site, was recording data that evening.

Its tracing showed a smooth line that erupted into a fit of wiggles, suggestive but inconclusive. Joining Dr. van der Vink in the tricky analysis were Dr. Christel B. Hennet of IRIS, Dr. Danny Harvey of the University of Colorado and Dr. Christopher Chyba of Princeton University.

Eventually, the IRIS team calculated that the event was 170 times larger than the largest mining explosion ever recorded in the Australian region, to helping rule out that possibility. The disturbance was calculated as having the force of a small nuclear explosion, perhaps equal to up to 2,000 tons of high explosives. In contrast, an atom bomb with a power of about 15,000 tons of high explosives leveled Hiroshima, Japan. But the signature of the disturbance seemed to be more that of an earthquake or a meteorite strike than a nuclear explosion.

Typically, the shock waves from nuclear blasts begin with a very distinct wave or spike as earth and rock are violently compressed. The signal then tends to become more fuzzy as surface rumblings and shudders and after shocks create a seismologic din.

With earthquakes, it is usually the opposite, with gentle jostling suddenly becoming much bigger and violent.

The main problem for analysis of the mystery event is that such clear distinctions tend to break down when the size of the disturbance under study is relatively small, as was the case in the Australian outback.

Nevertheless, the IRIS experts judged that the violent episode was probably natural in character rather than being a manmade blast, prompting official Washington to breathe a sigh of relief.

No mention of the seismic riddle was made in well-publicized hearings that Senator Nunn ran in late October and early November 1995 on Aum Shinrikyo as a case study of what fanatics with large financial resources can do to acquire weapons of mass destruction.

On Dec. 15, 1995, Mr. Nunn wrote the head of IRIS, David Simpson, thanking him for analytic aid. The scientific work helped Senate investigators "rule out certain terrorist activities," he said.

Still, one remote but still worrisome possibility remained. Aum Shinrikyo had apparently studied seismic warfare and artificially triggering earthquakes, a terrifying prospect for quake-prone Japan.

The cult apparently sent a party of its members to the former Yugoslavia to study the work of Nikola Tesla, the discoverer of alternating current who toyed with the theory of seismic weapons before he died in 1943. At the Tesla Museum in Belgrade, the members seem to have reviewed Tesla's thesis and other research papers concerning such weapons.

Many geophysicists view seismic warfare as a fantasy that is highly unlikely to ever materialize. Even so, the subject has been quietly studied for decades by governments worldwide, including the Soviet Union and the United States during the cold war.

So IRIS investigators kept pressing ahead to solve the Australian riddle, trying to determine if the event was an earthquake or a meteor strike. The team worked with computers and lengthy calculations, eventually showing

The IRIS team calculated that the event was 170 times larger than the largest mining explosion ever recorded in the Australian region, to helping rule out that possibility. The disturbance was calculated as having the force of a small nuclear explosion, perhaps equal to up to 2,000 tons of high explosives. In contrast, an atom bomb with a power of about 15,000 tons of high explosives leveled Hiroshima, Japan.

that an iron meteorite striking the earth at an oblique angle could have created the seismic upset. A meteorite five or six feet wide would have dug out a crater some 300 feet in diameter, the team calculated.

Despite preliminary searches, no impact crater has been found in the Australian outback.

Even so, Senate investigators are increasingly confident that the episode was natural in origin. "Eventually, we got information that led us to believe the group was out of the country at the time of the blast," said John F. Sopko, senior counsel to the subcommittee. "That pretty much eliminated the possibility of a weapons test."

The fall 1996 issue of the IRIS newsletter presents the analysis of the mystery event — the first public disclosure — and concludes that "the meteorite impact scenario is consistent with the eyewitness observations and with the energy levels derived from seismic records."

The team also estimates that such meteorite strikes on land occur at the rate of about once every six years, complicating the prospects for monitoring a comprehensive nuclear test ban.

In an interview, Dr. Hennet noted that IRIS had recently received readings from other seismometers in Australia that should help determine if the meteorite thesis is correct.

She also noted that in 1993 during the mystery event, IRIS had 63 stations in its Global Seismographic Network. Now it has more than 100, sharply increasing the group's ability to conduct its scientific sleuthing.

If the peacefulness of the Australian outback is suddenly shattered again, Dr. Hennet said, "we could probably identify the nature of the event with a high degree of confidence."

The main problem for analysis of the mystery event is that such clear distinctions tend to break down when the size of the disturbance under study is relatively small, as was the case in the Australian outback.

Opposite page: Near Ayers Rock in the Australian outback.

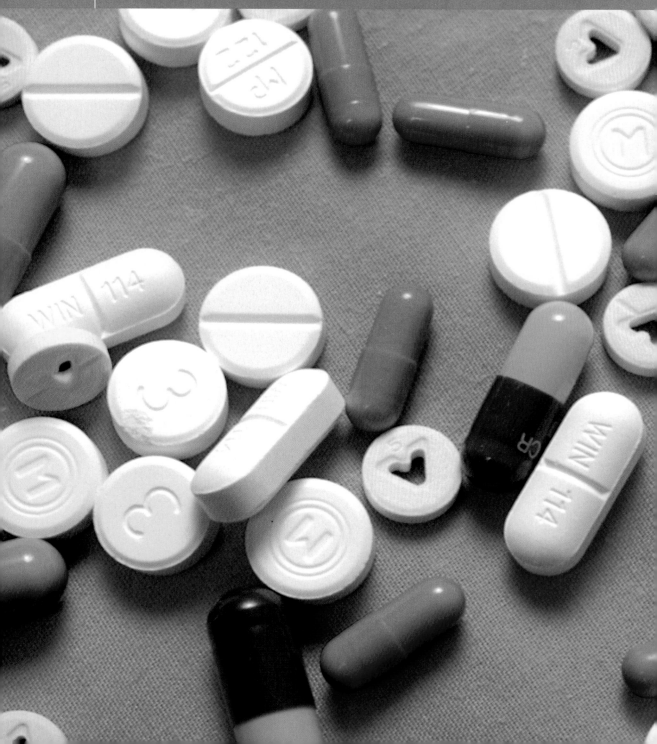

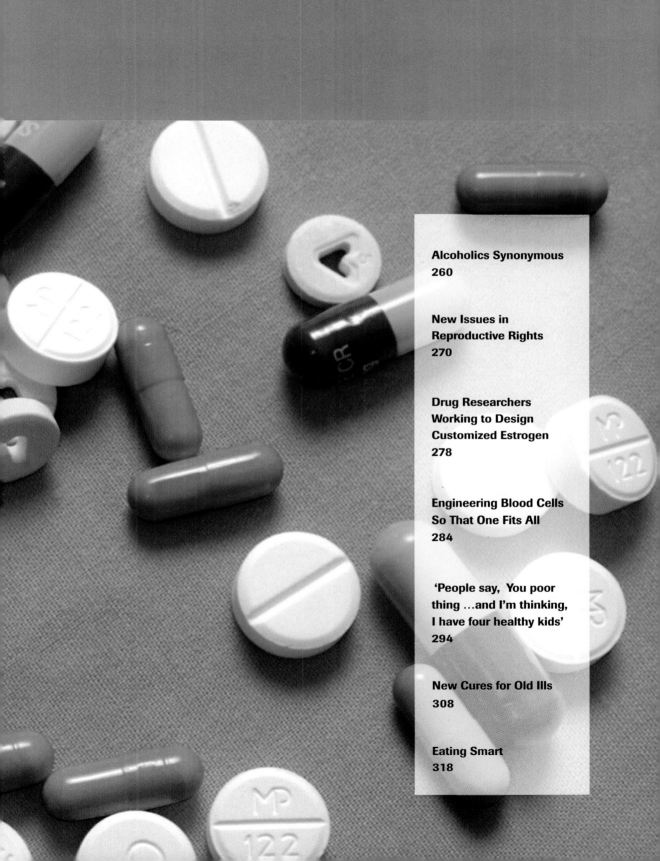

Alcoholics Synonymous

Heavy drinkers of all stripes may get comparable help
from a variety of therapies.

BRUCE BOWER

P sychotherapy studies rarely generate as much
anticipation as Project MATCH did. Mental
health clinicians and addiction researchers
anxiously awaited the results of this 8-year,
$27-million investigation that asked whether
certain types of alcoholics respond best to specific forms
of treatment. The federally funded investigation promised
to yield insights that would bring badly needed guidelines
to alcoholism treatment and perhaps allow clinicians to
tailor the current hodgepodge of approaches to the particular needs of each excessive imbiber.

The coordinators of Project MATCH have finally
served up their findings, but with a shot of disappointment and a twist of irony. At a press conference held last
December in Washington, D.C., they announced that alcoholics reduce their drinking sharply and to roughly the
same degree after completing any of three randomly
assigned treatments.

Trained psychotherapists administered the three
programs. In 12-step facilitation therapy, the therapist
familiarizes the client with the philosophy of Alcoholics
Anonymous (which treats alcoholism as an illness treatable only through abstinence, support from other addicts,
and personal surrender to God's spiritual authority) and
encourages attendance at AA meetings. Cognitive-
behavioral coping skills therapy focuses on formulating
strategies for avoiding or dealing with situations that
tempt one to drink. Motivational enhancement therapy
helps clients to identify and mobilize personal strengths
and resources that can reduce alcohol consumption.

Treatment matching has operated on the assumption
that alcoholics fall into categories best served by particular
strategies. For instance, 12-step facilitation therapy and
AA might work best with alcoholics searching for spiritual

Project MATCH promised to
yield insights that would bring
badly needed guidelines to
alcoholism treatment.

and religious meaning in their lives, cognitive-behavioral therapy may suit alcoholics who display serious psychiatric symptoms and thinking difficulties, and motivational enhancement could act as a tonic for heavy drinkers who express little desire or hope for improvement.

The new findings, however, "challenge the notion that patient-treatment matching is necessary in alcoholism treatment," states Enoch Gordis, director of the National Institute on Alcohol Abuse and Alcoholism (NIAAA) in Bethesda, Md. "The good news is that treatment works. All three treatments evaluated in Project MATCH produced excellent overall outcomes."

Alcoholics reduce their drinking sharply and to roughly the same degree after completing any of three randomly assigned treatments. ▼

Despite Gordis' optimism, opinions diverge sharply regarding the study's implications and the adequacy of its design. Some alcoholism researchers agree with the NIAAA director. They view Project MATCH as a critical step toward the ultimate goal of developing sophisticated therapeutic approaches that thwart the suspected biological causes of uncontrolled alcohol use.

Others dub the federal effort an expensive dud. The absence of a control group of alcoholics who received no specific intervention raises the likelihood that volunteers improved because of intensive personal attention and encouragement rather than any specific treatment techniques, these investigators argue. At best, they contend, the data suggest that AA and other free self-help groups prove effective enough to replace professionally administered alcoholism treatments that command big insurance bucks.

A third perspective holds that flaws in the design of Project MATCH leave open the possibility that many alcoholics benefit from treatment matching or could abandon their addiction on their own, outside the world of clinical interventions and AA.

Scientific interest in developing treatments attuned to alcoholics' individual characteristics goes back at least 50 years. More than 30 small-scale studies published during the 1980s reported that treatment matching based on a number of individual characteristics held promise for alleviating alcoholism. In 1989, the NIAAA initiated

Project MATCH (which stands for matching alcoholism treatments to client heterogeneity) to examine closely the most promising of those leads.

A total of 1,726 people diagnosed as alcohol-dependent (a condition marked by daily intoxication or extended drinking binges that disrupt home and work activities) were recruited from outpatient clinics or facilities that provide care following hospital stays. The volunteers were randomly assigned to one of the three designated treatments, which were delivered over 12 weeks at 30 locations by 80 psychotherapists.

Individuals also dependent on drugs other than alcohol were excluded from the study, although more than one in three volunteers reported having recently used an illicit substance.

Recovering alcoholic helps himself to coffee at a meeting of Alcoholics Anonymous.

Alcohol use was monitored for 1 year after treatment ended, with particular attention paid to the influence of the following individual characteristics on recovery: sex, extent of prior alcohol consumption, the presence of psychiatric symptoms, aggressive and criminal tendencies, difficulties in thinking and reasoning, motivation to change, desire to find meaning in life, and number of family members and friends likely to promote continued alcohol abuse.

Comparably large drops in alcohol consumption occurred for participants after courses of either 12-step facilitation, cognitive-behavioral, or motivational therapy, according to the NIAAA investigation, which appears in the January JOURNAL OF STUDIES ON ALCOHOL. Before

Adults attending an AA meeting.

treatment, volunteers, on average, drank on 25 out of 30 days, a number that fell to 6 days of drinking per month by the end of the follow-up. The amount imbibed on drinking days also dropped markedly after treatment.

In the year of follow-up, 35 percent of volunteers reported not drinking but 40 percent still had periods of heavy drinking on at least 3 consecutive days.

Only one individual characteristic affected treatment responses, notes psychologist Gerard Connors of the Research Institute on Addictions in Buffalo, N.Y., a Project MATCH investigator. Alcoholics exhibiting few or no signs of psychological disturbance achieved abstinence through 12-step facilitation therapy more often than those with pronounced mental symptoms.

Recovery from alcohol dependence or milder alcohol abuse most often occurs outside the confines of hospitals, psychotherapists' offices, or self-help groups. ▼

It remains possible that treatment methods not included in Project MATCH, such as group or marital therapy, work especially well for certain types of alcoholics, Connors notes.

For now, Gordis contends, it appears that individual therapies based on a variety of philosophies make approximately the same dent in alcohol use. The development of new drugs that diminish alcohol cravings (SN: 3/16/96, p. 167) will add to the impact of current psychosocial approaches, he holds.

"Treatment matches may become apparent when we get to the core of the physiological and brain mechanisms underlying addiction and alcoholism," Gordis asserts.

Since the Project MATCH results were first openly discussed at a meeting of alcoholism researchers in Washington, D.C., last June, a dissenting interpretation of their significance has been advanced. Because encouragement to attend AA meetings achieves as much as the two professionally administered treatments under study, according to this view, free self-help groups for heavy drinkers may pack enough punch to justify abolishing insurance coverage for paid treatments. The self-help groups are organized by volunteers and supported through donations.

"The Project MATCH findings support the idea that selling treatment for heavy drinking alongside free self-help programs such as AA is like selling water by the river, to coin a Zen saying," contends psychologist Jeffrey A. Schaler of American University in Washington, D.C. "Why buy when the river gives it for free?"

Moreover, the lack of a nontreatment control group that received as much regular attention and support during the 1-year follow-up as the group given treatment makes it impossible to tell whether any of the Project MATCH interventions had a specific impact, asserts psychologist Stanton Peele, a clinician and writer in Morristown, N.J.

Even if the interventions did work, the findings apply only to the minority of alcoholics who voluntarily enter treatment in clinical settings, Peele argues. A majority of those who seek professional or AA-type treatment for substance abuse in the United States do so on the orders of judges (following arrests for drunk driving or other offenses) or employers, according to federal data.

Recovery from alcohol dependence or milder alcohol abuse most often occurs outside the confines of hospitals, psychotherapists' offices, or self-help groups, further undermining confidence in such treatments, Peele adds.

For instance, a pair of Canadian telephone surveys—one nationwide and one in Ontario—find that of the randomly selected adults, three in four who had recovered from an alcohol problem 1 year or more previously did so without any outside help or treatment. About one in three of those who recovered in the national sample continued to drink in moderation, a figure that rose to two in three in Ontario, report psychologist Linda C. Sobell of Nova Southeastern University in Ft. Lauderdale, Fla., and her coworkers in the July 1996 AMERICAN JOURNAL OF PUBLIC HEALTH.

Similar results emerged from an analysis of interviews conducted in 1992 with 4,585 U.S. adults who had at some time been diagnosed as alcohol-dependent. In the year before the interviews, about one in four still had mild to severe alcohol problems, a similar proportion had drunk no alcohol, and the rest had imbibed in moderation, asserts NIAAA epidemiologist Deborah A. Dawson.

Those who had received some sort of treatment were slightly more likely than their untreated counterparts to have had alcohol problems in the past year, Dawson reports in the June 1996 ALCOHOLISM: CLINICAL AND

In 12-step facilitation therapy, the therapist familiarizes the client with the philosophy of Alcoholics Anonymous (which treats alcoholism as an illness treatable only through abstinence, support from other addicts, and personal surrender to God's spiritual authority) and encourages attendance at AA meetings.

Cognitive-behavioral coping skills therapy focuses on formulating strategies for avoiding or dealing with situations that tempt one to drink.

Motivational enhancement therapy helps clients to identify and mobilize personal strengths and resources that can reduce alcohol consumption.

EXPERIMENTAL RESEARCH. For those whose recovery lasted 5 years or more, prior treatment raised the likelihood of abstinence, whereas lack of treatment upped the chances of drinking in moderation.

"Treatment studies may not be generalizable to alcoholics who do not seek treatment," Dawson concludes. Peele, who views alcoholism not as a medical disease but as a learned behavior employed to cope with life's challenges, goes further. Such evidence, combined with the fact that the expansion of treatment rolls during the past 20 years has failed to reduce substance abuse rates, indicates that professional and AA-type approaches often present more risks than advantages to alcoholics, particularly those coerced into treatment, he contends.

A majority of those who seek professional or AA-type treatment for substance abuse in the United States do so on the orders of judges (following arrests for drunk driving or other offenses) or employers, according to federal data. ▼

George E. Vaillant, a psychiatrist at Brigham and Women's Hospital in Boston and director of a 50-year study of male alcoholics (SN: 6/5/93, p. 356), takes a much less radical stance than Peele, although he still has reservations about the design of Project MATCH.

Alcoholics Anonymous and behavioral interventions such as those in the NIAAA investigation provide more help over the long haul than any other forms of treatment, without regard to the personal characteristics of alcoholics, Vaillant argues.

"The Project MATCH findings are exactly what I would have predicted," the Boston researcher says.

In his opinion, researchers need to examine differences between alcoholics who succeed in recovering and those who fail, rather than limiting themselves to a search for contrasts among professionally run treatments.

Sustained recovery requires at least two of the following experiences, Vaillant theorizes: some sort of compulsory supervision (such as parole) or a painful alcohol-related event (such as a bleeding ulcer or a spouse's departure); finding a substitute dependency, such as meditation or AA meeting attendance; forming new, stable relationships that diminish addictive behaviors; and reformulating personal identity and the meaning of one's life through religious conversion or self-help group participation.

Such factors went unexamined in Project MATCH, according to Vaillant. Most notably, large segments of all three treatment groups attended AA meetings (and were not discouraged by researchers from doing so), thus obscuring the role played by AA in successful recoveries, he argues.

"Project MATCH was poorly designed, to say the least," asserts psychologist G. Alan Marlatt of the University of Washington in Seattle, a pioneer in the development of behavioral treatments for alcoholism. "Everybody can now project their own views about alcoholism onto this study."

Aside from the lack of a control group, the federal study also failed to evaluate directly the practice of patient matching, Marlatt holds. Volunteers were assigned to certain treatments not according to specific personal characteristics but at random; researchers tried to ferret out traits linked to improvement after therapy began.

In addition, the relatively "pure" alcoholics recruited for Project MATCH may respond to treatment differently than the majority of alcohol abusers, who regularly use one or more illicit drugs as well, Marlatt says.

While many questions remain about the effectiveness of alcoholism treatments, several psychotherapy studies — including a large federal study of depression treatments (SN: 1/11/97, p. 21) — find that some therapists are far better than others at fostering improvement in their clients. The quality of the relationship between a therapist and an alcoholic client probably exerts a major influence on how well a particular treatment works, Marlatt suggests.

To put it another way, therapist-client matching may turn out to hold at least as much research promise as patient-treatment matching — especially since the value of patient-treatment matching, at least for now, remains unclear.

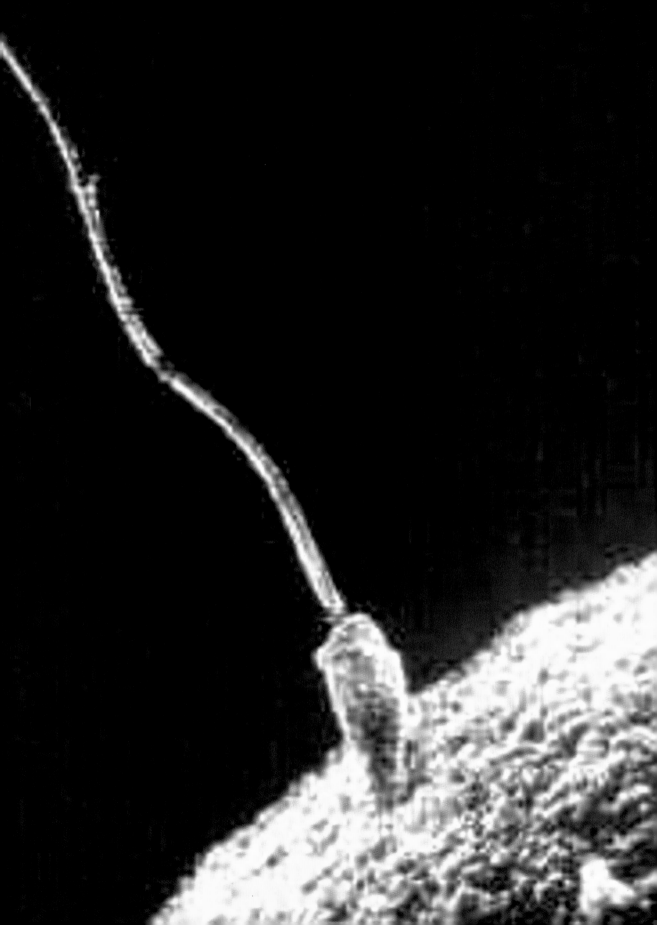

New Issues in Reproductive Rights

PAUL R. BOEHLKE

The phone rings. It interrupts the sad thoughts of an elderly couple living in a suburb of Milwaukee, Wisconsin. The woman tells her husband that she will answer the phone. It's someone from the hospital that treated their son for cancer, she says. The hospital had been unable to save him. "What could they want?" she thinks. The hospital worker asks about the $150 annual fee for storing their son's frozen sperm. The worker is unaware that the son has died. Just before the young man underwent chemotherapy and radiation treatments, the sperm was saved in case the young man should someday wish to have children. He was told that the treatments he would undergo involved a 50 percent chance of becoming sterile.

Surprised by this new information, the bereaved couple tell the hospital worker that they will get back to the hospital after considering this situation. The woman thinks about it and suggests to her husband that they could still enjoy being grandparents. He is seventy-eight; she is sixty-six. Her husband objects at first but later agrees. They call the hospital worker, informing her that their son has died. However, the sperm is not to be destroyed. The son has left all his property to them; surely that includes his sperm. They decide to find a woman who will agree to use the sperm to produce a grandchild for them. They have an unmarried daughter, age thirty-eight, and a son in a group home who suffers from a personality disorder. In their minds this could be their only chance for a grandchild.

At first the hospital refuses to release the sperm. The son had signed a standard form that said the sperm was for use by him and his future wife if he married. There is no mention of the grandparents. They suggest that the couple challenge the policy with a lawsuit.

Opposite page: Sperm entering ovum.

Instead of a lawsuit, the couple have their lawyer draft a liability release form absolving the hospital of any liability. The hospital then agrees. The dream of becoming grandparents goes forward.

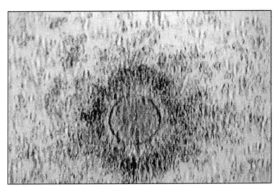

Female ovum (egg).

LEGAL ISSUES

The case described above occurred in 1997 and caused much concern among the general public, health services professionals, and those professionally concerned with medical ethics. This is uncharted territory, said R. Alta Charo, a law professor at the University of Wisconsin in Madison. The law does not say much about our rights to our cells and tissues, even when we are alive. Charo, one of eighteen members of U.S. president Bill Clinton's advisory committee on bioethics, says that as long as there is no conflict and no one is being harmed, the law is not going to intervene in a case like that in Milwaukee. Clearly, however, no one knows what the son would really think of all this, and what he would want done with his sperm.

Some of the questions are perplexing. For example, is sperm property? Can it be left to someone in a will? Is it covered by the Uniform Anatomical Gift Act? Most states have passed this gift law, which allows the next of kin to make decisions on the disposition of the remains of the deceased. Furthermore, do children conceived after a parent dies have equal claims with other children on the estate of the parent?

PUTTING YOUR SEX CELLS IN YOUR WILL

Sperm has been viewed as property. In the case of *Hecht v. Superior Court*, the children of William Kane took issue with Kane's lover. Kane committed suicide, but not before leaving fifteen vials of sperm in a sperm bank. In his will he left the sperm to Hecht, his girlfriend, so that she could conceive children by him afterward. Kane's children objected, fearing the birth of more heirs to the estate. In March, 1994, a judge ruled that the girlfriend should get the fifteen vials because a settlement agreement gave her 20 percent of all Kane's property. The judge treated the sperm as property.

Professor Bonnie Steinbock has analyzed the case and argues that sperm, eggs, and embryos should be treated as property. One argument is that this cellular material can be sold, and control of the cells can be transferred like any other property. Therefore, legal property rights do exist. Sperm and the like seem to qualify. Second, Steinbock finds that protection of unborn children from potential harm in the future is an inadequate reason to ban the practice. Third, the analysis suggests that concerns about commercial traffic in body parts and reproductive capacity (paid surrogate mothers) do not apply to the transfer of sperm. Steinbock concludes that concerns for individual autonomy and privacy in matters of reproduction justify the transfer of sperm by a will.

The number of new and odd reproductive cases is increasing. In Louisiana, a woman sued the federal government for Social Security death benefits for her four-year-old daughter. At issue was whether a child should be covered even if conception occurred after the husband died. The government was not sure that it wanted to open this door. The mother argued that the couple had been trying to conceive a child, and it was her husband's dying wish that she continue trying to get pregnant with his frozen sperm even after his death.

Are these odd cases? Maybe not. The time may be fast approaching when sperm, eggs, and embryos are routinely frozen for delayed pregnancy and genetic manipulation. People seem open to the idea of unfettered reproduction on demand. Our legal system will have to deal with an increasing number of cases in this area.

TAKING SEX CELLS AFTER DEATH

In 1994 in Titusville, Florida, a newlywed had sperm surgically removed from her husband and frozen two hours after he died in a car accident. Generally, sperm can be removed within twenty-four hours after death. She planned to try to become pregnant once the hormonal effects of the birth control pills she had been taking wore off. Nationwide, there have been about twenty-five cases in which sperm was actually removed from a man's body after he died.

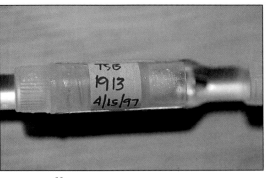

Vial of frozen sperm.

In England, a wife had sperm taken from her husband while he was in a coma on life support. It was frozen. He died in October, 1995. The woman then want-

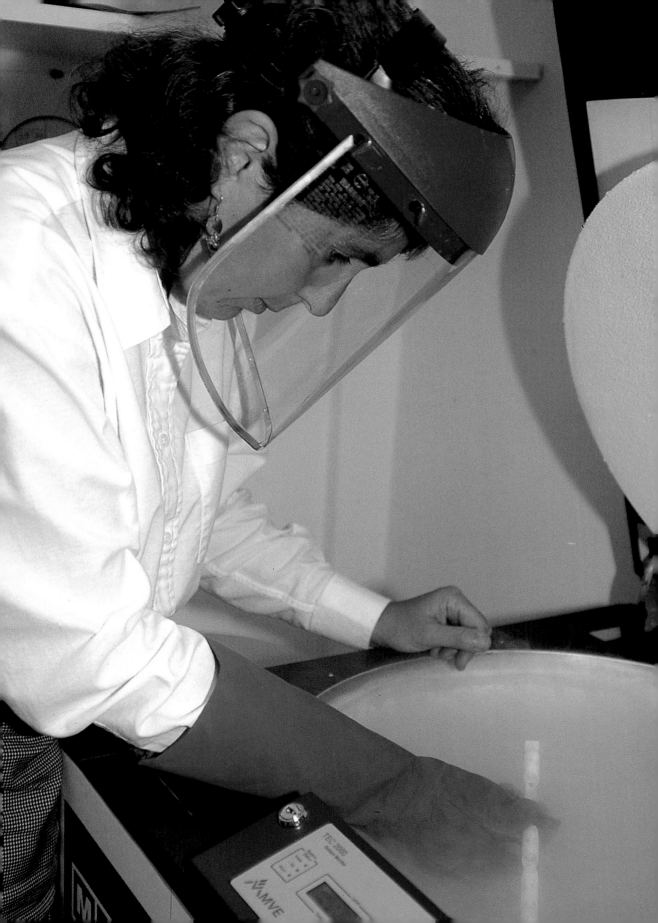

ed the sperm. A British court ruled against the woman because the husband had given no explicit consent. She then sued for the right to take the sperm to another country and won that case in 1996.

Arthur Caplan, a professor at the University of Pennsylvania and author of a book on ethics titled *Moral Matters*, calls sperm "harvesting" the ultimate invasion of privacy. Furthermore, he calls for people to give explicit directions for the use of frozen sex cells after death. Caplan believes that others cannot guess at what a deceased person would have wanted to do. Such speculation is a poor basis for public policy. Even when sex cells are viewed as property, the rights to that property are not automatically clear in all cases.

MORAL AND ETHICAL ISSUES

The Milwaukee couple whose son had died of cancer found no legal barriers to using his sperm once the liability questions were settled. Their son had not married, and there were no children to contest the plan to produce a grandchild. However, the legal system does not pretend to cover all issues concerning how we should act morally and ethically. In March of 1997 the story was reported in the Milwaukee *Journal-Sentinel* and was picked up by newspapers across the country. Reactions were strong and varied. Some women pleaded to be chosen as the mother. Some told the elderly couple that they had no business trying to do what they were doing. Talk shows and a film producer tried to contact the couple and were surprised that the couple did not want publicity. They rejected appearances on television but said they would be interested in a made-for-television movie if the payment for making it would be placed in a fund for their future grandchild.

By March of 1997 the Milwaukee couple had ten sperm samples left. Two attempts to impregnate a single woman by insemination had been made without success. They were considering including *in vitro* fertilization even though the cost was high. The couple was sympathetic to those who urged them to find a married couple to raise the child instead of a single woman. They continued to screen applicants through a blind mail box, looking for the right person to have their son's children. More than one would be fine, they said; they wanted to have as many grandchildren as possible.

The time may be fast approaching when sperm, eggs, and embryos are routinely frozen for delayed pregnancy and genetic manipulation.

Opposite page: checking on frozen sperm.

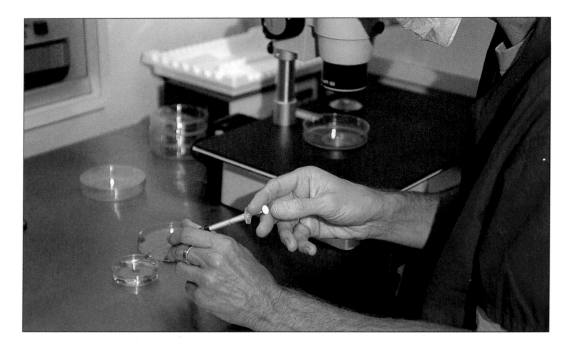

Placing egg in petri dish .

In a fairly similar case in California, a couple sought to use the frozen embryos of their daughter, who died of leukemia. The eggs were stored before her death after being fertilized by an anonymous sperm donor. The couple sought a woman to be a "gestational carrier." The woman chosen would have to agree to have an embryo implanted in her womb and to carry it until birth. In this case, the deceased daughter clearly agreed to this plan before her death. Moreover, her parents wished to raise the child, rather than restrict their role to that of grandparents.

POSTMENOPAUSAL PREGNANCY TRENDS

Menopause, the time when a woman loses her ability to produce viable eggs for fertilization and development into embryos, is usually reached between the ages of forty-five and fifty-five. At that time the ovaries quit maturing eggs, and the menstrual cycle stops. However, in 1997, modern fertility treatments, a donated egg, and some deception led to a sixty-three-year-old woman giving birth. The California woman, Arceli Keh, lied about her age in order to participate in a fertility program. She and her sixty-year-old husband had been childless. She is now the oldest known woman to ever become a mother. (The previous record was held by a sixty-two-year-old woman in Italy who had given birth shortly before Keh.) Keh had a normal pregnancy and breast-fed her daughter.

Delivery was by cesarean section because her blood pressure began to rise, a circumstance that is not unusual even during the pregnancies of younger women.

The Keh case is only the latest in a series in which women past their natural childbearing years have become pregnant. In these cases, eggs are removed from younger women who are paid as donors. Sperm is from the older woman's husband. Fertilization is accomplished in a glass petri dish, and a viable embryo is selected to be implanted into the postmenopausal mother.

Maintaining the pregnancy in such older women presents problems and higher risks to the mother's health as well as that of the fetus. First, the ovaries of postmenopausal women no longer produce high levels of estrogen and progesterone, which are necessary to build and maintain the uterine wall. Injections of the two hormones must be used. The technique works well enough, however, to bring the success rate for implanted eggs in postmenopausal women up to that of pre-menopausal women. Another concern arises from the stress that pregnancy may impose on the heart and other organs of older women; currently these effects are unknown.

Ethical concerns have been raised as well. Some argue that older parents may not live to see their children mature and that, even if they do, they may not have the energy to keep up with them. Parenting is filled with responsibilities, say these critics, and the energy to parent diminishes with age. Some children with older parents have expressed a wish that their parents were younger. Others reply that the ability to parent is not age-related. They point out that older parents may be able to offer their children greater financial stability and emotional maturity. Arceli Keh said that she and her husband feel young at heart, and they love their child.

The Milwaukee *Journal-Sentinel* urged caution and raised the issue of whether older pregnancies were not indicative of society's pressure on women to cling to eternal youth. As a practical matter, the editorial reported that the cost of the *in vitro* fertilization treatment was at least $50,000. If the trend toward such pregnancies continues, insurance companies will be asked to cover such costs. Society will have to ask if this is the best way to spend health care dollars. Such decisions, the editors concluded, should be made on a case-by-case basis. No general rules should be applied.

Drug Researchers Working To Design Customized Estrogen

Drugs that act like a rifle rather than a shotgun could help millions of women.

JANE E. BRODY

When it comes to estrogens, Nature seems to have given with one hand and taken with the other. In addition to making women women, these hormones help to protect the heart, bones and brain from the ravages of age. But they also stimulate the breast and uterus, increasing the risk of cancer in these tissues.

Now, however, researchers are hot on the trail of drugs that offer many of the benefits of natural estrogens without the serious risks that dissuade most women from taking replacement hormones after menopause. Their eventual goal is to produce a series of custom-designed compounds that could be prescribed to meet each woman's particular needs.

The research has thus far found that estrogen exhibits an extraordinary complexity and versatility that is at once intellectually challenging and enormously promising to those seeking practical solutions to some of the costliest and most devastating effects of aging.

As one researcher, Dr. Donald P. McDonnell of Duke University's department of pharmacology, put it, "With current hormone replacement therapy, we're walking a tightrope between positive and negative effects." While the current therapy gives women a mixture of estrogens that stimulate every estrogen-sensitive tissue in the body, for good and ill, he said, "we should be able to customize compounds that have different effects in different tissues."

One such drug, raloxifene by Eli Lilly & Company, is already in the final stages of clinical testing as an osteoporosis preventative that also protects the heart but does not stimulate cell growth in the breast or uterus. It is among several estrogen-like compounds in the pharmaceutical pipeline that can act selectively on estrogen-

Opposite page: Venus and Cupid are depicted in this painting.

sensitive tissues, although none is as far along the road to approval as raloxifene.

What made this development possible was the discovery that the various natural estrogens and synthetic estrogen-like compounds do not all act in the same way and that whether a cell is affected or not by a particular type of estrogen is not just a matter of yes or no. Researchers have found that the cells' receptor for estrogen is not a simple on-off switch with a static structure. Rather, the receptor turns out to be a malleable molecule whose shape is dictated by the substances it hooks up with, much like a water bed conforms to different bodies. The shape assumed by the estrogen receptor when it binds with a given molecule determines its ability to turn on different genes in the various body tissues that house these receptors. The ideal estrogenic compound would foster the growth of bone cells, protect arteries from clots and fatty deposits and preserve the vitality of the brain without triggering cell growth, and perhaps cancer, in the breast and uterus.

The ideal estrogenic compound would foster the growth of bone cells, protect arteries from clots and fatty deposits and preserve the vitality of the brain without triggering cell growth, and perhaps cancer, in the breast and uterus.

"We are moving toward a wonder drug," Dr. McDonnell said in an interview. "We're entering a new generation of hormone replacement therapy, and raloxifene will be the first to arrive." Raloxifene is not quite as potent as natural estrogen in protecting the bones and heart, and its potential to help maintain brain function has yet to be assessed, but it appears to be free of serious side effects, said Dr. John D. Termine, a biochemist at Eli Lilly who is overseeing the drug's development.

Critical to this practical research is a new understanding of how estrogens interact with genes in the cell nucleus. Estrogen receptors, the molecular locks into which estrogen keys fit, reside in the cell nucleus, acting like a telephone line between the caller, estrogen, and the receiver, the genes. In the receptors' quiescent state, they are covered by substances, called heat-shock proteins, that keep them in a state of readiness to bind to estrogen. Once estrogen hooks up with the receptors, these proteins drop off.

Until recently, Dr. McDonnell said, scientists assumed that the estrogen receptor was a simple switch that was turned on by various estrogens. The switched-on receptor could then activate genes by fitting into the nuclear proteins responsible for turning genes in the DNA on and off — the gene transcription apparatus. Such a straightforward switch would act the same in every tissue.

But Dr. Benita Katzenellenbogen and her colleagues at the University of Illinois have shown that different estrogenic compounds react with the receptor lock in different ways, resulting ultimately in different effects on neighboring genes. Dr. Katzenellenbogen, a professor of physiology and cell biology, has been studying estrogens and the estrogen receptor for a quarter-century. In an interview, she explained that the various estrogens and estrogen-like compounds — the ligands — fit into the binding pocket of the estrogen receptor a little differently, changing the conformation, or shape, of the receptor and producing an estrogen-receptor complex with a particular shape. That shape, in turn, determines how the complex interacts with the regulatory proteins and gene promoters needed to put the genetic machinery in motion.

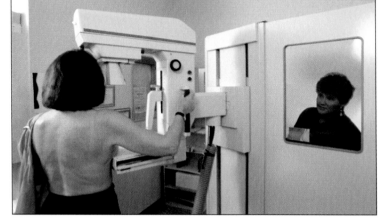

Patient undergoing a mammogram.

D r. McDonnell said: "It is now apparent that different ligands — hormones, drugs or other compounds — that bind to the receptor influence its overall structure and that different cells have the ability to discriminate between different shapes of the receptor. Thus, if the active end of the receptor assumed a square shape, it might fit into the transcription apparatus in bone cells but have no effect on the transcription apparatus in breast cells."

When these findings were first published, in the late 1980's, cell biologists immediately recognized their significance for hormone pharmacology. But it took the advent of tamoxifen, an estrogen-like drug that paradoxically blocks estrogen's action in the breast, to convince pharmaceutical companies of their practical potential, said Dr. Bert W. O'Malley, chairman of the cell biology department at Baylor College of Medicine in Houston. Tamoxifen, marketed by Zeneca Pharmaceuticals, is currently being used to prevent the recurrence of breast

cancer, but it stimulates cell growth in other tissues. In bone, for example, it fosters the production of the cells that form new bone, osteoblasts, which is good, and in the uterus, it stimulates the growth of endometrial cells, which is bad, because it can lead to uterine cancer.

Dr. O'Malley said the changing shape of the estrogen-receptor complex was not the only factor that accounted for its diverse actions in estrogen-sensitive tissues. He explained that certain proteins, called co-regulators, could make estrogen more or less potent in a particular tissue.

Once the receptor complex becomes tethered to the transcription apparatus of the gene, these co-regulator proteins—both co-activators and co-repressors—are drawn to the site. If co-repressors dominate the mix, the receptor complex may be unable to turn genes on or may have only a weak effect. If co-activators dominate, the genes are turned on and dictate the production of new proteins.

"There's a little battle between these enhancing and inhibiting factors going on all the time," Dr. O'Malley said. "The cell doesn't necessarily want genes to be turned on all the time so it has both an accelerator and a brake, just like a car."

Dr. O'Malley and his colleagues have calculated that 90 percent of the potency of the estrogen-receptor complex is determined by the particular combination of co-activators and co-repressors recruited by the complex. They have shown, for example, that tamoxifen's effects can be switched, changing it from an anti-estrogen to an estrogen, simply by changing the levels of co-activators and co-repressors.

The relative amounts of co-activators and co-repressors in a given tissue can vary from woman to woman, affecting each woman's sensitivity to the stimulatory effects of estrogenic substances, Dr. O'Malley said. Thus, tamoxifen may protect the breast or stimulate the growth of uterine cancer in one woman but not another.

"You can give 100 women the same amount of hormone," Dr. O'Malley said, "and the dose will turn out to be too much for some women and not enough for others. In the future, we should be able to measure the sensitivity to a particular hormone in a given tissue and predict the ideal dose for each woman."

However, as the experience with tamoxifen has shown, a woman's sensitivity can change with time, necessitating periodic monitoring of the effects of an estrogenic substance on a given tissue. Although tamoxifen initially acts as an anti-estrogen in the breast, blocking cell growth, breast cells in most patients begin to see tamoxifen as a stimulant, not a repressor, after five or more years of use, Dr. McDonnell said. That finding has prompted the National Cancer Institute to recommend that the drug be used for only five years, not indefinitely.

However, Dr. McDonnell added: "Resistance to the benefits of tamoxifen does not confer cross-resistance to other classes of estrogen. Therefore, it's likely that women who fail on tamoxifen can go on a different class of estrogenic drug and resume the preventive therapy."

A major challenge researchers face in looking for such drugs is that there is no short-term indicator to show whether a particular estrogen-receptor complex has the desired effect on breast tissue. For bone effects, substances in the blood can indicate the rate of bone formation, and for heart effects, levels of cholesterol — low-density and high-density lipoprotein — in the blood can be measured. But there is no direct marker for activity in the breast. Nor is there a simple biochemical indicator to show if a compound can get into the brain from the blood —crossing the blood-brain barrier—to stimulate the brain cells involved in memory and learning.

"The study of estrogen compounds that might benefit the brain is just getting started," Dr. McDonnell said. "We first have to determine what compounds will cross the blood-brain barrier and, if so, whether they will increase activity in the brain."

Researchers are hot on the trail of drugs that offer many of the benefits of natural estrogens without the serious risks that dissuade most women from taking replacement hormones after menopause. Their eventual goal is to produce a series of custom-designed compounds that could be prescribed to meet each woman's particular needs.

Engineering Blood Cells
So That One Fits All

PAUL R. BOEHLKE

A victim of a car accident is brought into the emergency room of a hospital. He is bleeding badly from an injury, and he has lost much blood. His blood is type A, but there is no time to determine that; neither will the emergency room staff be able to take time to do cross-matching, the process of mixing the patient's blood with donor blood to see if it is compatible. Following the standard procedure under such circumstances, the staff administer type O, "universal donor" blood.

Surprisingly, the transfused blood is immediately and vigorously attacked by the patient's immune system as foreign. The donated red blood cells are ruptured and spill out their hemoglobin molecules. These damaged cells block circulation in the smaller vessels. Fever and chills occur. The lack of circulating blood causes the patient to go into shock. The wounds to the tissues of the body initiate normal clotting mechanisms involving platelets and their blood-clotting chemicals. However, in this case, the damage is so widespread that the large reserves of platelets are soon used up. When platelet levels are reduced below 150,000 cubic millimeters, normal clotting in the circulatory system is affected. Integrity of the system is lost, and pinpoint leaks occur throughout the body. Every opening in the body bleeds. Even worse, the filtering of the kidneys is blocked by large amounts of hemoglobin that escape from the damaged red blood cells. The kidneys fail, and the patient dies.

The emergency room staff has never before seen this happen. The death is unexpected. As the universal donor blood, type O should not have caused such a reaction, no matter what the recipient's blood type is. Later investigation, however, shows that the blood administered was not type O, but type B, intended for another patient. Type B cannot be given to a type A person without tragic consequences. The victim was type A. As the donor blood mixed with the patient's, anti-B chemicals called antibodies in the blood of the type A person immediately attached to the entering red blood cells, causing the assembly of a set of proteins in the blood called complement. Complement molecules chemically bind to the antibodies and form holes in the type B cells (termed "hemolysis"), killing them—all this because of a human error.

BLOOD TYPING AND MISMATCHES: HOW SERIOUS IS THE PROBLEM?

Blood is a complex mixture of red blood cells, white blood cells, platelets that clot blood, proteins, antibodies, and ions. All are suspended in a fluid called plasma. Not all blood is the same, and not all blood types can be mixed. More than four million Americans receive blood transfusions each year. Most patients are typed and cross-matched, and their transfusions proceed without incident. Typing is done by mixing blood and antibodies while watching for agglutination (clumping) reactions. Cross-matching is essentially a "trial transfusion" in a test tube. Donor blood and recipient serum are mixed to see if there will be any serious reaction before the blood is actually transfused. Finally, if there is no time in an emergency situation, type O can be used.

Still, more than 330 people each year will get the wrong blood due to human error. A test, a label, or a chart may be misread or not read at all. Some believe that such mistakes may even be underreported. Fortunately, if blood intended for one person is given to another, it does not always cause harm. Only about 40 people will die from such clerical errors each year. Considering the number of people that are helped by transfusions, this is a relatively small number. It is, nevertheless, an intolerable number when one remembers that people are coming to a hospital to be helped, not to be harmed. The individuals involved will not be comforted by the statistics, and the hospital is likely to be held liable for the mistake.

Not everyone suffers a violent reaction when types of blood are mixed up, because some of the different types are compatible. There are four ABO types: A, B, AB, and O. They are grouped on the basis of two chemical compounds, called antigens. These may or may not be present on the membranes of the red blood cells. Type A red blood cells carry A antigens, and type B cells carry B antigens. Type AB has both the A and B antigens, but type O carries neither the A nor the B antigen.

Antigens activate the immune system in a person, combining with immune cells and their products, called antibodies. Antibodies are proteins that attach to foreign chemicals entering the body. Antibodies therefore work to protect us from disease.

When an unfamiliar ABO antigen is introduced into a person's body, it combines with specific ABO antibodies produced by the immune system. A person with a particular blood type can receive his or her own type because the immune system does not normally produce antibodies against molecules that are found in its own body. This allows type AB people to receive any of the ABO blood types, because the A and B antigens are not foreign to them. Type AB people are called universal recipients. Type A people can receive A or O, and type B people can receive B or O. Type O people can receive only type O. Blood donation is therefore like a one-way street. For example, O can give to A, but A cannot give to O: The O person has antibodies in the plasma against A antigens, but the A person has no antibodies against O blood. There are five major classes of antibodies which attack antigens. It is interesting that the natural antibodies against ABO antigens are class M

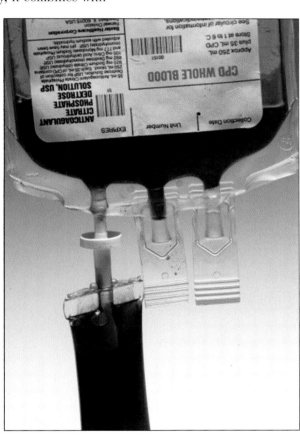

immunoglobins (IgM). IgM's are large compared to the other antibodies and very efficient at binding to foreign red blood cells. Fortunately, their size does not allow them to cross the placenta from the woman to harm a fetus of a different blood type. If the woman is, however, somehow exposed to an ABO antigen, smaller antibodies (mostly IgG's) will also be formed in her blood which can cross the placenta and cause problems.

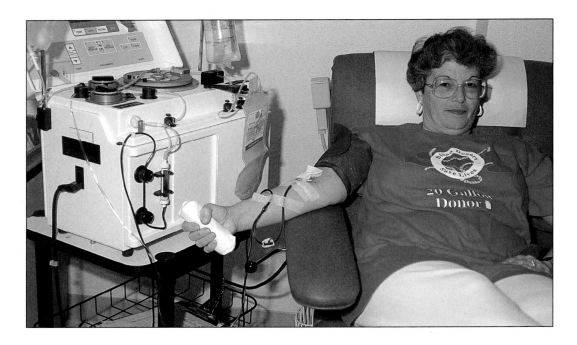

Above: Woman donating blood.

pproximately six hundred other antigens are present on blood cells in addition to ABO, and this fact might seem to discourage all transfusions. For example, a person would always have an ABO type but can also be classified by Rh, MN, Lutheran, Kell, Kidd, Duffy, Milwaukee, and other rare groupings. Fortunately, the other classifications like Rh are less critical in a first transfusion. People do not form antibodies against the non-ABO antigens unless they are initially exposed. Therefore an initial mismatch is required to form antibodies, and a second contact with the same antigen would be needed before severe trouble occurs. All the other types outside of ABO and Rh show weak or no reactions. The University of Wisconsin reports that ABO-Rh typing alone results in a 99.8 percent chance of a compatible transfusion. The addition of a screen for antibodies raises the odds to 99.94 percent, and a cross-match increases success to 99.95 percent.

The ABO classification remains most critical because people produce preformed antibodies for the A and B antigen (if they are foreign) without a prior mixing of blood. Rh and other groupings require initial contact before antibodies are formed. Then a second exposure is required before there is a negative reaction. Apparently, as far as anyone can tell, human immune systems have early contact with the A and B antigens (or sufficiently similar antigens) not by blood exposure but by some other means, perhaps through food or bacteria. The source of immunization must be very common in nature, because, although a baby is not born with these antibodies, they begin to appear at about the age of two months. Thus, humans go about their daily business already immunized against foreign ABO antigens. For this reason ABO typing remains fundamental to successful transfusions.

ONE TYPE FOR EVERYONE

As mentioned above, the universal donor blood is type O because it has no ABO antigens and is therefore the blood of choice in emergencies. Some hospitals stock only type O blood in emergency rooms and intensive care units to avoid mixups, but in many cases this causes a shortage of type O in the blood collection area. With greater understanding of the chemical structures of the ABO antigens, scientists have been pursuing the possibility of turning all blood into type O.

For more than fifteen years, researchers have pursued the possibility that A, B, and AB blood can be converted to universal donor type O by removing the A and B factors. The advantages are clear: Conversion of all blood to type O would eliminate clerical errors in the emergency room. Cross-matching would not be done. Third, all blood types could be used, eliminating oversupplies and storages. Presently, 5-10 percent of A and B blood is not used because its forty-two-day shelf life often expires first. Making all blood into type O would allow any unit of blood in a hospital to be used in an initial transfusion.

TRIMMING OFF SUGARS

A and B antigens on a red blood cell consist of chains of sugar molecules attached to lipids which are embedded in the cell membrane. The sugars are on the outside of the cell. The chains vary in kind, length, and direction. The chains on O cells are the shortest, with a galactose sugar linked to a fucose sugar at the end. The straight galactose-fucose chain does not function as an antigen. Other types are modifications of this basic structure. Type B also has the galactose and fucose but then has an additional galactose branching off on the side of the first galactose. Type A has an N-acetylgalactosamine on the galactose. In addition to this, three-fourths of the

More than four million Americans receive blood transfusions each year, and more than 330 people each year will get the wrong blood due to human error.

people with type A have an additional molecule of the type A three-sugar sequence. The type A and B sugar chains cause an immune response in someone not familiar with them. Type AB has both of them.

Under a microscope, the surface of a red blood cell looks very smooth. Nevertheless, if one could see the membrane at the molecular level, it would appear to have a jungle of sugar chains attached to it. Type A red blood cells have more than one million sugar chains on just one cell surface. Type B cells are less dense, each having about half as many sugar chains on its surface. The numbers seem overwhelming. How could one hope to change all those molecules?

The universal donor blood is type O because it has no ABO antigens and is therefore the blood of choice in emergencies. With greater understanding of the chemical structures of the ABO antigens, scientists have been pursuing the possibility of turning all blood into type O. ▼

According to *Science News* (January 11, 1997) Jack Goldstein of the Kimball Research Institute has been working on the problem for more than fifteen years. He believes that it is necessary to change most of the molecules, but not all of them, in order to change the blood's type effectively to O and has been working on a process for doing so. He is attempting to find a way to remove the extra sugar on the B antigen. Seeing that there are so many molecules to modify on just one cell, not to mention that there are 4-6 million cells in only one cubic millimeter of blood, Goldstein has also recognized the need to discover a chemical reaction that works quickly. He used an enzyme called alpha-galactosidase to remove part of the antigen (sugar) on the membrane of the red blood cells. (An enzyme is a protein that facilitates a chemical reaction—a catalyst. Enzymes can take chemicals apart or put them together.) Fortunately, enzymes in biochemical reactions are always specific and can repeat a reaction millions of times in mere seconds. In experimental trials, Goldstein's enzyme clipped off all the galactoses and reduced the structures to those found in type O.

Enzymes function because of their shape (conformation), which allows them to fit on target molecules. The acidity (pH) and temperature can change this shape and prevent enzymes from fitting on target molecules. Furthermore, the red blood cell has proteins in it that are also sensitive to pH and temperature. A key move for Goldstein, therefore, was to find a pH and temperature range at which the enzyme would work without harming the living red blood cells. His work has become easier because he no longer needs to extract his enzyme from natural sources such as coffee beans and chicken livers; his alpha-galactosidase enzyme can now be bioengineered.

A Massachusetts bioengineering company, ZymeQuest, has been licensed by Goldstein to apply his techniques. ZymeQuest has developed an automated machine to change type B blood into type O. Clinical trials are now under way to test the transformed blood, comparing it to natural type O. So far, no immune reactions have been seen. If the results of the trials remain positive and the Federal Food and Drug Administration gives approval, ZymeQuest may be able to market its synthetic type O blood by the end of 1998.

Goldstein is also working on converting type A to type O. This process will require a different enzyme. Type A is more difficult because many people in this group have the two forms of the antigen mentioned. Out of the million or so sugar chains on their cells, about fifty thousand have the extra copy of the final three sugars. In those cases two modifications will have to be performed. Furthermore, AB blood would have to be run through both processes.

REMOVING OTHER ANTIGENS

The Rh factor in blood, first discovered in the Rhesus monkey, may also be a target for biochemistry. Rh is quite complex; the factor, located on the red blood cell, is a protein with more than forty different forms, or isotypes. Part of it, not yet identified, acts as an antigen in people who have blood cells lacking this factor (Rh-negative).

Because 85 percent of the population are Rh-positive, mismatches for this factor do not pose as big a problem in blood transfusions. Also, because Rh-negative people do not carry preformed antibodies for this antigen, they will have no immediate reaction to a first transfusion of Rh-positive blood. On first contact, the Rh-positive

The hemolytic reaction to an inappropriate ABO transfusion can be severe...

Individual with group B Red Cells...

Receives transfusion of group A red cells...

Antibodies recognize A antigen as foreign...

The foreign cells are destroyed.

Toxic cell stroma & free hemoglobin released

• Fever, chills
• Kidney failure
• Death

Has naturally occurring antibodies to A antigens

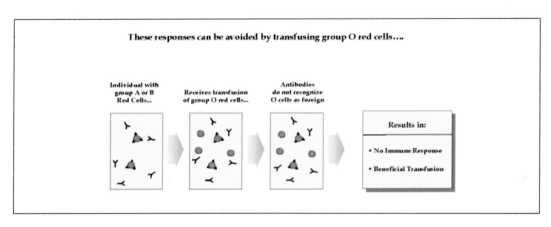

These responses can be avoided by transfusing group O red cells...

Individual with group A or B Red Cells...

Receives transfusion of group O red cells...

Antibodies do not recognize O cells as foreign

Results in:

• No Immune Response

• Beneficial Transfusion

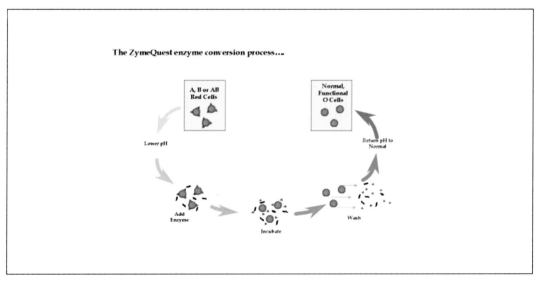

The ZymeQuest enzyme conversion process...

A, B or AB Red Cells

Normal, Functional O Cells

Lower pH

Return pH to Normal

Add Enzyme

Incubate

Wash

blood will stimulate the immune system of the Rh negative person, but the anti-Rh antibodies take several months to develop in that person. Red blood cells live an average life of 120 days, so most donor cells will have disappeared by the time the new antibodies are circulating. A second transfusion into the same person after antibodies have formed could be dangerous. If the person is a pregnant woman carrying an Rh-positive child, the child will be in danger because anti-Rh antibodies can cross the placenta.

ARTIFICIAL BLOOD

Some researchers have worked on producing a completely artificial cell-free blood. Such a fluid could be antigen-free, disease-free, and would not depend on availability of donors. The development of a successful artificial blood, however, seems to be further in the future. Physiologists agree that the form of the natural red blood cell is amazing in its ability to function in gas exchange. The shape of the red blood cell gives it a high surface-area-to-volume ratio for gas exchange. The cell's flexibility allows it to squeeze through small capillaries and the narrow places in the spleen.

Furthermore, imitating all the functions of blood is very difficult. Red blood cells carry the oxygen we breathe from our lungs to the cells of our body. As they do this, these same cells and the liquid plasma join to remove carbon dioxide from the tissues. The blood delivers nutrients and hormones throughout the body and removes wastes. These functions are vital.

At the present time the ability to save lives through transfusion still depends on healthy donors and careful typing and handling. In the near future transformed O blood will be available, allowing more efficient use of all types of available blood. It will also help guard against fatal human errors. Nevertheless, it is important to recognize that even with this new technology, the possibility of human error is always present.

Researchers have worked on producing a completely artificial cell-free blood. Such a fluid could be antigen-free, disease-free, and would not depend on availability of donors.

'People say, You poor thing, and I'm thinking, I have four healthy kids'

DONALD DALE JACKSON

Kirk Aymond has other identities—he's a chemical lab technician and a Renaissance enthusiast, to name two—but on this spring afternoon he is inhabiting the all-consuming role that has defined him to the world for the past several years: father of quintuplets. He has parked his 15-seat van at an entrance to the Cortana Mall in Baton Rouge, Louisiana, and he's unloading. Like everything else about parenting five 3½-year-olds, this is a character-building job. Also, inevitably, it attracts a lot of attention.

Kirk removes his homemade five-seat stroller from the back of the van while his wife, Denise, extracts their baby, 7-month-old Laura. As Kirk readies the stroller, a three-tiered quintmobile with two two-seat rows and a single chair on top deployed stairstep-style, the kids pile out of the van. Harley, the hugger, and bespectacled Connor climb into the stroller's bottom row. Dark-blond Garrett and Alyssa, who believes she and Harley are married, occupy the second tier. Krysta, who lost her vision when she was 10 weeks old but sometimes seems the most venturesome of the lot, takes the top seat. Laura gets her own vehicle. After 20 minutes of buckling, negotiating, toy-stowing and fielding questions from startled shoppers ("Uh, what do you call that, 'quartuplets'?"), everyone is ready.

Denise, in command of the small stroller, handles the stream of questions as if she hadn't heard them all several hundred times before. "How do you make it through the night?" "With my eyes half open." "How come they look different?" "Those two"—Denise points to Connor and Harley—"are identical; the others are fraternal." "Glad it's you and not me." "Me, too."

Weaving through the mall corridors, the Aymonds leave ripples of wonder in their wake. One woman stops, opens her eyes wide and, holding up four fingers and a

In the past ten years, as treatment for infertility has improved, the growth in multiple births has become almost a vertical line on the charts.

Opposite page: Austin, Kara, Justin and Julia Anderson, Norco, California.

thumb, soundlessly mouths the question "Five?" A teenage girl, possibly an aspiring teacher, halts the procession to poll the quints. "If you're happy, raise your hand," she demands. Harley and Connor obligingly lift their arms. Some people beam, others grimace and look away. "Twenty years ago," Denise says, "I might have been the one grimacing. I was never a baby person."

A woman with a missionary impulse waylays them as they head for a fast-food oasis. Blocking the stroller, she distributes blessings. "Oh my, they're gorgeous," she declares, smiling benignly. "Praise the Lord." Denise, whose passage through quint motherhood has been eased by a relentless sense of humor, lets her eyes rest on several women pushing single strollers. "I want you to know," she says, "that I don't look at their one pitiful little baby and think less of their trouble."

The escalation in the category known as "supertwins" began in the 1970s with the development of fertility drugs and techniques that stimulate ovulation. In the past ten years, as treatment for infertility has improved, the growth in multiple births has become almost a vertical line on the charts. ▼

After corn-dog nuggets, fries and Cokes all around, Garrett mounts a plastic chair and spreads his arms wide like a hopeful politician while Kirk ponders an obvious question: How do they cope with the multiple demands, the multiple *everything*, of raising quints? "Sure, I wondered at first how we could afford it," he says. "Then I realized that we had to take a day at a time. Things work out, you make do. You have to change your lifestyle, and you do. People turn up to help. You manage."

Denise agrees, in her fashion. "We went from DINK — that's Double Income No Kids — to SINK, Single Income Numerous Kids, and we're sinking fast," she says, retrieving a dropped coin for Krysta in mid-thought. "My whole mission is not to be just a mother, but to have a life. Friends help, family help, but sooner or later they leave. Me, I'm the crazy woman in the house who never leaves."

'SUPERTWINS' CLIMB THE CHARTS
The Aymonds are part of a phenomenon that has only recently begun to draw public notice — a population

explosion of triplets, quadruplets, quintuplets and even sextuplets (two sets in the United States and eight other known sets worldwide). The escalation in the category known as "supertwins" began in the 1970s with the development of fertility drugs and techniques that stimulate ovulation. In the past ten years, as treatment for infertility has improved, the growth in multiple births has become almost a vertical line on the charts.

Denise Aymond has evolved into a supertwins number-cruncher herself, to the extent that she is an acknowledged expert on quint totals. When her five were born in October 1992, they were the 23rd surviving set of quints in the country. As of April 1996, there were 39, with more arriving about once every eight weeks. Denise knows this because she makes a point of calling every quint mom, usually well before delivery, to offer support and advice on the many problems of multiple pregnancies. When she heard that a woman from upstate New York was carrying sextuplets (successfully delivered in March), Denise reached for the phone. "I asked her if her gums were bleeding yet. It's one of the strange symptoms you get. She asked how I knew. She hadn't even told her doctor."

The National Center for Health Statistics in Hyattsville, Maryland, has figures for multiple births in 1972-74 and 1989-93. In the earlier period, the number of surviving triplets born annually averaged 900 babies (not sets); from 1989-93, the average was 3,172. Quadruplets averaged 43 per year in 1972-74 and 241 in 1989-93. Quints went from 11 to 32. Experts estimate that a quarter of the women who receive fertility treatments and do get pregnant have more than one child.

The issues raised by this extraordinary flowering of multiple births are only now coming into focus. How good, for example, is the medical treatment available to women expecting three or more babies? How about the advice expectant mothers receive? They are often urged to undergo "selective reduction," the abortion of one or more fetuses to save the others, but they frequently have little to go on, besides fear, in making the agonizing decision. Supertwins are almost always premature and thus are more susceptible to fatal conditions and diseases, and other afflictions, such as Krysta Aymond's blindness. Hospital costs are astronomical—the Aymonds' insurers have paid more than half a million dollars.

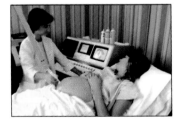

Beyond the medical questions, what is society's obligation to the new culture of multiples? Should there be a supertwin "safety net" to protect families from financial ruin? Special college scholarships? Should school officials keep the siblings together, separate them or let their parents decide? Studies show that child abuse is more common in multiple-birth families, in part, perhaps, because of sleep deprivation. "Unfortunately, these issues are not really part of our country's consciousness yet," says Patricia Maxwell Malmstrom, director of Twin Services, a resource agency for health and family service providers in Berkeley, California.

In the era before fertility drugs, quad and quint families were viewed as freaks of nature. Sometimes, as with the famous Dionne sisters of Canada, they were exhibited in glass-walled playgrounds, like zoo animals. The supertwins' best friend in those years was Helen Kirk of Galveston, Texas, whose interest was originally piqued by her work as an x-ray technician for a doctor who delivered quads. "Miss Helen" corresponded with supertwin families, sent the youngsters dollar bills on their birthdays, and collected souvenirs, pictures and information about them. Through sheer persistence, she eventually became a kind of maven of multiples and everyone's favorite authority. "Here's my black book," she offers, opening a small notebook. "It says I visited 15 sets of quints, 58 quads and hundreds of triplets."

Patty and Scott Shier, of Los Angeles, California, with 5-month olds Sarah, Joshua, Rachel, Hannah and Jonathan.

'PEOPLE LOOKED AT THEM THROUGH A WINDOW'

Now 80, Miss Helen maintains her supertwin archives in a 20-foot-long room lined with floor-to-ceiling shelves brimming with cardboard boxes. The boxes hold letters and photographs and posters, souvenir ashtrays and handkerchiefs, bumper stickers and dolls, books and magazines and clippings. "The Galveston quads were the Badgett girls," she recalls. "They were on view in their house for an hour in the mornings and afternoons. People looked at them through a porch window." Miss Helen's correspondence has tailed off since she suffered a stroke a few years ago, but she still hears from the media when supertwins are born.

"I always loved the alliterative names," she says. "Like the Badgetts—Jeraldine, Jeanette, Joyce and Joan. There were triplets in Oklahoma named Obie, Ocie and Odie, all girls. And, let's see, the Davises — Casey, Christa, Charla, Chanda and Chelsa." Her conversation is sprinkled with supertwin lore: "John-Boy Walton, you know, Richard Thomas, he has triplets…. During the war, people liked patriotic names for triplets. One set was named Franklin, Delano and Roosevelt. And there was Franklin D., Joseph S., for Stalin, and Winnie C., for Churchill. Winnie was a girl."

For a supertwin mother-to-be, the first hurdle is mental. Women who undergo fertility treatment have usually been trying to get pregnant for years. Doctors tell them that drugs like Pergonal increase the chance of a multiple birth and thus prematurity, with its higher risks, but the cautions don't always dampen the aspiring parents' enthusiasm. "You're on an emotional roller coaster when you're in treatment," says triplet mother Jody DeBussey of Westport, Connecticut. "We were so excited when we saw three heartbeats on the sonogram that we felt we could handle anything."

Denise Aymond, carrying five, was less confident. "They told me first that it was four. I thought, OK, two twin strollers, four car seats, fine—they'll fit in the car. Then they said five. I'm thinking, How do we do that? That was a whole different thing. The endocrinologist recommended reducing by two at ten weeks or so, but we knew we could lose all five if we did that. We spent a weekend absorbing this; then I decided that if we let them tamper and lost them all I'd never forgive myself. If we left it alone and it happened, I could live with that."

"We were in agony for two weeks with that decision, you feel so guilty," says Patty Czelada of Stamford, Connecticut, mother of four healthy 3-year-olds. "They took us to the hospital where they do it. Everything they told us about keeping them all was negative, that the chances of all four surviving were minimal. But God gave us four, so we kept four." The dangers are real. One study found the death rate either before or soon after birth was 19 times higher with triplets than with singletons. "The choice to reduce or not is a double bind," says Pat Malmstrom of Twin Services. "It's a risk either way."

Denise Aymond felt pessimistic even after deciding

In the era before fertility drugs, quad and quint families were viewed as freaks of nature.

against reduction. "I was just afraid it wasn't going to work, but Kirk was always optimistic. My girlfriends wanted to hose him down." At 13 weeks, she joined the two main nonprofit support groups for supertwin moms, the Triplet Connection in Stockton, California, and Mothers of Supertwins (M.O.S.T.) in Brentwood, New York. Both were founded by triplet mothers—the Triplet Connection by Janet Bleyl in 1983 and M.O.S.T. by Maureen Boyle in 1987—and took aim at the same void: an absence of reliable, accessible information on the problems that multiple-birth families confront.

A PEER GROUP HOMEPAGE ON THE WORLD WIDE WEB

Janet Bleyl had a particularly rocky ride through a triplet pregnancy after having already borne six kids. Like many supertwin mothers, she didn't feel the onset of preterm contractions, and by the time she was hospitalized at 26 weeks, doctors had to administer heavy doses of drugs to delay her labor in order to save the babies. For three more weeks, she couldn't eat or drink, and her kidneys actually shut down before she delivered three dangerously ill $2\frac{1}{2}$-pound boys. "I'll never forget that first horrifying sight of them," she says. "Their heads were like oranges; you could see all their veins; their chests were sunken in. Tubes and needles everywhere. They looked like 95-year-old men." The idea for the Triplet Connection stemmed from her experience.

The Connection sends new members a hefty packet of medical and child-rearing advice, along with a list of other supertwin mothers they can contact. There is also a homepage on the World Wide Web at http://www.inreach.com/triplets.

The support groups help women ask the right questions, such as which procedures are covered by insurance. Home uterine monitors, for example, which permit expectant mothers to keep track of contractions at home and which electronically transmit the data to a hospital, are covered by some insurers but not others. Insurers normally pay all or most of the tab for a premature newborn's stay in intensive care, which averages $255,000 for 34 days for triplets.

"Before the babies are born," Pat Malmstrom says, "supertwin parents have to answer these questions: Who is going to take care of the babies while we sleep? How much sleep do we need? How will we feed them seven or

Supertwins are almost always premature and thus are more susceptible to fatal conditions and diseases, and other afflictions.

eight times a day for three months? Who will help? Will they be breast-fed? And who's going to bring food into the house, prepare it, do the laundry and bathe the babies, in an age when even great-grandparents are working?"

Parents of multiples have to overcome any resistance they may feel toward asking for help. "It's hard; you have to humble yourself to admit you need help," Denise Aymond says. Most families use some combination of relatives, neighbors, volunteers and professionals, such as those sometimes provided gratis by local "respite" programs. "I had a list of a hundred people when the quints first came home," Denise says. "It was like a Motel 6 around here — the light was always on."

Elise, Allie and Lindsay Nedwin, Davis, California.

Quad and quint families often receive freebies from hometown and national businesses. "The Target store gave us 25 percent off on diapers," says quad father Randy Addington of Lodi, California. "Gerber sent us coupons. Mead Johnson gave two years' worth of formula. A motel donated a room so Dawn and I could get away for a night. We slept 15 hours." The Aymonds harvested free formula, a discount on a Ford van and $2,500 to start a college fund, among other largess.

The flip side of public generosity is public nosiness. Keith and Becki Dilley, parents of America's first surviving sextuplets (born in May 1993), were startled one day to see a tour bus packed with seniors idling in front of their house in a small Indiana town. A woman rushed to the door and demanded that the Dilleys wake the babies for a picture. "You get the most unfeeling questions," says Maureen Boyle of M.O.S.T. "A woman in a grocery line asked me if I had to 'do it' three times in one night." "They ask which child's the smartest, which do you like best and if the babies are 'natural,' as if they're not natural if we take fer-

tility drugs," Jody DeBussey says.

The full impact of adding three or more consumers to the family often doesn't hit right away. "The stress sometimes kicks in at about six months," Maureen Boyle says. "Until then you're mainly trying to keep the babies alive. When mothers call me for help, I tell them to focus on short-term goals, like shifting to a three-hour feeding at 7 pounds, sleeping through the night at 10 pounds, starting solids at 14. These are practical things they can look forward to. You can't imagine what a big deal it is to be able to take a shower without worrying."

But even for a supertwin mother who has Dad, Grandma or a neighbor working the midnight shift, the stress can be nerve-shreddingly intense. One researcher who studied families of twins found the risk of child abuse to be between 2 ½ and 9 times that in singleton families. This comes as no surprise to Dawn Addington, who has four 3-year-olds and still works part-time as a nurse. "I get to the point where I'm going batty. It's usually connected with lack of sleep," she says. The daunting "terrible twos" are the worst time. A British mother speculated to a researcher that quads learning to assert their personalities at that age have "the added handicap of trying to establish themselves within their own group as well as the family as a whole." Hers sometimes established themselves by galloping through the house like ponies. Denise Aymond was struck by her quints' different tantrum styles: "Garrett was a head banger. Alyssa holds her breath and turns blue."

Most schools have not yet addressed the escalation in multiples, but they can't delay much longer. "It won't be long before there will be triplets in most large school districts," Maureen Boyle predicts. Schools have traditionally separated twins to permit their individuality to flourish, but supertwin families and their advocates prefer a family-by-family policy. "Parents complain to us that their kids are forced into separate classes," says Pat Malmstrom, "but there's no one-size-fits-all solution. It should be case by case and year by year."

Hospitals and schools, Malmstrom believes, are often insensitive to the bonding that occurs among multiples. Nurses have found that putting two premature siblings together in a single incubator sometimes helps stabilize their heart rate and blood-oxygen level. Dawn

Most schools have not yet addressed the escalation in multiples, but they can't delay much longer.

Opposite page: identical twins.

Addington has seen the bond in her quads: "They're often tender with each other. When they wake up, they're always glad to see each other, and they read each other's moods. I'll discipline Haley, and Heather will go and get a blanket for her."

The flotilla of vans parked on the quiet residential street in Stamford, Connecticut, this weekday evening suggests a caucus of Little League coaches, but the drivers are supertwin moms gathered for their monthly share-and-support meeting. Six of the nine present are mothers of triplets, one is expecting triplets, two others have quads. Most are in their early 30s, fit, articulate; a few still work. There is no leader, so the conversation moves more or less naturally to toilet training, skipping along briskly from there.

"Competition doesn't work. You can't shame them by saying their brother or sister did it."

"I showed them underwear at a store and told them they'd be ready for it when they were trained. It worked that same day."

"We're entering my 5-year-olds in parochial school. I'll confess it, I played the triplet card. The school has never had triplets before. They want us. But they only have two classes, so we can't separate all three children. We're debating what to do. Tuition is $3,900 each."

"Do you find what I do, with strangers? They think they can ask you the most personal questions if you have triplets. They asked me if I had my tubes tied."

"I get sick of it. I told one woman I had to sleep with three men in one night. I think she believed it."

"What gets me is that people think they can *touch* my kids because they're triplets."

"By the way, did you hear that they're recalling certain vans? Something about the brakes."

"Can we all agree that triplet moms are better at setting limits?" All agree, with gusto. "I mean, singleton mothers let their kids get away with murder. We can't let that happen. Otherwise, *whap* — chaos! We can't fool around with little stuff."

"We were at a playground and another kid took a toy from mine. Being a triplet, my guy just got another one. I think they share better."

It continues this way for a couple of hours. One or two women peel off occasionally to get coffee or cake from the dining room. The hostess's husband has their quads under control. Not a hint of acrimony sullies the atmosphere. This is a confident, capable bunch. The others offer encouragement to the pregnant woman and the mother of 5-month-old quads. It is she who has the last word: "I should go. My first call is in about three hours." Cheerfully, they disperse to their vans.

Advocates for supertwin families contend that society ignores their special needs. "It's not a plot, it's a fact," Pat Malmstrom says. "Nobody in health care or social services is trained in the subject; there's nothing at medical schools or other grad schools."

The Council of Multiple Birth Organizations, an offshoot of the International Society for Twin Studies, issued a "statement of needs" for twin and supertwin families last year. The manifesto included improved education and care to avert preterm labor, better nutrition counseling during pregnancy, institutional encouragement of bonding among multiples and flexible policies that respect their unique relationship, such as placing twins and triplets on the same athletic teams. "We need a national policy," Pat Malmstrom believes. "There's no safety net. If a family's medical insurance pays only 80 percent, say, they're in big trouble."

"We have to recognize first that a multiple birth is a high-risk pregnancy," says Janet Bleyl of the Triplet Connection, "and that it needs to be managed by high-risk professionals. A high-level neonatal intensive care unit should be stan-

Jessianne, Juliette and Jenna Holder, Sylmar, California.

dard for multiple births. Insurers should recognize that preventive care is cheaper than treatment of sick, premature babies. If women have kids already and bed rest is prescribed, the health care provider should furnish help. It ought to be covered when it's necessary. So should home uterine monitors." Maureen Boyle of M.O.S.T., focusing on where the trouble begins, urges research and the development of programs that would educate doctors and prospective parents about the kinds of fertility treatments that so often produce multiples.

Nurses have found that putting two premature siblings together in a single incubator sometimes helps stabilize their heart rate and blood-oxygen level. ▼

It's Saturday morning at the Addington house in Lodi, California. Parents Dawn and Randy patrol quad-occupied territory: the kitchen and living-dining room. Their four 3-year-olds — Jared, Heather, Hannah and Haley — seem to drift apart and then bounce off each other like atoms under a microscope. Heather sits in a corner of the living room, methodically removing her clothes. Jared barrels through on a plastic trike. Haley does wind sprints. Hannah dives into a box of toys. Randy washes breakfast dishes, changes the television channel, referees a flare-up and helps Heather find her underwear, all within five minutes. Dawn moves at the same hectic pace. It's a four-ring circus. Two of the kids take turns shutting each other in a closet. Hilarity ensues. Randy picks up Haley and announces that she is a sack of potatoes. Haley giggles. "The best times are when we're all rolling around on the floor," Dawn says.

Action is nonstop in a quad household: eat, play, dress, play, snack, go out, play, eat, fuss, nap, play, eat. Time to go to the park. "Whose turn to sit in the front of the van?" "Mine," four voices reply. "Hannah, where are your shoes?" Hannah finds one, holds it up triumphantly. Addingtons spill out at the park and appropriate the swings. Randy and Dawn push. Bathroom traffic is heavy. "Sometimes I spend all my park time in the bathroom," says Dawn. Randy and the quads walk across a lawn. Something halts them, and for an instant the four toddlers and their father are frozen in a tableau, the kids' heads cocked at the same angle, like kittens. The moment passes and they break into a run toward their mom, who declares them all winners. "We don't get attention like we used to," she says. "Now we could be—who knows?—a day-care center." Randy warms Jared's hands, then Hannah and Jared hug.

Thirty minutes at the park, then off to McDonald's. Dawn takes orders in the car: "How many hamburgers and how many nuggets?" She orders "two hamburger Happy Meals for girls" and "two nugget Happy Meals, one boy, one girl." "You give the sex so you get the right toy," she explains. The clerk recognizes them. "Aren't you the…?" she begins. Dawn nods. Everyone eats except Heather, who spends her time spilling her fries and patiently replacing them in the bag, one by one. When she is scolded, her eyes glaze, apparently an ominous sign, and Dawn takes her outside for a time-out.

Fuss time starts on the way home. The toys—Jared gets a robot, the girls get horses—don't deflect it. Back home, the sleeping mats come out and the quads go down on the living-room floor. Mister Rogers sings softly on TV. Randy lies down next to Haley. Blessed quiet descends, two hours of peace. "Sometimes I think it's a miracle, you know," Dawn says. "I mean, for years I couldn't get pregnant, now I have four. I was afraid of losing them and afraid of having them. Now they're 3 years old. People say, You poor thing, and I'm thinking, I have four healthy kids. It's a miracle."

Elizabeth and Jeff Siebers of Grand Terrace, California, with Tommy, Peter and Molly.

New Cures for Old Ills

ELIZABETH D. SCHAFER

Historically, the neighborhood pharmacy has been a consistent source of remedies to soothe aches and pains. Modern pharmaceutical advances and medical research enable druggists to provide their customers state-of-the-art prescriptions to control and cure a variety of maladies. New molecular entities are being discovered as potential therapeutic drugs to battle aggressive diseases, such as cancer, that have challenged humans for generations, as well as new physiological foes such as acquired immunodeficiency syndrome (AIDS).

Before the professionalization of pharmacy, people relied on medicinal plants and herbs, potions, and folk traditions to ease their illnesses. Synthetic pharmaceuticals were first produced in the nineteenth century, when Hermann Kolbe synthesized salicylic acid, an antiseptic used in surgery. His drug was the catalyst for the modern pharmaceutical industry.

Scientists at chemical laboratories produced pharmaceuticals to combat diseases. Companies advertised their products to consumers, and patients did not have to have prescriptions to purchase the drugs. After penicillin was discovered in the 1920's and sulfa drugs in the mid-1930's, the commercialized pharmaceutical industry emerged.

The 1940's and 1950's witnessed intense research activity to identify and market new drugs. New compounds were created and patented as intellectual property, and companies competed, advertising their products directly to doctors. Pharmacy became a big business, and profits were used to fund new research. The Food and Drug Administration (FDA) approved new pharmaceuticals, indicating that they were safe for consumers, and regulation, prescriptions, and labeling of these controlled

Before the professionalization of pharmacy, people relied on medicinal plants and herbs, potions, and folk traditions to ease their illnesses.

substances became standards of the trade. The Centers for Disease Control and Prevention cooperated in the establishment of safe and effective drugs.

The United States has been a leader in drug research, but many companies maintain factories overseas, where regulations are not as stringent. Foreign manufacturers create drugs unavailable in the United States, and Americans have traveled to other countries to purchase these drugs, which are sometimes controversial, such as abortion pills, or merely extra strong, such as acne lotions.

As demand for pharmaceuticals to combat new bacterial strains, infections, and other diseases increases, pharmacologists are striving to discover, develop, and produce drugs that will improve the quality of life. ▼

As demand for pharmaceuticals to combat new bacterial strains, infections, and other diseases increases, pharmacologists are striving to discover, develop, and produce drugs that will improve the quality of life. It is expected that drugs to better treat, and perhaps even prevent and cure, diseases such as AIDS and cancer will someday be made available through laboratory research and medical advances.

RESEARCH AND DEVELOPMENT

Health care is a primary concern of most societies. Great debate has occurred over the crisis of accessible, affordable medical facilities. Pharmaceuticals must be available to help patients resist ailments and heal. Nonprescription, over-the-counter remedies provide health care for minor conditions, such as the common cold and rashes, offering relief when patients are unable to visit a physician and must treat themselves.

Through research and development, a variety of new, significantly beneficial pharmaceuticals have been produced. Pharmacologists often credit serendipity and luck with drug discovery. Others focus on specific diseases or problems and seek an effective therapeutic cure with minimal side effects.

The first stage in the drug development process is the discovery phase, when a chemist or pharmacologist initiates research by realizing a new organic reaction, synthesizing chemicals, studying their properties, and identifying further tests to be made. Researchers attempt to discover a new pharmacologically active compound that will be therapeutic or prevent illness. According to *Clinical Research in Pharmaceutical Development*, edited by Barry Bleidt and Michael Montagne in 1996, some chemists, to save money and time, use computer modeling to design drugs by planning and then envisioning the chemical structure on screen before synthesizing and testing it. Next, the drug is tested on animals for toxicity. In stage three, the company files the pharmaceutical as an investigational new drug, requesting authorization to begin testing with human subjects. During the fourth stage, human testing is pursued.

During phase I human testing, dosages of the drug are administered to healthy volunteers, usually in a double-blind study that includes a placebo group, to determine if the drug is toxic to humans. By phase II of the human testing, subjects with the pathological condition that the drug is designed to combat are given doses to see if it proves therapeutic. Next, in phase III of human testing, a large-scale, long-term test of human subjects is made to discover any adverse side effects the drug might cause. The drug not only must be safe and effective but also must be economical and satisfactory to patients. Scientists consider the drug's potential impact on patients according to their gender, ethnicity, and age. Pharmacokinetics (how the drug and body interact) and pharmacoeconomics (the economic and social impact of the drug) are also assessed.

In the next stage of drug development, long-term animal testing is pursued to determine any detrimental effects from lengthy exposure to the drug and how it might affect future generations. Thereafter, a new drug application is made to secure approval from the federal government for commercial marketing.

When the drug is released, it has at least three names. The first reflects its chemical molecular makeup; the second is a generic name, usually a shortened version of the chemical name; and the third is a brand name designated by the drug's creator and then trademarked. Marketing requires conformity to laws and regulations as well as ethical concerns. Companies carefully state what a pharmaceutical can be expected to achieve, recommend dosages and precautions, and stress hazards, risks, and pregnancy complications from taking the drug and contraindications with other pharmaceuticals and health conditions.

Under President William J. Clinton's direction, in 1995 the FDA streamlined its review process of drugs and medical devices to "Protect people, not bureaucracy." The new standards enabled the review process to occur more quickly, within two years. They also supported generic drugs, which are copies of brand-name pharmaceuticals (after the original twenty-year patent expires) and account for half of the 2.4 billion prescriptions issued yearly. In a speech delivered on March 16, 1995, in Arlington, Virginia, Clinton praised pharmaceutical manufacturers and federal employees, stating that "Americans don't have to worry about the safety or effectiveness [of medical products] when they buy anything—from cough syrups to the latest antibiotics or pacemakers." He explained that "the Food and Drug Administration has made American drugs and medical devices the envy of the world and in demand all over the world, and we should never forget that, either. And we are going to stick with the standards we have, the highest in the world."

PHARMACEUTICAL AND MEDICAL ADVANCES

New diseases, infections, and strains of bacteria that are resistant to current antibacterial drugs necessitate the development of novel vaccines and medicines. The drug industry creates entirely new compounds and formulations, improves current drugs to be more effective, and creates better coatings and delivery systems. Therapeutic agents, including blocking agents, anticoagulants, diuretics, and hormones, are produced in new dosage forms such as tablets, syrups, ointments, sprays, creams, and controlled-released pills.

In 1996, forty-one new drugs were released to the market for therapeutic and diagnostic uses by such industry giants as Merck, Upjohn, Glaxo Wellcome, Procter & Gamble, Pfizer, Bayer, and Bristol-Myers Squibb, as well as smaller companies. Some products had new indications, being designated for treating different conditions or released for nonprescription usages.

Chemotherapy for cancer has seen many new pharmaceutical developments. In 1971, scientists discovered

The drug not only must be safe and effective but also must be economical and satisfactory to patients. Scientists consider the drug's potential impact on patients according to their gender, ethnicity, and age.

taxol, a chemical in the bark of the Pacific yew tree, which has anticancer properties and have been synthesized into drugs called taxoids. Because the trees are endangered and each tree yields only one gram of taxol, which is half a treatment, synthesis of the chemical in the laboratory is crucial to assure an adequate supply. The taxoids are especially welcome because they offer hope to cancer patients whose cancer is resistant to traditional cancer therapies.

In tests, some patients' tumor cells were reduced in size, although others experienced side effects. Currently, researchers are attempting to make taxol water-soluble to increase quantity, enable new applications, and make it cheaper and more effective. Taxol investigators K. C. Nicolaou, Rodney K. Guy, and Pierre Potier wrote about their work in the June, 1996, issue of *Scientific American*, philosophizing that "in the discovery of new drugs, one

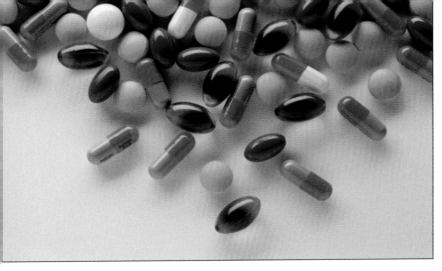

rarely cries 'Eureka!' Rather the process takes years of detailed research to determine how a drug works and how to improve its potency."

Numerous other anti-cancer drugs have been placed on the market to combat ovarian, prostate, and breast cancers. Other new treatments consider the possibility that bacterial microbes may cause stomach cancers. The *Helicobacter pylori* bacteria, which is present in one-third of the population's stomachs, is known to cause ulcers. Traditionally ulcers have been treated with surgery and stress-relieving techniques. Now, with the knowledge that acid-eating bacteria are present, new antibiotic drugs reduce gastric acid with histamine 2-receptor blockers. Ulcers are healed and rarely recur. In late 1995, the FDA approved clarithromycin (Biaxin), used with moeprazole (Prilosec) or ranitidine bismuth citrate (Tritec) for a monthlong treatment program.

Everyday pharmaceutical researchers are exploring possibilities for new drugs to save lives. These future drugs will make a difference in the quality of individuals' health as well as benefit society. ▼

Investigators have focused on drugs to aid memory retention in Alzheimer's patients, from which 30 percent of Americans over the age of eighty-five suffer, or to repress traumatizing memories in other patients. Donepezil hydrochloride was the second approved treatment after tacrine for Alzheimer's. In April, 1997, researchers announced that a combination of vitamin E and selegiline (Eldepryl), an anti-Parkinson's drug, slowed Alzheimer's symptoms for several months. Mary Sano of the Columbia University College of Physicians and Surgeons explained how she tested 341 patients for two years. The *New England Journal of Medicine*, however, warned that the test may not have been accurate and warned of possible side effects.

Another group of new drugs that are crucial in the late 1990's include the antiviral agents, which act against the human immunodeficiency virus (HIV) as protease inhibitors to prevent the HIV from replicating. In addition to drugs for adult HIV patients, pediatric pharmaceuticals have been developed for AIDS sufferers. The FDA approved two HIV protease inhibitors for children in March, 1997: nelfinavir (Viracept) pediatric 2-13 and ritonavir (Norvir). At that time, Health and Human Services secretary Donna E. Shalala praised researchers who "not only add another powerful weapon to our arsenal for treating HIV infection, but provide us with critical information on using these cutting edge drugs to help HIV positive children." Dr. Michael A. Friedman, the FDA Lead Deputy Commissioner, noted, "With each approval, we are providing more options in designing individualized treatment programs for adults and children."

Another pharmaceutical development was a more effective diabetes drug, troglitazone (Rezulin), that enabled patients to only take one injection daily of insulin plus Rezulin. In April of 1997, an anti-bone-thinning drug, Fosamax, was released to prevent bone fractures in osteoporosis patients. Fosamax was created as an alternative to hormone treatments which carried the risk of breast cancer. Researchers continue to work on bone-building drugs. Dr. Paula Stern, a pharmacologist at Northwestern University Medical School, stated, "The way I visualize the ideal future is that we'll be able to give Drug X that builds up bone to where it's stronger and the risk is no longer present, then Drug Y maintains it by preventing breakdown."

New drugs are designed to prevent strokes by dissolving clots. Recent antibiotics are designed to fight respiratory tract infections and new bacterial strains resistant to previous drugs. Ivy Block was the first drug designed to protect against poison ivy, sumac, and oak. The FDA's Orphan Products Program provides incentives such as grants and tax credits to ensure that drugs are created for diseases that affect fewer than 200,000 people. Rare disorders, including primary pulmonary hypertension and Lou Gehrig's disease, may be treated with drugs that are being examined in clinical trials.

Many drugstores carry both prescription and over-the-counter obesity drugs. Recently, fluoxetine hydrochloride was released as the first drug therapy for the eat-

Another group of new drugs that are crucial in the late 1990's include the antiviral agents, which act against the human immunodeficiency virus (HIV) as protease inhibitors to prevent the HIV from replicating.

ing disorder bulimia nervosa. New drugs such as dexfenfluramine (popularly known as fen-phen) reduce cravings for food, and chlorocitrate makes people feel full by slowing the release of serotonin.

In addition to drugs, new medical devices have been created that improve health care. A blood test that detects recurrence of breast cancer is called Truquant. The Ultramark 9 High Definition Ultrasound System makes possible high-definition ultrasound mammography and breast exams, and a semiautomatic system, known as the PAPNET Testing System, rescreens Pap smears. Photodynamic Therapy Units are the first tool to use laser light through fiber optics, activating a light-sensitive drug to treat esophageal cancer. An oral fluid HIV test has also been developed.

DRUGS FOR THE FUTURE

Everyday pharmaceutical researchers are exploring possibilities for new drugs to save lives. These future drugs will make a difference in the quality of individuals' health as well as benefit all society. Some investigators are currently pursuing combinatorial chemistry to produce and screen millions of molecules inside test tubes, hoping to discover previously unknown compounds to make new drugs.

Other experimenters are studying the 100,000 genes in human cells to identify genes that fight disease and maintain health. Knowledge of these genes will aid in the creation of therapeutic proteins and medicines. Through genetic research and engineering, deoxyribunucleic acid (DNA) can be manipulated to develop medicinal proteins from farm animals and other cell donors. Disease-resistant genes may help cure cancer and Alzheimer's. Additional anticancer research is determining how the telomerase enzyme in tumor cells rebuilds chromosome ends that usually are shortened during cell division.

At Cold Spring Harbor Laboratory, Tim Tully and Jerry C. P. Yin are examining the levels of the protein CREB in fruit-fly brains to study how the flies learn and remember. Other medical researchers are seeking drugs to prevent the release of oxygen-free radical molecules in the brain, which cause the tremors and immobility of Parkinson's disease. Some investigators are trying to inhibit enzymes from producing toxins that inflame tissues and cause arthritis.

From test tube to patient, drug development is a complicated biotechnological process. Medicinal chemists are innovative, arranging for pharmaceutical manufacture in zero gravity on the space shuttle as well as considering nontraditional sources for cures.

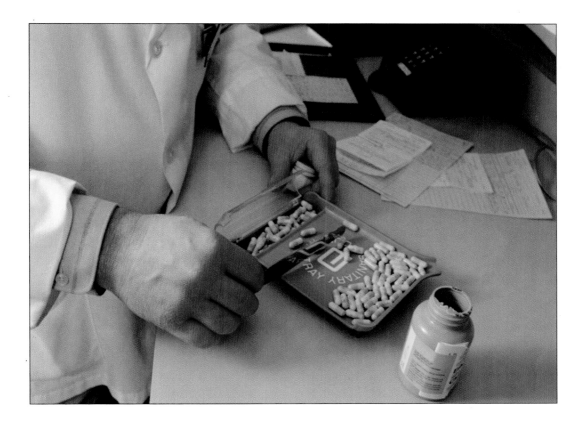

Dennis Chio at Washington University School of Medicine is working with an experimental drug K2528 to produce NAIP, a protein that reduces brain damage in clinical trials and may be applied to Alzheimer's, Huntington's disease, and epilepsy. "There is a barrier of inertia based on the historical notion that you could do nothing about brain damage," Chio reflected. "Now there is hope."

From test tube to patient, drug development is a complicated biotechnological process. Medicinal chemists are innovative, arranging for pharmaceutical manufacture in zero gravity on the space shuttle as well as considering nontraditional sources for cures.

The multivolume *Chronicles of Drug Discovery*, published by the American Chemical Society, consists of narratives by researchers who designed and synthesized novel drugs, and the FDA Internet home page (http://www.fda.gov) lists new drugs approved.

Eating Smart

ELIZABETH D. SCHAFER

H ave you ever heard the old wives' tale that eating fish can make you smart? The long-held belief that fish is brain food may prove to be more fact than fallacy. Nutritionists speculate that diets enriched with vitamins, minerals, and other crucial nutrients promote intellectual development and can even restore lost cognitive ability.

Currently, scientists are investigating the role of adequate nutrition in regard to intellect and health. Researchers agree that a well-balanced, low-calorie diet enhances longevity and life quality. However, they differ when considering the impact of malnutrition on brain growth and behavioral development. No one knows for sure how nutrition affects intelligence, and many experiments have been staged to examine various factors influencing mental aptitudes.

Scientists and pediatricians have studied malnourishment since the early twentieth century. Malnutrition has both human-made and environmental causes; children suffer nutritional deprivation due to droughts, famines, wars, poverty, abuse, and societal conditions. Starvation also occurs because of physiological complications, including food not being properly absorbed due to infections, irregular metabolism, or bodily rejection through vomiting and diarrhea.

Early nutritionists identified two primary types of malnutrition, kwashiorkor (protein deficiency) and marasmus (protein-calorie deficiency). Predominating in developing countries and also occurring in the Western Hemisphere, malnutrition affects growth and maturation, weakens the immune system, and delays mental development. Malnourished children encounter cultural disadvantages as a result of their lack of proper nutrition. Malnutrition is often linked to impoverished surroundings

Awareness of nutritional concerns has grown since World War II. During the 1950's, the United Nations Food and Agriculture Organization and World Health Organization analyzed world malnutrition and emphasized the need for vitamins, minerals, and protein in childhood diets.

and biological risks, including parasites, neglect, and lack of medical care, and it is difficult to isolate malnutrition as an experimental variable.

Awareness of nutritional concerns has grown since World War II. During the 1950's, the United Nations Food and Agriculture Organization and World Health Organization analyzed world malnutrition and emphasized the need for vitamins, minerals, and protein in childhood diets. Since that time, the problem has worsened. In 1992 an estimated 195 million children under the age of five were malnourished worldwide, and approximately 12 million American children consumed nutritionally poor diets.

FOOD FOR THOUGHT

Intelligence is determined by many factors, including genetic and environmental variables. Each individual is born with a genetic range for mental ability which is shaped by external stimuli. The relationship between malnutrition and behavioral development in children has been a primary concern of nutritionists. Concepts about the influence of malnutrition on cognitive development have changed drastically in the last thirty years.

David A. Levitsky and Barbara J. Strupp of Cornell University are currently leading researchers in this field.

In 1992 an estimated 195 million children under the age of five were malnourished worldwide, and approximately 12 million American children consumed nutritionally poor diets.

In a supplement to the August, 1995, *Journal of Nutrition,* published by the American Institute of Nutrition, they outlined research theories and hypotheses since the 1960's. During that decade, scientists believed that malnutrition during childhood caused irreversible brain damage. When children were denied proper diets, the cessation of brain development resulted in retardation and impaired brain function, creating behavioral problems.

These scientists researched the effect of malnutrition on animals. Depriving rats and pigs of adequate nutrition hindered brain growth and resulted in permanently smaller brains in test subjects. The researchers noticed neural changes, including emotional reactions such as anxiety, depression, lack of motivation, and impaired learning ability and long-term memory.

Their hypothesis that malnutrition caused brain damage, however, was difficult to apply to humans because they would have to study and test malnourished human subjects for accurate assessments. Researchers wrote many scientific articles, mostly inconclusively speculating about the problems instigated by undernutrition in humans as based on observations of animals. The focus on malnutrition was considered crucial because at least half of the world's children suffered from some degree of starvation.

Although studies of human malnourishment were difficult to interpret because of other factors, scientists emphasized that poor diets affected mental development in numerous ways as well as stunting body growth and causing chronic health problems and that poverty exacerbated these conditions. Scientists feared that impaired intellectual functions would hinder the children's success and survival in the rapidly industrializing world.

From 1969 to 1977, researchers studied the long-term effect of Protein Energy Malnutrition (PEM) in Guatemala. They gave children two nutritional supplements: Fresco, a fruit drink with no protein, and Atole, a high-protein food. Both groups were provided iron and vitamins. The children consuming Atole performed better on cognitive tests even if

Passive parents who do not insist on investing time and money for adequate nutrition cause much of the malnutrition among children.

they suffered socioeconomic deprivation. The scientists concluded that protein mitigated poverty's effect on Guatemalan children's cognitive development.

Because children's brains attained 80 percent of adult size between conception and age two, the researchers emphasized that the nutritional supplements were best if given during this period of rapid growth. To assure full intellectual and physical growth, toddlers needed vast quantities of nutrients and calories. Malnourishment during the first two years of life was believed to cause permanent and severe brain damage, but some researchers questioned this theory, considering it a simplistic explanation.

At Cornell, Levitsky and Richard H. Barnes conducted tests with malnourished rats in the 1970's. The rats performed poorly on tests of mental ability, but Levitsky and Barnes concluded that the rats' failures were not attributable to brain damage. Instead, the scientists reasoned that the rats lacked energy because of their limited diet. As a result, they did not interact with their peers. The absence of contact with people and things in their environment prevented them from being intellectually stimulated and becoming independent. Levitsky and Barnes hypothesized that malnourished children could develop cognitive skills through social interaction and experiences.

Researchers began considering the possibility of restored cognitive ability in previously starved children. With adequate nutrition and stimulation, a reversal of brain damage was feasible. Scientists began to realize that malnutrition temporarily halted brain growth but that when an adequate diet became available, growth resumed. After being on hold, brain growth continued, and nutritionists stressed that adequate nutrition was vital throughout childhood, not just to age two.

Nutritionists speculated that undernourished children were delayed, not damaged, intellectually. Their learning was interrupted and acquisition of information interrupted. Denied nutrients and sensory stimulation, they lost learning time during crucial periods of development. As a result, they had difficulty solving problems. While properly nourished children approached problems with logic and experience, explaining when necessary that they lacked enough information or competence, malnourished children avoided the problem by asking for water or to leave. Exposure to an

Eleven Food Groups Defined in the "Nutrition Revolution"

- animal foods/eggs
- milk/yogurt/cheese
- grains
- bread/crackers/ingredients
- legumes/nuts/seeds
- vitamin-C fruits/vegetables
- fats
- sweets
- herbs/spices/condiments/flavorings

Because the brain is resilient, malnourished children are able to heal and process information given nutrients, educational support, and psychosocial stimulation.

improved educational environment and enriched diet restored many lost cognitive skills, including altered speech, vision, hearing, and coordination.

In the 1990's, researchers focused on the biochemistry of the brain in malnutrition. They determined that children were most vulnerable to malnutrition when certain neurons were organizing during prenatal brain growth in addition to postnatal development. Studies of laboratory animals revealed that malnutrition caused decreased protein synthesis during brain growth, lesions, amino acid deficiencies, and reduced numbers of neurotransmitter receptors. Fewer brain cells were produced, and their distribution was altered.

Significantly, the cerebral cortex, crucial for intellect and cognitive reasoning, was smaller, and cortical structures were affected. Cortical neurons were less dense than normal, and their synapses were reduced. Although the total number of cerebral neurons was not diminished, microstructures were damaged. Nutritional rehabilitation, however, promised some recovery. In rats, rehabilitation restored cell density and synapses. Some neural aberrations, such as reduced brain myelin, did not recover. Myelinated axons (cell message transmitters) in the brain transmitted information more quickly than non-myelinated cells.

Currently, nutritionists believe that malnutrition may briefly alter neurotransmitter metabolism, affecting mental acuity. They note that brain levels of two crucial monoamines, serotonin and norepinephrine, return to normal with proper nutrition. Because the brain is resilient, malnourished children are able to heal and process information given nutrients, educational support, and psychosocial stimulation. Scores on intelligence tests are normal or above, but children who have been malnourished are often plagued with attention disorders and impulsive behavior.

Without intervention, the cycle of malnutrition, poverty, and limited cognitive development will be perpetuated. Although current theories and research that malnutrition causes intellectual impairment are controversial and have not been definitely proven, the scientific indications that adequate nutrition not only assures normal brain development but can even restore and reverse

Necessary Amino Acids:
- Arginine releases growth hormone
- Glycine calms
- Histidine stimulates brain growth
- Isoleucine fights mental retardation
- Methionine decreases stress
- Taurine supports memory
- Tyrosine improves intelligence
- Valine strengthens the mind and thoughts

damage should be seriously considered. Malnutrition is a critical social, political, and humanitarian concern, and the detrimental effects of nutritional deprivation can be countered with vitamin- and mineral-rich diets to help every child reach his or her full genetic potential.

MENUS FROM CONCEPTION TO ADOLESCENCE

Each human infant is born with ten billion neurons in the fetal brain. No additional neurons are produced after birth. Nutritionists and physicians encourage women planning pregnancies to realize that their nutritional habits will influence their future children. Everything the mother eats and drinks affects the fetus in her womb. Before pregnancy, women are urged to consume folic acids and vitamins. During pregnancy, nutrients are vital to embryonic development.

Amino acids are necessary for forming fetal brains, which need food to grow billions of cells. In particular, the glial-cell complex, which provides brain power, needs nutritional energy. Protein is also crucial, because it is the component of neurons, the basic brain cell. Vitamin B-6 is important during the formation of the central nervous system and in brain development, as well as long-chain essential fatty acids for growth of neural membranes. Adequate fetal nutrition assures the normal biochemical creation and development of axons (cell message transmitters), dendrites (cell message receivers), and neurotransmitters (the catalysts for messages).

This nutritional bond between mother and child continues after birth. In the 1980's, Dr. Jean-Pierre Changeux, a neurobiologist at the Collège de France, Paris, was one of the first researchers to note that newborn brain cells organize from a fetal mass into the organ with which we are familiar. Components of the brain especially tied to intelligence—the glial-cell complex, dendrites, and neurotransmitters—expand, requiring glucose, proteins, fats, cholesterol, vitamins, and minerals to thrive.

Children undergo their fastest growth before the age of five, when they are most reliant on care givers. They depend on these people to provide them with essential foods and nurturing for development. Nutritionists adamantly promote breast-feeding for infants and young toddlers. Considering human breast milk the best nutrient for children, scientists have analyzed its nutritional content and stated that breast milk optimizes mental development in children. Some researchers even claim that breast-fed children score higher on intelligence tests.

Nutritionists speculate that diets enriched with vitamins, minerals, and other crucial nutrients promote intellectual development and can even restore lost cognitive ability. ▼

Nutritionists also stress that the brain needs substances it cannot manufacture. The brain receives nutrition from food carried to cells through the bloodstream. Metabolism physiologically provides nutrients to the brain and the central nervous system; these nutrients are important for control and coordination of the body.

Nutrition and digestive chemical processes provide energy to power the body and brain. Amino acids, minerals, and fatty acids maintain neurons in the brain. Numerous amino acids perform other tasks: Arginine releases growth hormone; glycine is calming; histidine encourages brain growth; isoleucine fights mental retardation; methionine resists stress; taurine strengthens memory; tyrosine improves intelligence; and valine reinforces the mind and thoughts.

Proteins are broken down into amino acids, which are then used to make needed proteins in body cells for chemical processes and structures. If insufficient calories have been consumed, however, proteins are utilized for energy, not for restoring the body. Researchers now know that the consumption of supplements will also reinforce the body. Vitamins and minerals, including iron and iodine, aid proteins to strengthen vision, grow bones and teeth, fight infections in the central nervous system, and transport oxygen to tissues in hemoglobin. Nutrition experts urge parents and children to eat plentiful servings of protein, vitamins, and minerals and sufficient calories, recommending diets of vegetables, fruits, enriched breads, pasta, rice, lean meat, poultry, fish, beans, milk, and cheese.

Although Francine and Harold Prince's book, *Feed Your Kids Bright*, was published in 1987, its main points resemble current research. They promote sound childhood nutrition from conception to adolescence to nurture brain growth and performance. Suggesting that an enriched diet can raise an IQ score by as much as thirty-five points, the Princes also claim that nutritious diets can battle hyperactivity and help children with learning and mental disorders. They emphasize that vitamin and mineral supplements can reverse symptoms of brain damage and help slow learners. They insist that parents should eliminate "brain-harmful foods" such as sugar and additives, from children's diets. Junk food, a teenage staple, lacks the minerals and vitamins that growing bodies crave. These foods and their ingredients harm brains and bodies, reacting hostilely with cells and tissues and impeding chemical functions. In particular, salt, sodium compounds, saturated fats, chemical colorings, flavorings, and preservatives impede intellectual growth. Full of empty calories, like alcohol, junk and fast food unfortunately fuel many children.

Some school lunch programs have removed these non-nutritious foods from menus; students' scores increased after eating improved diets, including morning meals provided by the National School Breakfast Program. Passive parents who do not insist on investing time and money for adequate nutrition cause much of the malnutrition among children. Also, teenaged mothers lacking sufficient nutrition give birth to infants at risk of mental deprivation.

Additional risks to mental development tied to nutrition include eating disorders, such as anorexia nervosa and bulimia. In these syndromes, victims view food emotionally as an enemy, stripping themselves of vital nutrients through purging or starving. The American cul-

Scores on intelligence tests are normal or above, but children who have been malnourished ar often plagued with attention disorders and impulsive behavior.

ture's emphasis on body image and its association of beauty with extreme thinness have resulted in this different form of malnutrition among an affluent populace. Internationally, malnutrition ravages poorer populations, in which almost half of infant mortalities are due to starvation.

FEEDING A STRONGER, SMARTER WORLD

Nutritionists agree that the best diet to maintain mental vigor consists of healthy foods with ample fiber and nutrients. Unfortunately, in developing countries, many micronutrients, such as vitamin A, iodine, and iron, are in short supply, causing detrimental long-term effects. In 1993, a World Bank report, "Best Practices in Addressing Micronutrient Malnutrition," estimated that two billion people worldwide suffer from lack of these nutrients. The report warned, "When moderate or severe deficiencies coincide with critical developmental stages, they can cause prolonged or permanent dysfunction."

Malnutrition is a critical social, political, and humanitarian concern, and the detrimental effects of nutritional deprivation can be countered with vitamin- and mineral-rich diets to help every child reach his or her full genetic potential. ▼

The report noted that iodine deprivation could cause retardation, neurological problems, and deafness; lack of vitamin A could result in blindness and low birth weights; and absence of iron could weaken immune systems and alter motor skills. Calculating a minimum financial loss of $1 billion annually (based on lost wages, lost time learning, and lost lives), the report outlined solutions. Iron, vitamins, and iodine should be distributed and people educated about their benefits and foods they should eat.

Cultural and political values, however, often interfere with such instructional programs. Many societies believe pregnant women should resist weight gain and not eat, denying themselves and their unborn children of nutrients. Also, even though nutritious foods are available and funding provided, many people make poor food choices. Moreover, some food-processing procedures strip produce of vitamins and minerals necessary in daily diets

according to the Recommended Dietary Allowances by the Food and Nutrition Board, National Academy of Sciences-National Research Council.

At the 1990 Summit for Children, 1991 Ending Hidden Hunger Conference, and 1992 International Conference on Nutrition, goals were set for micronutrients to be available to every child by the year 2000. A February, 1996, *Scientific American* article, "Malnutrition, Poverty, and Intellectual Development," written by J. Larry Brown, director of the Tufts University Center on Hunger, Poverty, and Nutrition Policy, and Ernesto Pollitt, of the School of Medicine, University of California, Davis, reiterates the need for protein in childhood diets. They stress the strengthening of our world society through the proper nutritional investment in each person on earth.

Some school lunch programs have removed these non-nutritious foods from menus; students' scores increased after eating improved diets, including morning meals provided by the National School Breakfast Program.

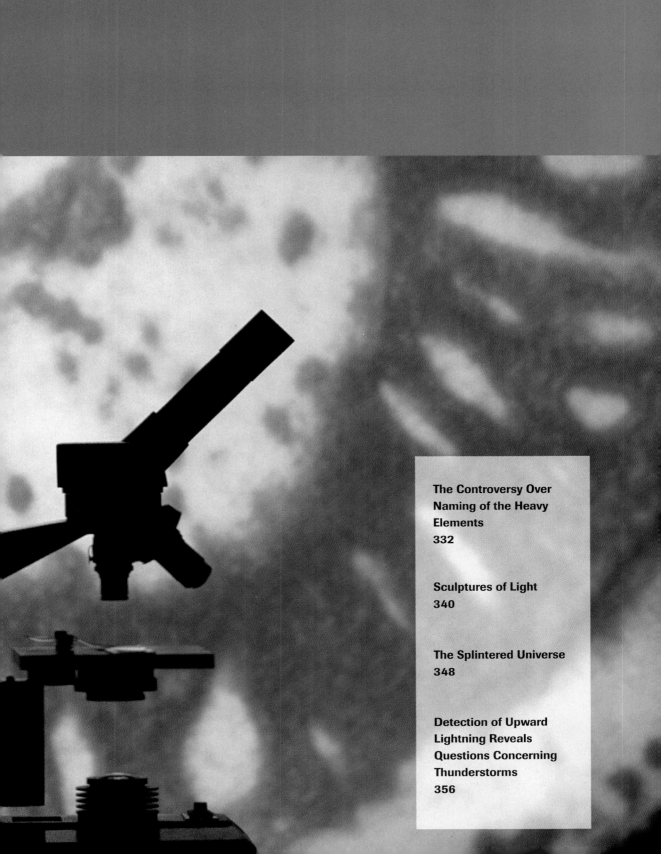

The Controversy Over Naming of the Heavy Elements

JOHN R. PHILLIPS

B y the 1940's, the chemists' periodic table contained 92 different elements, arranged in order of their increasing atomic numbers. The atomic number of an element does not merely locate it in the periodic table; it also denotes the number of positively charged protons and negatively charged electrons in the atom. The protons, together with uncharged particles called neutrons, are concentrated in a tiny region of unimaginably large density called the atomic nucleus. The number of neutrons plus protons is called the mass number. Most elements consist of several varieties ("isotopes") with different mass numbers but the same atomic number. The electrons orbit around the nucleus, forming a diffuse cloud of negative charge, and electron clouds on neighboring atoms interact to produce the characteristic chemical properties that are associated with each element. Chemical reactions—even explosions or fires—do not involve enough energy to alter atomic nuclei. Substances can be changed into other substances, but only by rearranging the patterns of their atoms, not by altering the atoms themselves.

Marie Curie [Curium].

CHANGING ONE ELEMENT INTO ANOTHER

Elements toward the end of the periodic table, with atomic numbers greater than 83, exhibit natural radioactive decay. Particles such as helium nuclei (called alpha particles) or electrons are emitted by the element, and a new element is formed. This process is known as transmutation: conversion of one element into another. Radium emits alpha particles and decays eventually into lead. Alpha particles can be used to produce artificial transmutation, as demonstrated by Ernest Rutherford in 1919, in an experiment in which nitrogen nuclei reacted with alpha particles to produce an isotope of oxygen.

Opposite page: Glenn Seaborg points out seaborgium on the periodic table of elements.

Albert Einstein [Einsteinium].

Enrico Fermi [Fermium].

Cylde Thombaugh [Plutonium].

Transmutation reactions also occur when uncharged neutrons are captured by atomic nuclei, producing neutron-rich species that can then decay by emission of an electron to form an element of increased atomic number. Nuclear fission, or the splitting of the nucleus into roughly equal fragments, can occur during neutron bombardment of uranium. Controlled fission reactions, first demonstrated in 1942, were then used as powerful neutron sources, enabling large-scale transmutation of uranium into elements with atomic numbers greater than 92: the "transuranium" elements. By 1944, four transuranium elements had been synthesized: neptunium, plutonium, americium, and curium. Names for the new elements were suggested by the discoverers and officially adopted by the International Union of Pure and Applied Chemistry (IUPAC).

After the end of World War II, the Lawrence Radiation Laboratory at Berkeley, California, became a world leader in isolating and characterizating new elements. During the period 1945-1958, the next six elements after curium were added to the periodic table: berkelium, californium, einsteinium, fermium, and mendelevium (atomic number 101). The same time period saw the emergence of the Soviet Union as a nuclear power and a serious competitor with the United States in basic nuclear research, including element synthesis. The most prominent Soviet (Russian) laboratory was at the Joint Institute for Nuclear Research in Dubna, outside Moscow, now called the Flerov Laboratory for Nuclear Reactions (FLNR).

WHY SYNTHESIZE NEW ELEMENTS?

The effort to synthesize new elements was originally motivated by the need to develop atomic weapons. Plutonium, for example, is an element that readily undergoes nuclear fission, with energy as a by-product. Thousands of tons of plutonium were made and used for the construction of nuclear warheads. New elements after plutonium were available in smaller quantities and tended to have uses related to their emissions of radiation. Thus californium (mass 252 isotope) can be used as a portable neutron source for doing neutron activation analysis in remote locations. The transfermium elements are so rare that practical uses are hard to conceive, but scientific interest now motivates further extension of the periodic table.

Nuclear scientists seek fundamental information about the structure of the nucleus and the origin and nature of its stability. The nuclear shell theory, proposed in 1950, provides the framework for current studies. In this model, neutrons and protons occupy energy levels that can accommodate definite numbers of particles, in pairs. Filled shells are particularly stable. Calculations based on the shell model are used to predict the stability of new elements with respect to spontaneous fission and other decay schemes. A particularly tantalizing prediction is the "island of stability" concept. Super-heavy elements around atomic number 114 may be much more stable than the immediately preceding elements. By pushing forward into discovery of these super-heavy elements, researchers can test the shell theory and if necessary modify it.

Mercury is a heavy silver-white metallic element.

Chemists are always eager to compare groups of elements and examine the systematic changes in chemical properties that occur. The heavy elements are especially interesting in light of relativistic effects that can stabilize oxidation states not seen with lighter elements in the same group. The study of new synthetic elements can help to clarify these effects.

Up through mendelevium (atomic number 101), the new elements were made by incrementing atomic numbers one unit at a time. As each element was discovered, atoms of it were accumulated until enough were available to use as a target for bombardment by small particles such as neutrons or alpha particles. This strategy got progressively more difficult to implement as succeeding elements became rarer and shorter-lived. In the quest for elements 102 and beyond, it proved more advantageous to use larger ions to bombard smaller (and more plentiful) target atoms. Thus element 102 was sought through bombardment of curium (atomic number 96) with ions of carbon (atomic number 6).

Dmitiri Mendeleev [Mendelevium].

DISPUTES ARISE

In 1959, the first evidence was obtained for element 102, for which the name nobelium was suggested by the

Alfred Nobel [Nobelium].

E.O. Lawrence [Lawrencium].

Ernest Rutherford [Rutherfordium].

discoverers and soon accepted by IUPAC. The first work unfortunately could not be repeated, and conflicting claims of priority were made by the Soviet group at Dubna and the group at Berkeley. The Soviets proposed the name joliotium (after Pierre and Irène Joliot), but the tide of common usage flowed against them. Nobelium was universally accepted as the name, even though IUPAC eventually concluded that priority belonged to the Dubna group. The principle of the discoverer's having the right to name the element then seemed compromised.

The nobelium work at Berkeley was done using a new device called HILAC (Heavy Ion Linear Accelerator), which permitted the use of heavier bombarding ions and improved detection systems for the reaction products. The Dubna group continued to use a cyclotron.

When it came to element 103, Berkeley and Dubna made conflicting claims of priority, with the Americans suggesting the name lawrencium for E. O. Lawrence, inventor of the cyclotron and nuclear science pioneer at Berkeley. The Dubna group preferred the name rutherfordium, for Ernest Rutherford, discoverer of the nucleus, but IUPAC ruled in favor of lawrencium, although stating that both groups shared priority of discovery. At Berkeley, the reaction of californium (atomic number 98) with ions of boron (atomic number 5) yielded lawrencium. A special system was used for trapping the recoil products from the californium target on a moving metalized tape that carried them rapidly to detectors.

ENTERING THE FOURTH TRANSITION SERIES

With lawrencium came an important milestone: Element 103 was the last of fourteen elements in the periodic table constituting the actinide series, so called because it begins with actinium, element 89. These elements resemble one another chemically and have closely related electron configurations. Element 104 was expected to be the first element in the fourth transition series, and therefore to resemble its congener hafnium (element 72). Element 104 began to be referred to as eka-hafnium ("beyond hafnium"). This type of naming followed the usage of Dmitri Mendeleef, the Russian chemist who in 1871 proposed a periodic table predicting elements 31 and 32, which he called eka-aluminum and eka-silicon (now known as gallium and germanium).

As early as 1964, the Dubna group reported detection of what they considered to be a very short-lived isotope of element 104. They bombarded a plutonium target (atomic number 94) with ions of neon (atomic number 10). Later experiments at Dubna and elsewhere failed to confirm the reported half-life of the product, which the Soviets decided to call kurchatovium after Igor V. Kurchatov, leader of the Russian nuclear weapons program. At Berkeley, the Soviet work was considered inconclusive, local work being deemed more reliable. The Americans had used the reaction of californium (atomic number 98) with ions of carbon (atomic number 6) and suggested the name rutherfordium for element 104. At this point, everyone involved agreed that Rutherford should be honored with an element but disagreed on who should decide which element it would be.

Element 105 (isotope of mass 260) was produced at Berkeley in 1970 and identified by its emission of alpha particles, forming known daughter species. The successful experiment was done using HILAC to accelerate ions of nitrogen (atomic number 7) aimed at a target of californium (atomic number 98). The name hahnium was suggested, after German nuclear chemist Otto Hahn. The Dubna group claimed to have made an earlier discovery of an element 105 isotope that decayed by spontaneous fission. This work produced one atom of the new element after twenty hours of irradiation of americium (atomic number 95) by a beam of neon (atomic number 10) ions. The name nielsbohrium was put forth by Dubna for element 105, after the Danish Nobel laureate Niels Bohr.

Niels Bohr [Nielsbohrium].

Evidence for element 106 was obtained nearly simultaneously by the American group at Berkeley and the Dubna group in 1974. No name was suggested by either group. Both experiments involved using ion beams to bombard heavy metal targets. In Berkeley, ionized oxygen (mass 18 isotope) reacted with californium (mass 249 isotope) to make a mass 263 isotope of element 106. The Dubna group used a lead (atomic number 82) target bombarded with ions of chromium (atomic number 24). The target was mounted on a disk that rotated, carrying the irradiated target out of the ion beam and into a bank of detectors — thus enabling more rapid detection of the evanescent reaction products. The lead target and relatively heavy chromium ions were used in order to produce a form of element 106 that would be stabler toward spontaneous fission, and more certainly identifiable.

[Table 1]

Atomic No.	Name
104	unnilquadium
105	unnilpentium
106	unnilhexium
107	unnilseptium
108	unniloctium
109	unnilenium

[Table 2]

Atomic No.	Name (IUPAC)	Name (ACS)
101	Mendelevium	Mendelevium
102	Nobelium	Nobelium
103	Lawrencium	Lawrencium
104	Dubnium	Rutherfordium
105	Joliotium	Hahnium
106	Rutherfordium	Seaborgium
107	Bohrium	Nielsbohrium
108	Hahnium	Hassium
109	Meitnerium	Meitnerium

By March, 1997, the IUPAC had introduced a revised list of names for elements 104-109 which represented a compromise with the ACS:

Atomic No.	Name
104	Rutherfordium
105	Dubnium
106	Seaborgium
107	Bohrium
108	Hassium
109	Meitnerium

It appears likely that these names will be ratified by all concerned sometime late in 1997. The three most recently discovered elements (atomic numbers 110, 111 and 112) remain unnamed.

INTERNATIONAL COMMITTEES ATTEMPT TO MEDIATE

With the increasing number of disputes between Berkeley and Dubna, the need for mediation became apparent. An unsuccessful attempt was made by the IUPAC and IUPAP (International Union of Pure and Applied Physics) to organize a committee to resolve the controversies. Although the committee was established in 1974, it never met, and another committee was not formed until 1986.

In 1977, a system of naming new elements was proposed that allowed the generation of systematic names by simple rules starting from the atomic number. This approach resulted in cumbersome names that were not aesthetically pleasing but that could be used immediately while questions of priority were being sorted out. Examples of such names include those shown in Table 1. These names did not attract widespread usage among researchers but made their appearance in some university textbooks, and the practice of giving nonsystematic names to new elements continued.

GSI ENTERS THE FRAY

In the search for element 107, German workers at the Gesellschaft für Schwerionenforschung (Society for Heavy Ion Research, or GSI) at Darmstadt apparently succeeded first in 1981. Earlier work at Dubna must be regarded as inconclusive. GSI combined its Universal Linear Accelerator (UNILAC) with a special detection system using a velocity selector called SHIP (Separator for Heavy Ion Reaction Products). This apparatus, combined with the so-called cold fusion technique (use of stable target elements such as lead bombarded with relatively heavy ions), has allowed the discovery at GSI of single atoms of elements with atomic numbers up to 112.

ANOTHER INTERNATIONAL COMMITTEE

In 1986, IUPAC and its physics counterpart IUPAP formed a committee called the Transfermium Working Group (TWG) to consider conflicting claims of priority and to suggest criteria that would have to be satisfied before the discovery of a new element could be recognized. The IUPAC Commission on Nomenclature of Inorganic Chemistry would have the responsibility for naming transfermium elements. After a thorough study of the discovery profiles of elements 101-109 and solicitation of responses from Dubna, Berkeley, and Darmstadt, TWG and IUPAC recommended names for the elements in 1994.

The name for element 109 honored Lise Meitner, co-discoverer of fission with Otto Hahn. The originally suggested "nielsbohrium" for element 107 was changed for consistency with other names. The attempts of TWG to adjudicate claims of priority of discovery met great criticism from scientists at Berkeley and, to a lesser extent, from Dubna and GSI. The Americans believed that TWG, by not having a nuclear chemist in its ranks, had failed to give proper consideration to the chemical work done at Berkeley. The American Chemical Society (ACS) formed a committee to consider names for the elements and produced the alternative slate shown in Table 1. The ACS chose to forsake Otto Hahn in favor of Hassium for element 108, after the Latin name for the province of Hesse, where GSI is located. Also, the ACS broke with tradition by honoring Glenn T. Seaborg with the name seaborgium for element 106, the first time a living person had been so honored. The two alternative slates of names are shown in Table 2.

By March, 1997, the IUPAC had introduced a revised list of names for elements 104-109 which represented a compromise with the ACS (see Table 3). It appears likely that these names will be ratified by all concerned sometime late in 1997. The three most recently discovered elements (atomic numbers 110, 111, and 112) remain unnamed.

Lise Meitner [Meitnerium].

[Table 3]
Individuals Honored by an Element

Marie Curie (1867-1934)

Albert Einstein (1879-1955)

Enrico Fermi (1901-1954)

Alfred Nobel (1833-1896)

Dmitri Mendeleef (1834-1907)

E.O. Lawrence (1901-1958)

Ernest Rutherford (1871-1937)

Niels Bohr (1885-1962)

Lise Meitner (1878-1968)

Glenn T. Seaborg (1912-)

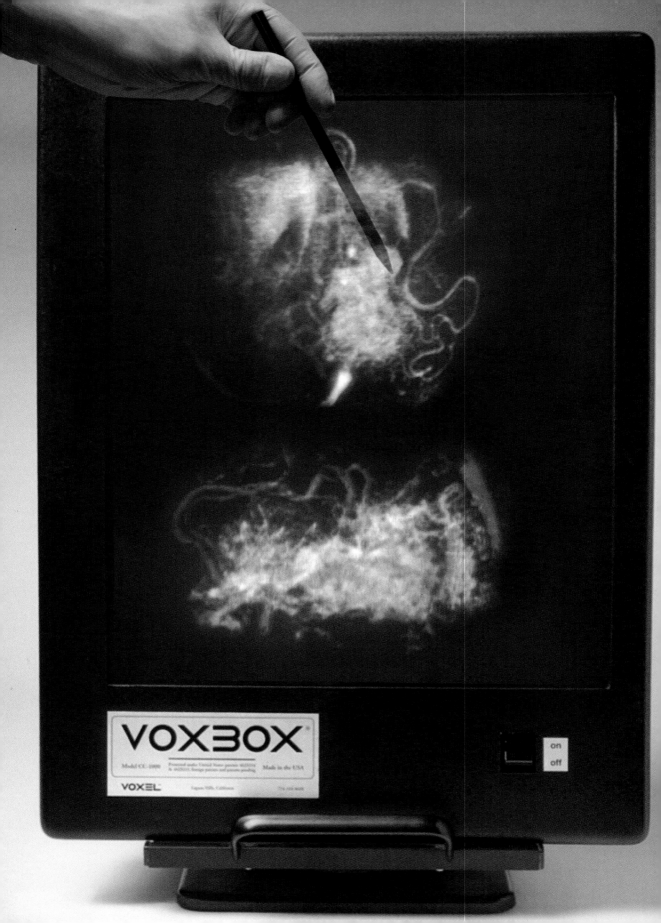

Sculptures of Light

A new three-dimensional display turns on the imagination.

CORINNA WU

There's something deeply satisfying about wresting a three-dimensional image from a two-dimensional picture. Witness the recent popularity of computer-generated "Magic Eye" art: Wherever one of these pictures hangs, throngs of people gather around to stare, squint, and cross their eyes in an attempt to make the concealed 3-D form leap out.

For those 3-D pictures, looking for the images is part of the fun. For 3-D techniques being developed for medical imaging, however, the fewer ocular and mental acrobatics required, the better. Existing approaches, such as computer images that can be rotated at will, work well in many cases, but they often give only a limited viewing angle or require clumsy headgear. Their fundamental drawback is that they are still essentially flat.

Recently, a group of researchers took a major step toward true 3-D visualization. Elizabeth Downing of 3D Technology Laboratories in Mountain View, Calif., and her colleagues have designed a three-color, 3-D display that generates what appear to be solid objects rather than creating an optical illusion on a computer screen. They describe their creation in the Aug. 30 *Science*.

Though still a few years away from practical use, the invention created a flurry of excitement among scientists who foresee its potential applications. "It's an approach which is unique in what it can deliver and the way it goes about displaying information," says study coauthor Roger Macfarlane, a physicist at IBM Almaden Research Center in San Jose, Calif.

The device is the culmination of 8 years' work by Downing while studying mechanical engineering at Stanford University, and now she's determined to see her display through to the marketplace.

The prototype display consists of six small lasers

Opposite page: The holographic lightbox, Voxbox ®, generates a special spectrum of light which interacts with the information on the film to produce the Voxgram.

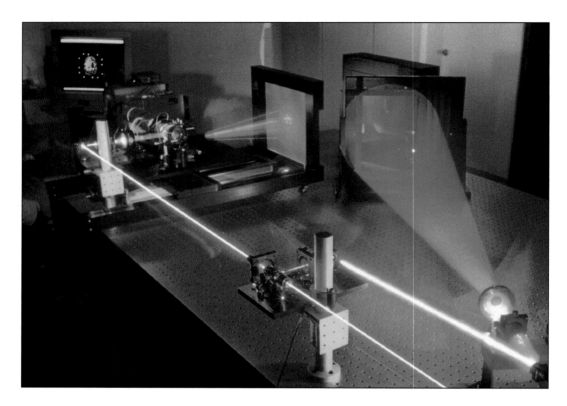

Digital Holography System: provides hospitals the capability of producing 14" x 17" holograms, called Voxgrams ®, of their own clinical data in-house.

aimed at a block of fluorescent fluoride glass about the size of a sugar cube. At points where the lasers intersect within the glass, the fluorescence they provoke traces out shapes and patterns. During one demonstration, a red loop and green and blue squares glow from the interior of the cube.

The ghostly, transparent images can be viewed from any angle, Downing says, which is an improvement on available imaging technologies. One, for example, renders 3-D objects on a computer screen through realistic lighting effects and shading. "It's very sophisticated and actually pretty good for most things," she says, but the illusion changes if a viewer's head moves. This problem of a restricted viewing angle also plagues other techniques, such as stereoscopic displays.

In principle, Downing's display works much like a television screen, which is coated with phosphorescent chemicals that glow when scanned by an electron beam. Downing sandwiched together three layers of glass to form the cube, each layer doped with a rare earth ion that provides one of three colors: red (praseodymium), green (erbium), or blue (thulium).

Each ion fluoresces only when excited by light of two different wavelengths, a process called upconversion. Two excitation photons are converted up to emit a single photon of combined energy, Macfarlane explains. One laser beam enters the sample and excites an ion to a higher energy level. When the other beam hits the ion, it gets kicked up to an even higher energy. Only then does the ion fluoresce, as it falls back to the ground state and emits light of a specific wavelength.

Moving the two beams traces out a 3-D shape, in the same way that twisting the two knobs of an Etch-A-Sketch toy draws an outline. The lasers redraw the image 30 to 100 times a second, a rate that refreshes the display fast enough for the eye to see a static figure. The spot, or voxel (from volume-pixel), where the lasers cross is only about 100 micrometers in diameter.

Downing assembled the display on a shoestring budget, spending a lot of time "begging for equipment and sometimes stealing it," she jokes. John Ralston of SDL Corp. in San Jose, also a coauthor of the Science article, gave her the lasers she needed. Macfarlane steered her toward the fluoride glass, which had been invented by French scientists Michel Poulain, Marceau Poulain, and Jacques Lucas.

Although she would have preferred buying it, she says, Downing ended up making the glass herself, experimenting with different proportions of ingredients to optimize the fluorescence.

Fine-tuning the fluorescence proved tricky. If the concentration of rare earth ions in the glass was too low, the material didn't glow enough. If the concentration was too high, the ions would reabsorb the emitted light, either quenching the fluorescence or causing the material to glow outside of the targeted voxels.

Downing likens the glass-making process to baking chocolate chip cookies. "If there aren't enough chips, the cookies don't taste good. But if there are too many, that doesn't work either."

One immediate goal of the researchers is to get erbium to do double duty by glowing both red and green. The fewer elements needed, the simpler the ultimate display design. In that scheme, as before, one laser would push erbium to the first energy level. The wavelength of the second laser excitation would determine the resulting

Each ion fluoresces only when excited by light of two different wavelengths, a process called upconversion.

color. "If you don't climb so high, you get red light. If you climb higher, you get green light," Macfarlane explains.

They need to fine-tune the excitation wavelength and perhaps tweak the composition of the glass to get the greatest efficiency for each color, Macfarlane says. Eventually, they will also have to increase the size of the glass block to make the technique practical.

Downing conceived of the idea for the 3-D display on June 21, 1988, according to an entry in her notebook. She later learned that similar work had been done nearly 20 years earlier. In the early 1970s, J.D. Lewis, C.M. Verber, and R.B. McGhee, then at Battelle Laboratories in Columbus, Ohio, used xenon lamps to excite an erbium-doped crystal but produced only a faint glow.

Downing's success became possible only through recent advances in laser technology and materials. The Battelle scientists were ahead of their time, she says.

Though still a long way from being able to display that kind of information, the new technology may allow doctors to see, for example, heart valves working or blood flowing in the brain.

When Downing started her project, the equipment available to her was barely adequate. Just 3 years ago, she and her colleagues had to rely on several pitifully inefficient, 5-foot-long lasers to stimulate the glass. Now, they use compact solid-state lasers similar to the ones found in compact disc players. These lasers can be bought in a wide range of wavelengths and give exceptionally good output. The prototype display fits on a 1-foot-square breadboard. "You can literally hold it in your hand," Macfarlane says.

Other scientists in the imaging field are impressed. Guy A. Marlor of West End Partners Imaging in Fremont, Calif., says he saw her demonstrate the system. "I was totally fascinated," he says.

The technology has caught the fancy of the medical imaging community because of its potential for displaying data from computerized tomography (CT) scans, ultrasound, and magnetic resonance images (MRI) in three dimensions. At present, these techniques, for all their

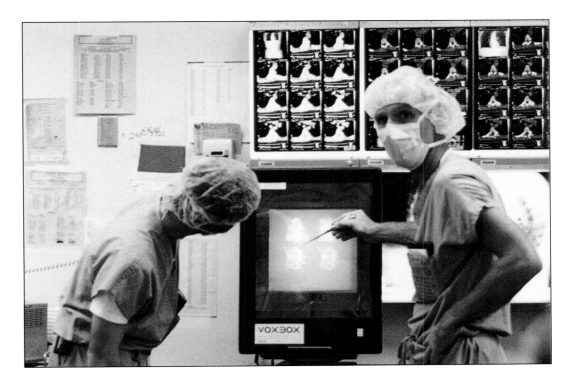

Voxgrams are used in the operating room to assist in surgical procedures.

detail, show only flat slices of very solid human bodies. Doctors must mentally reassemble the slices to get a coherent picture of the body part.

Though still a long way from being able to display that kind of information, the new technology may allow doctors to see, for example, heart valves working or blood flowing in the brain, Marlor says.

Many groups are now experimenting with ways of displaying reassembled data slices on a computer screen, but one of the 3-D methods that has already penetrated the medical imaging market is digital holography, developed by Voxel of Laguna Hills, Calif. Exposing holographic film to multiple CT, MRI, or ultrasound scans builds up a composite image. The resulting hologram—a floating "sculpture of light"—can be viewed through a special light box.

Surgeons can insert instruments into the hologram to gauge distances, and they can overlay holograms of different tissues—a network of blood vessels over a tumor, for example—to see how they relate. The technique can't portray movement within the body, however.

Digital holography is especially valuable for seeing abnormalities in the spine and the brain, says William

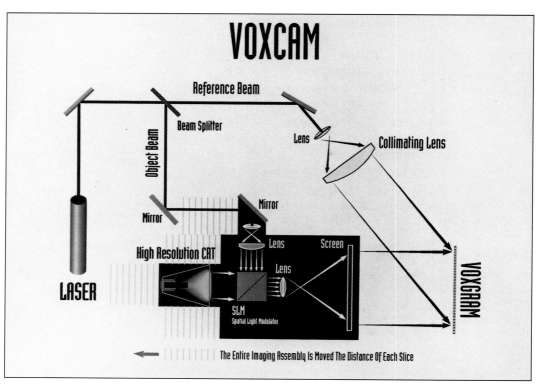

VOXCAM

Reference Beam

Beam Splitter

Object Beam

Lens

Collimating Lens

Mirror

Mirror

High Resolution CRT

Lens

Screen

Lens

LASER

SLM
Spatial Light Modulator

VOXGRAM

The Entire Imaging Assembly Is Moved The Distance Of Each Slice

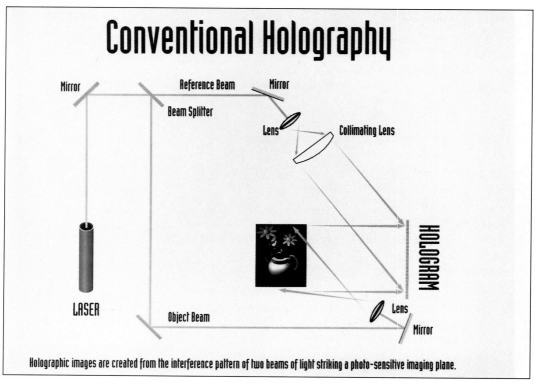

Conventional Holography

Mirror

Reference Beam

Mirror

Beam Splitter

Lens

Collimating Lens

LASER

Object Beam

Lens

Mirror

HOLOGRAM

Holographic images are created from the interference pattern of two beams of light striking a photo-sensitive imaging plane.

Orrison, director of the New Mexico Institute of Neuroimaging in Albuquerque. After his first look at a hologram, he says, the 20 years he has spent studying neuroanatomy became instantly clear. "If a picture is worth a thousand words, then a hologram is worth a million," he says.

For the past 2 years, the institute has sent MRI and CT data to Voxel for processing. The first on-site camera, which can take and develop such digital holograms in less than half an hour, is scheduled to be installed there this month.

All 3-D technologies have their advantages and disadvantages, says Raymond A. Schulz, a spokesman for Voxel. Downing's technology is "done in a solid cube, so it's not a piece of film you can transport from one place to the other," he says. "You can't stick a surgical screw in it." But it has the potential to show motion where holography does not, he adds.

"She's got a lot of technical hurdles to overcome yet, but it's certainly very interesting."

The big limitation of using this technique for medical imaging, Downing and Macfarlane acknowledge, will be the time it takes to transfer the enormous amount of data contained in multiple scans to the display. "You know how long it takes to write graphics on a computer screen in 2-D," Macfarlane says. "There's an awful lot of picture elements involved when you add a third dimension." Data compression techniques and arrays of lasers, each responsible for scanning smaller areas of the glass, might reduce the burden.

Downing estimates that 3D Technology Laboratories is 4 or 5 years away from having a salable product. "Our goal is to push a new technology into the marketplace," she says. "We want this in hospitals, schools, anywhere it can help engineers solve problems."

For now, though, the next step is simply to get the device to produce more complicated figures: the Eiffel Tower, a jumping frog, and Herbie the Love Bug, to name a few on the drawing board.

Those further investigations are temporarily on hold, however. Downing has gotten so much interest in the technology that she has been spending most of her time on the phone talking to reporters and potential investors rather than in the lab.

The big limitation of using this technique for medical imaging, Downing and Macfarlane acknowledge, will be the time it takes to transfer the enormous amount of data contained in multiple scans to the display.

The Splintered Universe

Physicists model the early universe in droplets of superfluid helium.

DAN VERGANO

I f there were a cosmic complaints department that honored warranties on the Big Bang, the universe would have been returned shortly after it exploded into existence. Most physicists believe that the primordial fireball shuddered through several breakdowns within the very first moments of time. These collapses may have splintered the young universe, riddling it with defects.

One might argue that this is just the sort of thing that discourages big consumer purchases, but some cosmologists contend we're lucky to have had cracks in creation. Without matter clumping together in the wake of these cosmic defects, no stars would have formed (SN: 3/24/90, p. 184). Without stars, there would have been no Earth. No Earth, no earthlings.

A neat theory, but proving it presents a large obstacle, says one of its originators, Thomas W.B. Kibble of Imperial College in London. "Obviously, the problem with the early universe is you can't do experiments on it."

Twelve years ago, however, one physicist proposed a novel method of modeling the early universe in the laboratory. Several teams have now applied his scheme and are drawing lessons about what may have happened immediately after the Big Bang.

Wojciech H. Zurek's idea for recreating the early universe grew out of his eavesdropping at an interdisciplinary physics meeting in 1984. "I was listening to people talk about Big Bang cosmology. I didn't understand what they were saying," recalls Zurek, a physicist at the Los Alamos (N.M.) National Laboratory.

The cosmologists were puzzling over the aftermath of the Big Bang. Following the initial explosion, they asked, why wasn't the sky paved with smoothly distributed hydrogen? How did galaxies come together in the

Opposite page: Lagoon nebula.

first place, and what herded them into grouped clusters (SN: 9/23/95, P. 202)?

Zurek read halfway through one of Kibble's papers, and he began to understand: The cosmologists were saying that as the early universe cooled, it went through phase transitions.

As a condensed-matter physicist, he had studied these phenomena. They occur when matter suddenly changes its structure because of alterations in the pressure or temperature around it, such as when water freezes into ice.

Where there are phase transitions, there are often defects. Just as cracks frequently appear in ice cubes as they form, so flaws sprang up in the early universe. According to cosmological theory, these imperfections were whirlpools of primordial matter that spun off at moments of cosmic transition. Alongside other oddly shaped blemishes, the vortices would have spanned the length of the early universe with a distorting mass whose gravity pulled nearby matter into its fast-moving trail.

VOILA, CLUMPS OF GALAXIES

Zurek didn't finish the paper. Instead, he began thinking about the way whirlpools, or vortices, spread through fluids and how to model these whirlpools in the laboratory.

Publishing his ideas in 1985, he first suggested that researchers mimic the vast emptiness of space by using a superfluid—an extremely cold liquid that lacks friction. Like the interstellar void, superfluids offer no resistance to motion (SN: 4/9/94, p. 239). A canoe paddle dipped into a superfluid pond would fail to move the boat.

Next, he suggested that when superfluid helium undergoes a phase transition to form liquid helium, vortices would spring up, just as spiraling defects erupted in the decay of the Big Bang. Physicists studying these eddies would, in essence, watch a replay of the early universe.

In 1985, a group of physicists at Los Alamos began trying Zurek's proposed experiment with liquid helium-4, a heavy isotope of the element. They found that lowering the substance to superfluid temperatures—a few degrees above absolute zero—while looking for tiny defects in the liquid was beyond their ability. When one of the group's leaders died in 1987, the effort ended.

Just as cracks frequently appear in ice cubes as they form, so flaws sprang up in the early universe.

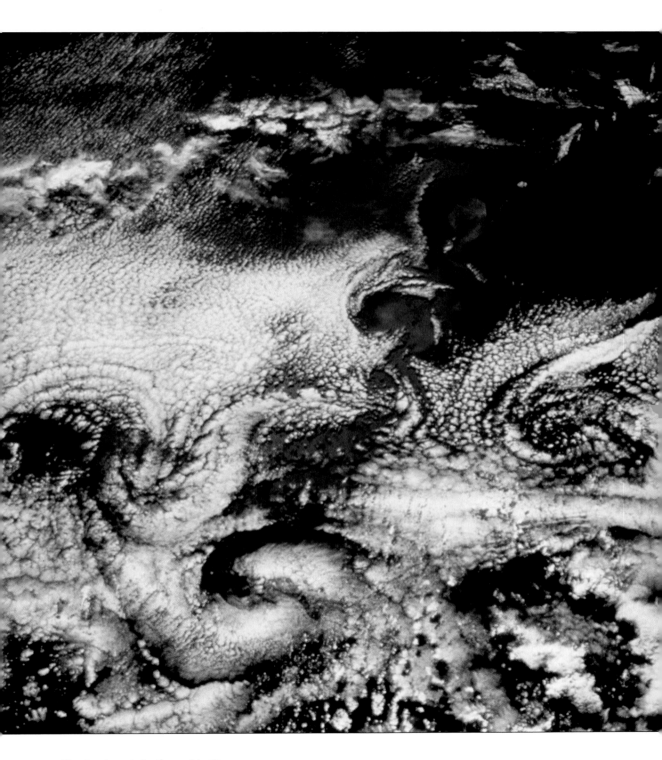

Cloud vortexes in the Canary Islands

"Since no one was doing these experiments, I thought I'd give it a go," says Bernard Yurke of Lucent Bell Laboratories in Murray Hill, N.J. (SN: 6/1/91, p. 344). In 1991, he and theorist Neil Turok of Princeton University modeled cosmic defects by using liquid crystals, the orderly liquids that line up to form numerals in digital watches.

The molecules of liquid crystals can undergo a phase transition that causes them to line up in one direction. When Yurke triggered such a transition by abruptly increasing the pressure on the liquid crystals, he observed alignments in several locations at once, all pointing in different directions. All sorts of defects sprang up at the intersections of these liquid crystal lines. Vortices whirled apart and then rejoined. Pulsating dots appeared and then annihilated one another. Curious, knotlike flaws rippled for a time and then faded.

The researchers observed more than 20 defects in the liquid crystals. "How the defects move mimics what may have happened at early times," says Yurke.

Although this experiment did not include the frictionless environment of a superfluid, it had two advantages: The vortices could be observed through a microscope rather than a nuclear magnetic resonance imaging instrument, and their phase transition took place at room temperature. "It's a marvelous idea," says Zurek, who is excited that these early tests supported at least part of his theory.

Meanwhile, Peter McClintock of the University of Lancaster in England had read Zurek's original paper and become fascinated by the idea of modeling the early universe in a superfluid. He decided against trying it "because I thought somebody is bound to do it in 6 months. And then nobody did, so I thought, perhaps we'll have a go at it," he says.

In 1994, his group finally carried out Zurek's original suggestion by using helium-4 to study analogs of cosmic defects. The physicists placed a milligram of liquid helium inside a bronze bellows cooled to $2° C$ above absolute zero. Expanding the bellows, they induced a pressure drop in the helium that caused it to shift to a superfluid state. At the same time, the investigators fired sound waves into the helium.

Unable to look directly at the invisible vortices, they relied upon distortions in the movement of the sound waves to reveal the swirls. The results verified Zurek's predictions. "We showed you get enormous defects after transition," says McClintock.

It's not so outlandish to use a drop of liquid helium to model the entire universe, McClintock explains. According to theory, cosmic defects developed 10-/34 seconds after the Big Bang sprang forth from an infinitesimally small point. "At the time we're talking about, the universe was very small — perhaps the size of a golf ball," says McClintock.

Despite the success of the experiment, superfluid helium-4 frustrated researchers because they could not peer directly at vortices. They began eyeing the other helium isotope, helium-3, whose atomic nuclei spin in such a way that the substance is readily visible to nuclear magnetic resonance imaging instruments. Experimental physicists had avoided the isotope heretofore because it turns into a superfluid at only a few tenths of a degree above absolute zero, making it very difficult to handle.

One exciting feature of helium-3 is that it absorbs neutrons, says Kibble. Working at the Helsinki University of Technology in Finland, he and physicists from Europe and the United States fired neutrons into superfluid helium-3 contained in a 5-millimeter-wide cylinder. With each heat-producing impact, small pockets of normal fluid bloomed in the frictionless reservoir. As the liquid cooled back down to superfluid status, the researchers observed cigar-shaped vortices in the remnants of the pockets.

By rotating their apparatus, the researchers lured these defects into the center of the cylinder long enough to count them. In the July 25 *Nature*, the team reported finding the same number of vortices Zurek had predicted in 1985.

That issue of Nature also contained an experiment that complemented and extended the Helsinki study. Researchers a the Center for Very Low Temperature Research in Grenoble, France, cooled superfluid helium-3 to 160 millionths of a degree above absolute zero. At this temperature, vortices stabilized as soon as they formed.

Lacking nuclear magnetic resonance imaging equipment, the second group rigged a system of sensitive wires within the superfluid and then shot a neutron of known energy into the chamber. By looking at how much energy the fluid absorbed, the physicists from Grenoble and

According to theory, cosmic defects developed 10-/34 seconds after the Big Bang sprang forth from an infinitesimally small point.

Lancaster could determine the strength of the resulting vortices. The two helium-3 experiments, like McClintock's, agreed with Zurek's prediction.

"The fact that we have three experiments in superfluids, with totally different ways of doing effectively the same thing, is nice because it's added confirmation," says Alasdair Gill of the University of Geneva, who participated in the Helsinki experiment.

Dimitri Nanopoulos, a physicist at Texas A&M University in College Station, cautions that the studies test only a model, not the actual early universe. Still, he calls the experiments "a remarkable achievement."

If cosmic defects existed just after the Big Bang, the recent studies could shed some light on them. These strange beasts would have roared through the universe as extraordinarily thin, dense strings 10-/31 meters in diameter. Each meter of their length would have weighed 1019 kilograms and had a huge gravitational pull. "If you were to have one go down the street, you'd see the houses on both sides pull in behind it at something close to the speed of light," says Gill. Such aggregation of matter in the wake of a cosmic defect's passage is what scientists speculate started the formation of galaxies.

In two of the experiments, the vortices contained viscous liquid helium, trapped at a temperature just above that of the superfluids. These results suggest that cosmic strings preserved remnants of primordial matter, seething at the high temperature of the Big Bang, long after the birth of the universe.

A competing theory of cosmology, called inflation, posits that galaxies grew out of gravitational shock waves in the expanding universe (SN: 5/8/93, p. 296). Gill believes that inflation lost some of its adherents this summer after the helium-3 experiments lent support to the cosmic defects model.

"It's getting to the stage where it seems very plausible," he says. "You obviously want to push it further—to know not just how many vortices or cosmic strings there were, but also if they are all in loops or long, straight strings. You want to know all the patterns of strings."

Astronomers are starting to study photographs of stars, searching for distinctive gravitational effects caused by cosmic strings.

To settle the argument between inflation and cosmic strings, many physicists await studies of the cosmic back-

To settle the argument between inflation and cosmic strings, many physicists await studies of the cosmic background radiation — heat left over from the Big Bang. Finding uneven radiation would argue for the cosmic defect theory. Current studies measure only slices of sky more than 10° across, not fine enough to decide the issue.

ground radiation — heat left over from the Big Bang. Finding uneven radiation would argue for the cosmic defect theory. Current studies measure only slices of sky more than 10° across, not fine enough to decide the issue.

Until physicists build instruments capable of resolving the background radiation in fine detail, they will have to content themselves with recreating the universe in liquid helium. Zurek sees a benefit to bringing together cosmology and low-temperature physics — the two fields enrich each other's perspective.

"The interesting thing is that people saw masses of vortex lines in liquid helium for years and wanted to get rid of them," says Zurek. "We only got to ask questions about them by thinking about cosmology."

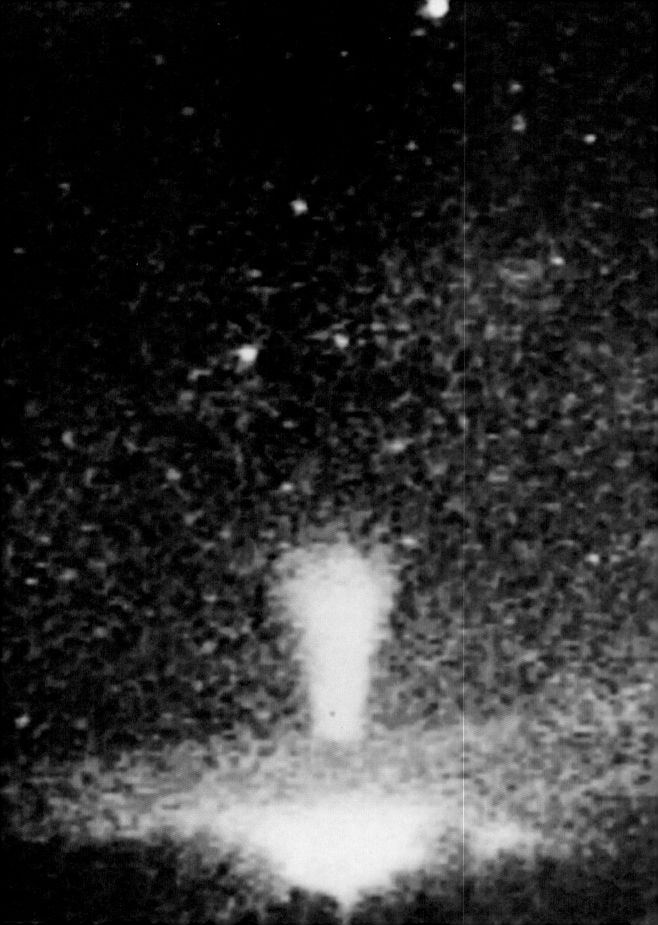

Detection of Upward Lightning
Reveals Questions Concerning Thunderstorms

CHRISTOPHER KEATING

I n 1989 researchers from the University of Minnesota in Minneapolis trained a low-light camera on thunderstorms over the Great Lakes and unknowingly set into motion a series of events that they could not have foreseen. People had been reporting for years that they had observed lightning shooting upward from the top of thunderstorms, but scientists had always scoffed at such reports for lack of evidence. That evidence, however, finally came in the conclusive form of video images of upward lightning accidentally captured by the Minnesota team. This documentation has sparked new discoveries, and controversies, concerning the nature of thunderstorms.

NEW KINDS OF LIGHTNING DETECTED

The upward lightning they observed is now referred to as sprites. Sprites are weak but massive red flashes that appear directly over thunderstorms and extend upward to about 95 kilometers (about 60 miles), lasting only a few thousandths of a second. Sprites often appear in clusters and will frequently reappear in the same area. These phenomena were then observed from the space shuttle in 1990. Sprites have been reported for years, and the historical record indicates they may have even been reported for centuries.

It is possible to see sprites by going to a region at night with little light pollution when there is a thunderstorm near the horizon. Because sprites shoot upward from the tops of the clouds, they can be seen just above the thunderstorm as a faint, brief flash of red. Because the sprites are so faint, it is important that the viewing area be as dark as possible.

Shortly after this discovery came another. Two jet aircraft operated by the National Aeronautics and Space

Opposite page: Blue jet, one type of upward lightning.

Administration (NASA) were circling an intense thunderstorm over Arkansas in 1994 while studying sprites when they observed what are now called jets. Jets are another type of "upward" lightning but are distinct from sprites. Jets are blue in color and shaped like large, narrow cones, shooting upward from the tops of thunderstorms at about 100 kilometers (62 miles) per second and reaching altitudes of 40 to 50 kilometers (25 to 30 miles).

Then, in 1995, yet another form of upward lightning was discovered. Called elves, they are immense, green, doughnut-shaped flashes that occur on the bottom of the ionosphere 100 kilometers (62 miles) up and can be up to 400 kilometers (250 miles) across.

ENERGETIC SIGNALS DETECTED IN THE ATMOSPHERE

Strange, new lightning was not the only thing detected in the upper regions of the atmosphere in recent years. In 1993 a NASA satellite designed to detect gamma-ray bursts in space instead detected isolated instances of gamma-ray bursts originating in Earth's atmosphere. Gamma rays are associated with the most energetic events in the universe, and the detection of these rays from Earth's atmosphere was very surprising. In 1996, X rays were also detected coming from Earth's atmosphere. While less powerful than gamma rays, X rays are still very energetic, and before these recent discoveries it was not expected that any event in the atmosphere would produce them or gamma rays.

Also in 1993, huge radio pulses were detected coming from the atmosphere. These radio pulses were similar to radio pulses produced by normal lightning activity but were about ten thousand times as strong. It was suspected that these events were coming from thunderstorms and probably from the upward lightning, but it could not be demonstrated at that time.

SCIENTISTS DEVELOP CONFLICTING THEORIES

This flood of newly discovered phenomena has resulted in scientists all over the world reexamining previously held theories concerning thunderstorms. Determining exactly how these phenomena form has sparked a debate in the scientific community. One theory has been developed by the team of Robert Roussel-Dupre and Yuri Taranenko, physicists at Los Alamos National Laboratories, and Alex Gurevich of Russia's Lebedev

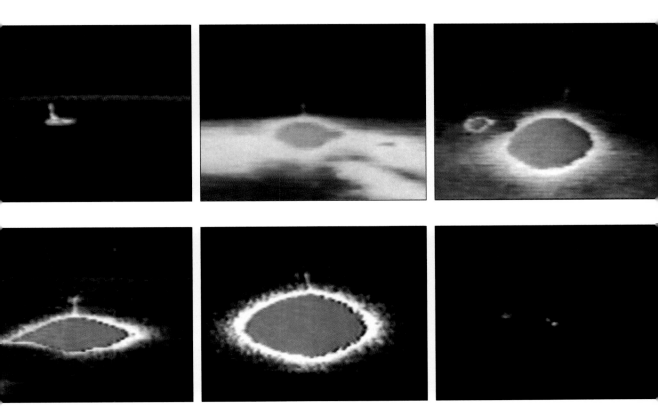

Above: Another form of upward lightning called "elves."

Institute of Physics in Moscow. They claim that sprites and jets result when electron avalanches occur in the powerful electrical fields over thunderstorms.

An electron avalanche is an event during which moving electrons acquire very high energy levels in the form of velocity. Normally, an electron would lose most of its energy when it collides with an atom, but in an electron avalanche the electrons have acquired so much energy that they lose only a small percentage of their energy in a collision. Instead, they knock loose another electron and continue to hit yet another atom. Meanwhile, the electrons that are knocked loose this way are in turn accelerated to very high energies and are able to knock loose other electrons. This phenomenon is called the "runaway breakdown model," and computer modeling of this theory has produced lightning at the same altitudes and with the same color as those observed in sprites and jets.

In this model, the initial high-energy "seed" electrons are provided when cosmic rays from space, extremely high-energy particles, collide with atoms and molecules

Above: Red sprite.

in the atmosphere. The electron avalanche can occur only when these seed electrons are found in the large electric fields that exist above thunderstorms. Further, the event must occur immediately after a normal cloud-to-ground lightning stroke.

Thunderclouds contain powerful, but oppositely charged, electric fields in their tops and bottoms. As long as both fields are present, the forces arising from these fields compete with each other and partially cancel each other out. However, when a cloud-to-ground strike occurs, one of the fields is temporarily removed, leaving only the opposite field. Free electrons that would previously experience opposite forces from the two electric fields now are accelerated by only one electric field, allowing them to attain high velocities. This field will then project them toward the ionosphere, the charged region of the atmosphere starting at altitudes of about 100 kilometers (62 miles). As they speed upward they collide with air molecules, releasing even more electrons. In a few thousandths of a second a huge flash of light will form, either towering red sprites or the cones of blue jets, depending on exactly where in the atmosphere the collisions are occurring.

A different theory has been proposed by V. P. Pasco, Umran Inan, and T. F. Bell at Stanford University. They are skeptical of the need for a cosmic-ray trigger and believe the electrical fields existing in thunderstorms are sufficient to accelerate the electrons. They also believe the environment existing in the cloud immediately after a positive cloud-to-ground strike is sufficient in itself to accelerate electrons to high enough velocities to create jets and sprites. This is called the normal air breakdown model. The cosmic-ray-induced runaway breakdown occurs, they believe, only infrequently. This model is consistent with detailed observations.

Roussel-Dupre and Taranenko argue that the air in the thunderstorm is too dense to allow this to occur. The field strength required for a normal air breakdown is ten times as large as the field strength required for the runaway breakdown. Optical measurements taken during 1996 showed that the colors of sprites and jets were the result of electron collisions with the air molecules present at that altitude. While this does not indicate which method is present in the clouds, it does show that high-energy electron collisions are responsible.

In contrast to theories about sprites and jets, there appears to be little disagreement concerning the nature of green elves. When a large upward lightning discharge occurs, in addition to the light display it also releases a large electromagnetic pulse. This pulse expands as it moves outward, acquiring something of a doughnut shape. When it strikes the ionosphere the charged particles absorb this energy and reemit it as light. Thus the ionosphere acts much like the screen on a television that is bombarded with electrons from behind.

The presence of green elves would seem to support another theory about sprites and jets that suggests that the electron breakdown is caused by large electromagnetic pulses originating within the thundercloud. This is called radio frequency breakdown.

UPWARD LIGHTNING AND GAMMA-RAY BURSTS LINKED

What about the gamma-ray bursts? Are they associated with upward lightning?

First, scientists had to demonstrate that gamma-ray bursts were originating in the area of upward lightning. The problem with demonstrating this is that initially, while sightings of upward lightning were common, they all took place over North America while the NASA satellite used to detect the gamma-ray bursts flew only over the equatorial regions. Hence, there was no proof that gamma-ray bursts could even be found in the same area as upward lightning. This question has been answered with worldwide observations that showed that jets and sprites do occur in the tropical regions. The question remained: Is upward lightning occurring in the same area as the gamma-ray bursts?

A team consisting of Inan and Steven C. Reising at Stanford and Gerald J. Fishman and John M. Horack at NASA's Marshall Space Flight Center has been able to demonstrate that gamma-ray bursts are associated with lightning-producing storms. Using detectors at Palmer Station in Antarctica, the team was able to identify electromagnetic pulses produced by large thunderstorms. These pulses are also associated with sprites. Measurements of these pulses allowed them to identify where the storms were occurring. They then compared these data with data collected by the Burst and Transient Source Experiment (BATSE), which is flying on NASA's Compton Gamma Ray Observatory in space. It was this instrument that first detected the gamma-ray bursts originating within Earth's atmosphere. This comparison allowed them to demonstrate conclusively that at least some of the atmospheric gamma-ray bursts are produced by sprites.

The next question to answer is just how does lightning produce bursts of highly energetic electromagnetic waves. These gamma-ray bursts are believed to be created at the same time as the upward lightning by the same electron breakdown. When the electrons are accelerated to high velocities, some of them avoid collisions and continue to accelerate. In this way they are able to obtain velocities near to the speed of light. When they do finally strike a molecule in the air, the resulting collision releases tremendous amounts of energy in the form of highly energetic gamma rays. This same process, at slightly lower speeds, is probably also responsible for the X-ray emissions that have been detected.

WHY SHOULD WE CARE?

Understanding these newly discovered electrical processes within our atmosphere will present a challenge to scientists for years to come. Currently, scientists believe the upward lightning is just one piece to the global electrical circuit. This circuit begins on the surface of the Sun and travels outward through space via the thin, charged plasma called the solar wind. This plasma con-

Scientists are now wondering if sprites, jets, and elves can be detected on other planets with lightning, such as Jupiter and Venus. If it can be confidently determined whether these planets have this upward lightning, we may be able to make one more comparison between our planetary system and the systems of those planets.

sists of principally free electrons and protons traveling at hundreds of kilometers per second. Earth is protected from these energetic, charged particles by the planet's magnetic field, which deflects the particles. This deflection creates a region around Earth known as the magnetosphere. However, some of the solar wind particles can follow the Earth's magnetic field lines down into the upper atmosphere in the polar regions, creating the auroral lights when they collide with molecules in the air.

This movement of charged particles within our atmosphere sets up a system of currents within the charged ionosphere, resulting in a series of currents circulating in the charged regions of our atmosphere high above our heads, the global electrical circuit. Scientists have detected a possible connection between thunderstorms at our level and the currents that exist at altitudes of more than 100 kilometers (62 miles).

The importance of these discoveries is that these currents of charged particles in our atmosphere affect such devices as electrical power systems, satellites, radio and radar systems, and even pipes in the ground (causing corrosion). With the existence of upward lightning we have to wonder what kind of connection, if any, exists between the global electrical circuit and weather. If there is a connection, understanding it may allow us to make better forecasts of certain weather events such as thunderstorms and tornadoes.

Scientists are now wondering if sprites, jets, and elves can be detected on other planets with lightning, such as Jupiter and Venus. If it can be confidently determined whether these planets have this upward lightning, we may be able to make one more comparison between our planetary system and the systems of those planets. This method, called comparative planetology, allows us to understand our own planet better by learning more about other planets. Exactly what role upward lightning plays is still not clearly understood, but inevitably more surprises will be found in the regions over thunderstorms.

Jeffry Jensen

Obituaries

Sagan

Purcell

Leakey

Khariton

Tombaugh

Salam

Auerbach, Oscar (1905, New York, New York – January 15, 1997, Livingston, New Jersey). Although he never graduated from high school, Auerbach eventually studied at New York University and received a medical degree from the New York Medical College in 1929. During the 1930's and 1940's, he worked on Staten Island at Sea View Hospital and then at Halloran Hospital. In 1952, Auerbach went to work for the Veterans Administration hospital located in East Orange, New Jersey. As a respected pathologist, he was the first medical investigator to find evidence of the link between smoking and cancer. During the 1960's, his research came to national attention when the Surgeon General's 1964 report on the dangers of smoking cited Auerbach's work. Because he was considered a very disciplined and thorough researcher, the medical community became convinced that the link between smoking and cancer was on solid scientific footing. From 1966 until his death, he taught at the New Jersey Medical School. Married twice, Auerbach is survived by two sons, a brother, a sister, and five grandchildren. The cause of death was unreported.

Calvin, Melvin (April 8, 1911, St. Paul, Minnesota – January 8, 1997, Berkeley, California). His parents emigrated from Russia and settled in St. Paul, Minnesota. He attended Michigan College of Mining and Technology and received a B.S. degree in chemistry in 1931. He continued his studies at the University of Minnesota, where he received a Ph.D. in chemistry in 1936. Calvin became an instructor at the University of California at Berkeley in 1937. He became a full professor at Berkeley in 1947. During the 1950's, Calvin began tracing the phases of photosynthesis. For his research into photosynthesis, he was awarded the 1961 Nobel Prize in Chemistry. Over the years, he received numerous honors. He published seven books, including Following the Trail of Light (1992). Calvin is survived by two daughters, a son, a sister, and six grandchildren. The cause of death was unreported.

Dicke, Robert Henry (May 6, 1916, St. Louis, Missouri – March 4, 1997, Princeton, New Jersey). After attending the University of Rochester, he transferred to Princeton University, where he received a Ph.D. in nuclear physics at the University of Rochester. During World War II, he assisted in the development of radar at the Massachusetts Institute of Technology (MIT). Dicke was one of the first scientists to support the big bang theory. He also challenged Albert Einstein's general theory of relativity. Although controversy surrounded his argument against Einstein's theory, Dicke was a highly respected physicist. He was the author of several books, including Introduction to Quantum Mechanics (1960), Theoretical Significance of Experimental Relativity (1965), and Gravitation and the Universe (1970). He is survived by his wife of fifty-five years, two sons, and a daughter. He suffered from Parkinson's disease for many years. Complications from that disease caused his death.

Herman, Robert (August 29, 1914, New York, New York – February 13, 1997, Austin, Texas). He received a B.S. degree from the City College of New York in 1935 and his M.S. degree and Ph.D. in physics from Princeton University in 1940. From 1942 to 1955, he worked at the Johns Hopkins University in its Applied Physics Laboratory. While at Johns Hopkins, he collaborated with Ralph A. Alpher on research into the big bang theory. Herman calculated that somewhere in space there were echoes of the big bang. While working at General Motors Research Laboratories during the late 1950's, he was in the forefront in constructing methods to analyze city traffic flow. He taught at various academic institutions, including, after 1979, the University of Texas at Austin. He is survived by his wife, three daughters, and two grandsons. The cause of death was lung cancer.

Huggins, Charles Brenton (September 22, 1901, Halifax, Nova Scotia, Canada – January 12, 1997, Chicago, Illinois). After receiving a B.A. from a small Nova Scotia institution, Acadia University, Huggins entered medical school at Harvard University. He was only nineteen years old when he began his medical studies. Four years later, Huggins received both his M.A. and medical degree from Harvard. In 1927, he became an instructor in surgery at the University of Chicago. Six years later, he was promoted to associate professor and became a naturalized citizen of the United States. He taught and did research at the University of Chicago until his retirement in 1969. During the 1940's, he first published findings from his research on the manipulation of hormones for the purpose of hindering the reproduction of cancerous cells. In 1966, he and virologist Peyton Rous were awarded the Nobel Prize in Physiology or Medicine. Huggins' research helped to prove a link between hormones and breast and prostate cancer. A new form of cancer therapy was developed in which hormones were used to retard the growth of the cancerous cells. The cause of death was unreported.

Khariton, Yuli B. (February 27, 1904, St. Petersburg, Russia – December 19, 1996, Sarov, Russia). Between 1926 and 1928, Khariton was a pupil of the noted British physicist Ernest Rutherford at the Cavendish Laboratory of Cambridge University. During the 1940's, he was one of the few Soviet physicists who was selected to work on the Soviet Union's atomic weapons program. With Khariton's help, a secret weapons complex was founded at Sarov (also known as Arzamas-16) in April, 1946. He served as the complex's scientific director for forty-five years. Khariton is considered one of the fathers of the Soviet nuclear weapons program. For his work on nuclear weapons, he was awarded the Soviet Union's highest civilian honor, the Hero of Socialist Labor. The cause of death was unreported.

Leakey, Mary (February 6, 1913, London, England – December 9, 1996, Nairobi, Kenya). Born Mary Douglas Nicol, she first became interested in archaeology after being taken to see European Cro-Magnon cave paintings by her father. In 1936, she married the noted archaeologist Louis Leakey. They traveled to Africa to begin a lifelong quest to discover the origins of humankind. In the late 1940's, she discovered a skull that was estimated to be twenty-five million years old. The skull was found on an

island in Tanzania's Lake Victoria and was identified as an apelike ancestor of humans known as Proconsul africanus. In 1959, she came upon a skull of a hominid. This find was estimated at being almost two million years old. She and her husband became world-famous. In 1978, she discovered footprints in Tanzania that confirmed that humans walked on two feet more than three million years ago. Her husband died in 1972. She continued working in the field until 1982. Leakey is survived by three sons and ten grandchildren. The cause of death was unreported.

Mark, J. Carson (July 6, 1913, Lindsay, Ontario, Canada – March 2, 1997, Los Alamos, New Mexico). In 1935, he earned a B.A. degree from the University of Western Ontario. Mark continued his studies at the University of Toronto, where he received a Ph.D. in mathematics in 1938. From 1938 to 1943, he taught mathematics at the University of Manitoba. He worked for the Canadian National Research Council from 1943 to 1945. As a member of the British Mission to the Manhattan Project, he went to Los Alamos Scientific Laboratory in May, 1945. He began working there full-time in 1946. While working at the laboratory, Mark helped to develop a number of weapons systems. In 1947, he was named head of the theoretical division (commonly known as the T Division) of the laboratory. Mark remained a division leader until his retirement in 1973. He is survived by his wife, three daughters, three sons, and thirteen grandchildren. Mark struggled with a nerve paralysis for about a year before his death.

Purcell, Edward Mills (August 30, 1912, Taylorville, Illinois – March 7, 1997, Cambridge, Massachusetts). In 1933, he received a B.S. degree in electrical engineering from Purdue University. He continued his studies at Harvard University and received a Ph.D. in physics in 1938. From 1940 to 1946, Purcell worked at the Radiation Laboratory of the Massachusetts Institute of Technology (MIT). He then went to teach physics at Harvard. Purcell would remain on staff there until his retirement in 1977. In 1952, he and Felix Bloch were awarded the Nobel Prize in Physics. Purcell had discovered a way of detecting the magnetic waves that came from the nuclei of atoms. His research helped to make it possible for unknown substances to be analyzed. He is survived by his wife, two sons, and a brother. The cause of death was respiratory failure.

Sagan, Carl (November 9, 1934, Brooklyn, New York – December 20, 1996, Seattle, Washington). Studying at the University of Chicago, Sagan earned four degrees from that institution, including an A.B. in 1954, a B.S. in 1955, an M.S. in physics in 1956, and a Ph.D. in astronomy and astrophysics in 1960. In 1968, he began teaching and doing research at Cornell University. Because of his thirst to understand the planetary universe, Sagan became heavily involved in doing research, writing, and assisting in several National Aeronautics and Space Administration (NASA) missions. He became nationally known for his unique ability to communicate complicated scientific concepts to the public. His many books were eagerly read and his television series Cosmos (1980) was watched by hundreds of millions of people from around the world. He is survived by his wife, four sons, a daughter, a sister, and a grandchild. After suffering with the bone marrow disease myelodysplasia for two years, Sagan died of pneumonia.

Salam, Abdus (January 29, 1926, Jhang-Maghiana, India – November 21, 1996, Oxford, England). After studying in India, Salam won a scholarship to continue his studies at Cambridge University, where he received a B.A. degree in 1949 and a Ph.D. in theoretical physics in 1951. In 1957, he became a professor of theoretical physics at the University of London's Imperial College of Science, Technology, and Medicine. The recipient of numerous awards, Salam was awarded the 1979 Nobel Prize in Physics along with Steven Weinberg and Sheldon Glashow. Each of these physicists had constructed independently a theory that explained how two of the four basic forces of nature, the weak nuclear force and the electromagnetic force, were in reality unified.

Spitzer, Lyman, Jr. (June 26, 1915, Toledo, Ohio – March 31, 1997, Princeton, New Jersey). Educated at Yale University and Princeton University, Spitzer began teaching physics and astronomy at Yale in 1939. He left Yale in 1947 to begin teaching at Princeton, where he would remain until his death. Known as a visionary astrophysicist, he inspired the building of the Hubble Space Telescope. The telescope began as a mere idea in 1947. The idea finally became a reality when the telescope was sent into space in 1990. President Jimmy Carter awarded him the National Medal in Science in 1979. He is survived

by his wife, three daughters, a son, and ten grandchildren. The cause of death was heart disease.

Todd, Sir Alexander Robertus (October 2, 1907, Glasgow, Scotland – January 10, 1997, Cambridge, England). Educated at Glasgow University, the University of Frankfurt, and Oxford University, Todd joined the staff of Edinburgh University in the mid-1930's. In the late 1930's, he began important research on nucleotides at the University of Manchester. From 1944 until his retirement in 1971, Todd was a professor at Cambridge University. In 1954, he was knighted for his scientific achievements and for his work on behalf of the British government. In 1957, he was awarded the Nobel Prize in Chemistry. His research shed light on the makeup of genes. The cause of death was unreported.

Tombaugh, Clyde William (February 4, 1906, near Streator, Illinois – January 17, 1997, Las Cruces, New Mexico). While growing up on a farm, Tombaugh showed an early interest in astronomy. Although lacking any formal training in astronomy, he was given a job at the Lowell Observatory in Flagstaff, Arizona. On March 13, 1930, it was officially announced that he had discovered a new planet. It was called Planet X at the time, but it was eventually given the name of Pluto. Pluto was the ninth planet to be discovered in our solar system, and the only one to be found in the twentieth century. In addition to working at Lowell, Tombaugh taught at Arizona State College and New Mexico State University. He is survived by his wife, two children, and five

grandchildren. Respiratory problems led to his death.

Wald, George (November 18, 1906, New York, New York – April 12, 1997, Cambridge, Massachusetts). Educated at New York University and Columbia University, Wald joined the faculty of Harvard University in 1934. He would remain there until his retirement in 1977. In 1967, he was awarded the Nobel Prize in Physiology or Medicine along with Ragnar Granit and Haldan Keffer Hartline. Wald's research had led to a better understanding of how images are passed from the eye to the brain. Over the years, he spoke out against the Vietnam War and the building of weapons of mass destruction. He is survived by his wife, three sons, a daughter, and nine grandchildren.

Wu, Chien-Shiung (May 31, 1912, Liuho, China – February 16, 1997, New York, New York). Educated at the National Central University in Nanking, China, Wu emigrated to the United States in 1936 in order to continue her studies at the University of California at Berkeley. In 1940, she earned a Ph.D. at Berkeley. She joined the faculty at Columbia University in 1944. In 1954, Wu became a naturalized citizen of the United States. Considered an experimental physicist, her research contributed to the understanding of nuclear forces and structure. In 1975, she became the first woman to be elected president of the American Physical Society. The recipient of many awards, Wu also had an asteroid named in her honor in 1990. She is survived by her husband and son. The cause of death was a stroke.

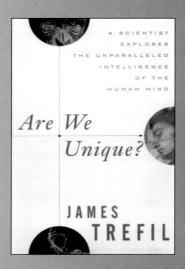

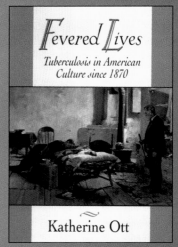

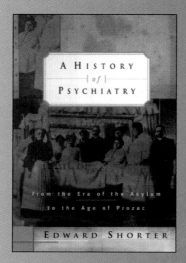

Baskin, Yvonne. *The Work of Nature: How the Diversity of Life Sustains Us*. Washington, D.C.: Island Press, 1997. 288 pp.

An engaging overview of the concept of biodiversity, one that explains how the loss of animal and plant species can have unexpected and often calamitous consequences for the underlying biological processes that support life on Earth. Baskin's work includes a foreword written by Paul Ehrlich.

Chadwick, Douglas H., and Joel Sartore. *The Company We Keep: America's Endangered Species*. Washington, D.C.: National Geographic Society, 1996. 157 pp. Illustrated.

A wildlife biologist collaborates with a wildlife photographer to produce this extensively illustrated work that examines the sociopolitical, ethical, and scientific issues surrounding the species and ecosystems protected under the 1973 Endangered Species Act. A chart folds out to display all of the species listed under the act and chronicles the main causes of their decline.

Gallagher, William B. *When Dinosaurs Roamed New Jersey*. New Brunswick, N.J.: Rutgers University Press, 1997. 180 pp.

Although commonly associated with the arid regions of the West and Southwest, dinosaur remains have been found in many other areas of the United States. Gallagher's work offers a comprehensive history of fossil deposits found in New Jersey, ranging from Benjamin Franklin's inspec-tion of a fossil duckbill foot discovered in 1787 up through amber deposits that have preserved more delicate remains from the bird and insect world.

Groves, Julian McAllister. *Hearts and Minds: The Controversy over Laboratory Animals*. Philadelphia: Temple University Press, 1997. 221 pp.

An intriguing study of the ongoing conflict between animal researchers and animal-rights activists and the impact of their emotional clash on the scientific community. Groves attempts to provide insights into the common ground that exists between the opposing sides and how these common interests may serve to direct efforts toward a more productive solution to the problem of laboratory testing.

Mayr, Ernst. *This Is Biology: The Science of the Living World*. Cambridge, Mass.: The Belknap Press of Harvard University Press, 1997. 327 pp.

An emeritus professor of biology at Harvard, Mayr has the necessary scholarly credentials to produce this overview of biological thinking from Aristotle to Darwin and beyond.

ASTRONOMY AND SPACE SCIENCE

Dyson, Freeman. *Imagined Worlds*. Cambridge, Mass.: Harvard University Press, 1997. 192 pp.

Combining his familiarity with science fact and science fiction, Dyson offers an intriguing chronicle of the perils that arise when science and technology are forced to serve questionable political and economic ends. Voicing his support for the safe disposal of all nuclear weapons, Dyson also offers his hopes that the creation of space colonies may alleviate many of the pressures that currently threaten to overwhelm civilization on Earth.

Ferris, Timothy. *The Whole Shebang: A State-of-the-Universe(s) Report*. New York: Simon & Schuster, 1997. 464 pp. Illustrated.

Popular science writer Timothy Ferris assesses the current state of the cosmos and explores the new theories that have arisen from the conjunction of modern astronomical discoveries and particle physics theories. A challenging work, but one that benefits from Ferris's clear writing style and sensitivity to the needs of lay readers.

Goldsmith, Donald. *The Hunt for Life on Mars*. New York: Dutton, 1997. 256 pp. Illustrated.

A somewhat flawed but informative popular account of the search for scientific evidence confirming that life has existed on Mars. Goldsmith is particularly adept at explaining the scientific processes involved and at conveying the excitement generated by the August, 1996, discovery of tantalizing clues to life in a Martian meteorite.

Grinspoon, David Harry. *Venus Revealed: A New Look Below the Clouds of Our Mysterious Twin Planet*. Reading, Mass.: Helix Books, 1997. 368 pp. Illustrated.

An astrophysicist involved in the Magellan space probe mission to Venus, Grinspoon discusses the various scientific findings gathered by observatories and space probes that have provided tantalizing glimpses of conditions on Venus and the geological and atmospheric forces that operate on Earth's sister planet.

Mann, Alfred K. *Shadow of a Star: The Neutrino Story of Supernova 1987A*. New York: W. H. Freeman, 1997. 192 pp. Illustrated.

Mann provides a readable description of the scientific information gathered in 1987, when neutrinos were detected in the emissions from a dying supernova. These discoveries confirmed long-held scientific theories and supplied new ideas about the life and death of stars.

EARTH AND ENVIRONMENT

Barker, Rodney. *And the Waters Turned to Blood*. New York: Simon & Schuster, 1997. 352 pp.

An engrossing account of JoAnn Burkholder's discovery of a new species of dinoflagellate and the impact that toxins traced to this microorganism had on the river and ocean ecology of North Carolina. Although Barker has a penchant for exaggerating the drama of this account, the actions and responses of the public health officials who were informed of Burkholder's studies speak for themselves.

Broad, William J. *The Universe Below: Discovering the Secrets of the Deep Sea*. New York: Simon & Schuster, 1997. 368 pp.

Written by a Pulitzer Prize-winning science writer, this work provides an overview of various forms of deep-sea

technology — ranging from vehicles to instrumentation to satellites — that have allowed humans to explore what has become one of the last scientific frontiers of "innerspace."

McSween, Harry Y., Jr. *Fanfare for Earth: The Origin of Our Planet and Life*. New York: St. Martin's Press, 1997. 272 pp. Illustrated.

A well-reasoned and informative history of life on Earth, pulling together details from various scientific disciplines and offering a convincing argument for the unique position that this planet holds in our understanding of the universe.

Schneider, Stephen H. *Laboratory Earth: The Planetary Gamble We Can't Afford to Lose*. New York: BasicBooks, 1996. 174 pp.

Stanford professor Stephen H. Schneider provides a scientific assessment of the problems of global climate change and the long-range consequences of human influences on Earth's climate.

Takacs, David. *The Idea of Biodiversity: Philosophies of Paradise*. Baltimore: The Johns Hopkins University Press, 1996. 393 pp.

A timely analysis of the history of conservation strategies and the possibility of maintaining and protecting Earth's biodiversity. Takacs strives for a balanced approach, voicing his concern that extremists are polarizing the debate over biodiversity in much the same way that the antinuclear movement has with

nuclear research, failing to consider the complex issues and ethical values that are involved.

HUMAN SCIENCES

Glasser, Ronald. *The Light in the Skull: An Odyssey of Medical Discovery*. New York: Faber & Faber, 1997. 210 pp.

A pediatric specialist and science writer, Glasser offers a densely detailed study of medical research and progress—a work that is made accessible to general readers by the author's facility in summarizing and humanizing the stories behind the medical discoveries he chronicles.

Keizer, Bert. *Dancing with Mister D: Notes on Life and Death*. New York: Doubleday, 1997. 336 pp.

A Dutch physician recounts his experiences working in a nursing home for the terminally ill, some of whom choose the legal alternative of physician-assisted suicide. Keizer offers an incisive look at both side of the euthanasia debate while providing profiles of his patients that are poignant, but never saccharine.

Marsa, Linda. *Prescription for Profits: How the Pharmaceutical Industry Bankrolled the Unholy Marriage Between Science and Business*. New York: Scribner, 1997. 292 pp.

Marsa charts the meteoric rise of biotechnology companies in the 1980's and 1990's and the impact that corporate greed has had on the race to discover a cure for AIDS. She offers useful summaries of the scientific research involved while encouraging readers to consider the human consequences of pharmaceutical companies' concern for the bottom line.

Nuland, Sherwin B. *The Wisdom of the Body*. New York: Alfred A. Knopf, 1997. 416 pp.

Nuland explores the complex processes by which the human body maintains itself, introducing challenging scientific concepts in this highly readable work. The book serves as an interesting companion to Nuland's National Book Award-winning work How We Die: Reflections on Life's Final Chapter (1994).

Ott, Katherine. *Fevered Lives: Tuberculosis in American Culture Since 1870*. Cambridge, Mass.: Harvard University Press, 1996. 256 pp. Illustrated.

A wide-ranging social history that explores the impact of tuberculosis on American lives and culture from early attempts to halt its spread and treat its victims to modern concerns about its recurrence.

Rensberger, Boyce. *Life Itself: Exploring the Realm of the Living Cell*. New York: Oxford University Press, 1997. 290 pp. Illustrated.

Washington Post science writer Boyce Rensberger casts cells as the heroes in his story of modern cell science and the physical basis of life.

Rhodes, Richard. *Deadly Feasts: Tracking the Secrets of a Terrifying New Plague*. New York: Simon & Schuster, 1997. 259 pp. Illustrated.

Although written on a topic ripped from current newspaper headlines, Rhodes avoids taking a sensational approach to so-called mad cow disease and a host of other afflictions (including Creutzfeldt-Jakob disease) that have spread primarily as the result of unsafe practices in agribusiness. He presents a cautionary tale, warning readers of the fatal consequences of these practices if not banned by the Food and Drug Administration and other government agencies.

Ryan, Frank. *Virus X: Tracking the New Killer Plagues — Out of the Present and into the Future*. Boston: Little, Brown, 1997. 448 pp.

Following the success of his 1993 work on tuberculosis, The Forgotten Plague, Ryan profiles the scientists involved in the investigation of new viral disease, including the Ebola and hanta viruses as well as AIDS, and explains the methodologies employed in this search. This riveting and highly readable account joins a growing shelf of works that explore the viral frontier.

Sapolsky, Robert M. T*he Trouble with Testosterone: And Other Essays on the Biology of the Human Predicament*. New York: Scribner, 1997. 288 pp.

Stanford biologist Sapolsky offers a thought-provoking collection of essays on subjects that explore the biological dimensions of human behavior and the concept of biological determinism. Eleven of these essays first appeared in Discovery magazine, to which Sapolsky is a regular contributor.

Shorter, Edward. *A History of Psychiatry: From the Era of the Asylum to the Age of Prozac*. New York: John Wiley & Sons, 1997. 448 pp.

Shorter's work explores two centuries of psychiatry — from nineteenth century attempts to segregate those with mental illnesses in asylums through attempts to provide more effective treatment of so-called nervous conditions and twentieth century efforts to treat patients through counseling and medication. His account lacks objectivity, however, with respect to the contributions that psychoanalysis has made to the treatment of mental illness.

Trefil, James. *Are We Unique? A Scientist Explores the Unparalleled Intelligence of the Human Mind*. New York: John Wiley & Sons, 1997. 256 pp.

In his latest work, prolific science writer James Trefil grapples with the intricacies of human consciousness and intelligence, bringing together discoveries made by biologists and theories propounded by computer scientists in an effort to explain the current state of knowledge in the field of cognitive science.

PAST, PRESENT, AND FUTURE

Wynn, Charles M., and Arthur W. Wiggins. *The Five Biggest Ideas in Science*. New York: John Wiley & Sons, 1997. 208 pp. Illustrated.

Two science professors explore five fundamental science concepts — the big bang theory, plate tectonics, the periodic law of chemistry, the model of the atom, and evolution — to reveal the scientific methods that led to their discovery and demonstrate how these ideas are undergoing constant revision and rethinking in the light of new scientific evidence and theories.

**PHYSICAL SCIENCES
AND TECHNOLOGY**

Amato, Ivan. *Stuff: The Materials the World Is Made Of*. New York: BasicBooks, 1997. 304 pp.

Amato explores the world of engineering and materials science, showing how twentieth century advances ranging from cellular telephones to bullet trains to medical imaging technology have their foundation in the discovery and fabrication of polymer plastics, silicon chips, and fiber optic materials that have been developed by engineers and designers in the field of materials science.

Brennan, Richard P. *Heisenberg Probably Slept Here: The Lives, Times, and Ideas of the Great Physicists of the Twentieth Century*. New York: John Wiley & Sons, 1997. 288 pp. Illustrated.

In addition to Heisenberg, science writer Brennan profiles physicists ranging from Max Planck and Albert Einstein to Richard Feynman and Murray Gell-Mann, providing capsule summaries of their contributions to the field of physics in text that is easily accessible even for readers whose math skills are less than perfect.

Dewdney, A. K. *Yes, We Have No Neutrons: An Eye-Opening Tour Through the Twists and Turns of Bad Science*. New York: John Wiley & Sons, 1997. 171 pp. Illustrated.

Written in a debunking vein, Dewdney's work cleverly exposes the research flaws behind cold fusion and several other alleged discoveries from the twentieth century. With wit and a wry sense of humor, Dewdney wisely offers readers a solid grounding in the basic scientific principles that helped expose the shortcomings of these theories and discoveries.

Fölsing, Albrecht. *Albert Einstein*. Translated by Ewald Osers. New York: Viking, 1997. 928 pp. Illustrated.

In this biography, first published in Germany in 1993, Fölsing takes readers on a fascinating journey through the famed physicist's life, allowing a glimpse of the inner man and his emotions while offering ample evidence of his scientific genius.

Gullberg, Jan. *Mathematics: From the Birth of Numbers*. New York: W. W. Norton, 1997. 1120 pp. Illustrated.

Although readers may be daunted by the size of Gullberg's book, it contains a wealth of diverting anecdotes, puzzles, and drawings along with its compendium of basic math formulas, equations, proofs, and functions. Gullberg's enthusiasm for all types of mathematical thinking is infectious and is sure to overcome the math phobia experienced by many of his readers.

Kevles, Bettyann Holtzmann. *Naked to the Bone: Medical Imaging in the Twentieth Century*. New Brunswick, N.J.: Rutgers University Press, 1997. 400 pp. Illustrated.

An accessible history of medical imaging technologies from X rays to mammography to CT scans and how these technologies have contributed to various revolutions in the diagnosis and treatment of disease, allowing doctors and other medical professionals to examine the inner-workings of their patients' bodies.

Marshall, Ian, and Danah Zohar. *Who's Afraid of Schrödinger's Cat?* All the New Science Ideas You Need to Keep Up with the New Thinking. New York: William Morrow, 1997. 395 pp. Illustrated.

A lively encyclopedia of two hundred concepts from the physical sciences with thought-provoking links that will lead readers to related topics of interest to science-fiction readers and science undergraduates alike.

Murray, Charles J. *The Superman: The Story of Seymour Cray and the Technical Wizards Behind the Supercomputer*. New York: John Wiley & Sons, 1997. 256 pp.

This informative biography chronicles the life of Seymour Cray, the pioneer in the field of supercomputing who diligently focused on engineering and design even after the personal computer revolutionized the world of computer technology. Murray does a fine job of placing Cray's achievements within the historical context of the growth of the computer industry.

Pais, Abraham. *A Tale of Two Continents: Physicist's Life in a Turbulent World*. Princeton, N.J.: Princeton University Press, 1997. 520 pp.

This autobiography chronicles Pais's experiences from

his years spent hiding from the Nazis during World War II up through his interaction with many of the leading figures in twentieth century physics as a result of his work at Princeton's Institute for Advanced Study. Known for his biographies of Niels Bohr and Albert Einstein, Pais is somewhat less adept at framing the story of his own life, although the vignettes he provides give tantalizing glimpses of the man behind the scientist.

Rochlin, Gene I. *Trapped in the Net: The Unanticipated Consequences of Computerization.* Princeton, N.J.: Princeton University Press, 1997. 256 pp.
   A science professor at the University of California, Rochlin invites readers to contemplate the unforeseen consequences arising from our increased reliance on computers in all aspects of modern life. Although he offers somewhat grave predictions, Rochlin is reluctant to endorse a Luddite position, acknowledging the stiff costs and near-impossibility of "pulling the plug" on computer technology.

Index

378

THE ANIMAL AND PLANT WORLDS

The Trouble with Clones
© 1998 by Webster's Unified, Inc.

The Dolphin Strategy
Carl Zimmer/©1997. Reprinted with permission
of *Discover* Magazine

**Horses, Mollusks and the
Evolution of Bigness**
Copyright © 1997 by The New York Times Co.
Reprinted by Permission.

**Snow Geese Survive All Too Well,
Alarming Conservationists**
Copyright © 1997 by The New York Times Co.
Reprinted by Permission.

The Wired Butterfly
Mark Caldwell/©1997. Reprinted with permission
of *Discover* Magazine

APPLIED SCIENCE AND TECHNOLOGY

CalTech's Motley Crew
Copyright ©1997, *The Chronicle of Higher
Education*. Reprinted with permission.

Chinks in Digital Armor
Reprinted with permission from SCIENCE NEWS,
the weekly newsmagazine of science, copyright
©1997 by Science Service.

Materials in the Magic Kingdom
Reprinted with permission from SCIENCE NEWS,
the weekly newsmagazine of science, copyright
©1996 by Science Service.

**Command of the Air
in the Twentieth Century**
© 1998 by Webster's Unified, Inc.

**Undaunted by Failure,
Balloonists Vow to Try Again**
Copyright © 1997 by The New York Times Co.
Reprinted by Permission.

**Peering into the Earth's Critical Layer
with GPR**
© 1998 by Webster's Unified, Inc.